The New
CALIFORNIA
Cook Book

For Casual Living
All Over the World

The New
CALIFORNIA
Cook Book

For Casual Living All Over the World

By
GENEVIEVE CALLAHAN

DECORATIONS BY PHILIP LITTLE

BONANZA BOOKS · NEW YORK

My Thanks to You

To generous friends all over the country—and all over the world—go my sincere thanks for helping to produce this book. There are not enough pages to list all of you who have contributed recipes and ideas to the first edition and to this new one. But I am mindful of each of you—and forever grateful.

A special thank-you, too, to all you newspaper food editors in cities large and small, who have continued to recommend The California Cook Book to your readers.

To each of you I say, as I frequently write when inscribing copies of the book for friends: Here's good cooking to you, California-style—and fun doing it!

Sincerely,
Genevieve Callahan

Contents

What's New About This Revised Edition

Since its initial publication in 1946, The California Cook Book has gone through several additional large printings. In this printing, I have made the following important changes:

1. Put in an entirely new chapter on Outdoor cooking (see pages 331 to 361).
2. Added outstanding new recipes and ideas to every chapter. (Note particularly the new ways with vegetables in Chapter Seven.)
3. Brought old favorite recipes up-to-date to coincide with newer cooking techniques and baking temperatures.

In brief, this is the best of the original California Cook Book, plus! I hope you like it.

G. C.

About This Book

"CALIFORNIA IS MORE THAN A STATE—it's a way of life." That is what designers of sports clothes say. Architects and decorators recognize the fact. Visitors from other parts of the country feel it, comment upon it.

Just what is this California way of life? As I see it, it's a pleasant mixture of outdoor and indoor living, with emphasis on the out of doors. It's a blending of comfort and style, casualness and care, functionalism and fun.

That way of living explains why we demand clothes that are comfortable, casual, colorful, good-looking, suitable for indoors and out; why we make the garden or patio or terrace an integral part of the house we live in. It explains, too, why we Californians like to eat so many of our meals under the skies; why we are constantly figuring ways to cut down kitchen time indoors to give us more time outside; why we like to substitute informality for formality, imagination for elaboration, flavor for fussiness.

In this *California Cook Book for Casual Living All Over the World,* I have tried to capture some of the flavor of California living, and to interpret it in terms of food. I have tried to pack the pages full of favorite California recipes and ideas that good cooks everywhere will turn to when they want something to give a new lift to the meals they serve. I have tried to do a book which will be equally inspirational and usable in Philadelphia and Pasadena, in Seattle and San Antonio, in Des Moines and Dayton.

Everything in this book has been selected for downright eating pleasure. The menus are for the sort of meals we like to serve our friends from the East and the South and the Northwest when they visit us in our Russian Hill apartment in San Francisco, or in our little red cottage in Inverness, where we spend our week ends. The recipes are the kind that friends so frequently ask us to write out for them.

It's an informal cook book, you will find—as informal as patio living. But for all its informality and its uninhibited, undictatorial attitude toward recipes and cookery, I think you will agree that this is a gourmet cook book in the true sense— a book for the connoisseur of good food. As every good home economist, nutritionist, and dietitian knows, food simply has to taste good, otherwise it won't be eaten. And no matter how vitamin-saving the method of cooking may have been, or how beautiful the arrangement on the serving plate, most of the effort has been wasted if the food is lukewarm, or is poorly seasoned. (You'll note, however, that the rules of sound nutrition are observed throughout this book, though the word "nutrition" rarely appears.)

A few of the recipes given may at first glance look a bit extravagant. I have included them because they are so well worth making. And remember, you can always balance a rich, glamorous dish in both cost and digestibility by keeping the rest of the menu on the simple side. (Like Lou Richardson's dream of the "perfect balanced menu"—sparkling Burgundy balanced with hamburgers!)

Whether you live in California or Maine or Washington or Florida, then, or anywhere in between; whether you cook in an apartment kitchenette or a suburban kitchen; whether you are man or woman, expert grill-master or amateur egg scrambler, you will find here many a recipe, many a helpful idea that has been put in especially for you. I hope you find and use every one of them, and through them find new fun in cooking and eating—and living—California style.

Genevieve Callahan.

The New
CALIFORNIA
Cook Book

For Casual Living
All Over the World

By-laws of Salad Making

1. Pick the right salad to fit in with the meal you are serving. That means a light salad with a light dressing to serve as the first course for dinner, or to go with the meat course; a heartier salad, with perhaps a richer dressing, to serve as the main course at luncheon, or to build up a slim dinner or a picnic or barbecue meal; a rich or not-so-rich fruity or frozen salad to serve as dessert. Put the emphasis on greens and raw vegetables and fruits, because of their crisp textures, fresh flavors, and their vitamin and mineral values.

2. When you bring salad makings into the kitchen, wash them at once, quickly—don't soak them. Remove wilted outer leaves of lettuce or cabbage, but don't separate the leaves at this time. Scrub the carrots and other roots with a stiff brush. Don't scrape or pare or shred anything in advance of salad-making time: exposing cut surfaces to the air means loss of vitamins. Store washed raws in a covered pan in the refrigerator to crisp them.

3. When you cook vegetables in advance to use in salads, drain and give them a quick dip into ice water the minute they are tender; then store, closely covered, in the refrigerator. If feasible, pour a little French dressing over them before storing; the dressing not only adds flavor but helps to preserve color and vitamins.

4. Mix and fix your salad immediately before serving, doing whatever dicing or shredding is necessary then. Don't chop things too fine—you don't want hash. And don't labor over any salad. The light quick touch, important in all good cooking, is especially essential in salad making.

Chapter 1

California Ways with Salads

IT IS fitting that this California cook book should begin with a chapter on salads, just as so many California dinners begin with salads. It is natural that it should be a big and important chapter. For all over the country, salads—especially green salads—are becoming more important in everyday meal planning and serving.

I said that many dinners here begin with salads. That is particularly true in restaurants and tearooms. At home dinners the salad is more likely to accompany the main course in order to simplify serving for the no-help hostess. At luncheons and suppers, whether for family alone or for guests, the salad frequently *is* the main course.

When you use recipes from this chapter, remember that

salad making in the California style is pretty much free hand, as an artist works, rather than painstakingly accurate, as a scientist proceeds. Don't hesitate to change any salad recipe according to your inspiration, your sense of taste, and the current contents of your refrigerator!

THE TOSSED GREEN SALAD

No matter where you live you can have just the kind of green salad you want. Chances are you'll decide you like best a combination of some crisp, firm greens—such as head lettuce; romaine, if you can get it; endive; escarole—with some softer-textured ones, such as leaf, or local or Bibb lettuce; butter lettuce; oakleaf or Australian lettuce; watercress.

Certainly you can find in the markets almost any type of French dressing you want, ready to use. Or you may choose to mix a special dressing in advance, ready to pour over and toss with the greens the last minute. Or—and this is especially likely if you are a man—you may elect to bring the bowl of greens to the table and make the dressing, right on the salad, as described in the following paragraphs. (One friend of ours always does this, at the candle-lighted table, with so much ceremony that his cousin, a priest, refers to "Joe's Solemn High Salad.")

STEPS IN MAKING GREEN BOWL SALADS

Use a good-sized bowl, preferably a wooden one, big enough to mix and toss the salad without mishap. Rub the inside of bowl thoroughly with a cut clove of garlic. Tear rather than cut the well-washed and drained greens into not-too-small pieces, and put them into the bowl. Over them, dribble salad oil—olive oil, or one of the vegetable oils, or a mixture of these. Add enough so that the leaves will be well coated when they are tossed. Sprinkle lightly with salt and coarse black pepper (freshly ground in your little pepper grinder, if possible), add a handful of chopped chives or green onions with their tops; then mix and toss gently but thoroughly with fork and spoon, using an over-and-over motion, until every leaf glistens. Taste, to check on seasonings. Just before taking to table, sprinkle lightly with wine vinegar, plain or flavored with tarragon or shallot or basil, or a mixture of these, using about 1/4 to 1/3 as much vinegar as you used of oil. Don't pour on too much! Toss again until well mixed or "fatigued," as French salad makers say, but not tired out! Taste again, and add whatever it needs, if anything. Serve at once.

If you are using a ready-mixed dressing, choose a thin one, shake well, and sprinkle it over the greens just before serving time, using just enough to coat the leaves well. Toss until well mixed, and serve at table.

FIESTA SALAD

When you're having a big gang for a barbecue or buffet, you'll find this big bowl salad as convenient as it is different and good. You can have all the makings fixed in advance, ready to put together, toss, and serve.

1 head iceberg lettuce
1 head romaine or curly endive
2 peeled ripe tomatoes
1 big mild onion (preferably red)

2 tender cucumbers
1 green pepper
1 (6 1/2 or 7 ounce) can tuna, chunk-style or solid-pack

Dressing:

1/2 cup salad oil
1/4 cup wine vinegar
1/2 teaspoon salt
1/4 teaspoon coarse black pepper
3 or 4 dashes of Tabasco sauce

1/2 teaspoon finely chopped fresh marjoram (or pinch of dry marjoram)
1 cup dairy-packed sour cream
1/2 cup crumbled Roquefort cheese

Rub your biggest wooden salad bowl with garlic. Break up the lettuce and romaine into the bowl. Peel tomatoes, cut up coarsely, and let drain a bit while you slice the onion, cucumber, and green pepper on the bias, and arrange over the lettuce. Break up the tuna and scatter over all; add the drained tomato. Mix the dressing, pour over the salad and toss gently. Season to taste while mixing. Serves 8.

ABOUT GARLIC

Garlic in a salad is what you miss if it isn't there! Every tossed green salad, every vegetable salad, every hearty salad needs at least a whiff of it to round out and harmonize the various flavors.

There are three chief ways of using garlic in salads. First, and commonest, probably, is to cut an unpeeled clove of garlic in two and rub the cut surfaces over the inside of the wooden salad bowl just before mixing the salad. (I use a small wooden masher, like a potato masher, to crush the garlic and rub it over and into the wood.)

Second is the way suggested in the recipe for Romaine Salad Superb, which follows. For this, you add plenty of peeled and chopped garlic to a bottle or jar of salad oil, and let stand a few hours before using.

Third is the method that professional chefs frequently use. For this, you peel the garlic cloves, place them on a chopping board, and chop coarsely with a big knife. Now cover the garlic with plenty of salt; continue chopping, and mashing with the side of the blade, until the garlic has entirely disintegrated and mixed with the salt. Use this freshly garlicked salt in the salad or other mixture. Commercially prepared garlic salt and garlic-flavored wine vinegar are convenient short-cuts for including the flavor of this pungent root in salads.

For ordinary family use, a little garlic will go a long way. Though it is sold by the pound in California markets, I usually buy just one head or root of garlic, and break off one bulblet or "clove" at a time. An average root is made up of at least ten to fifteen bulblets, good for that number of salads. I like, too, to grow a few roots of garlic in the window box herb garden. Through the summer I snip off bits of the green tops and use as chives or shallot tops would be used. When the tops die down, I pull the roots, dry them, and have the matured heads for winter salad making.

ROMAINE SALAD SUPERB

This is the "Caesar Salad" you've probably eaten and exclaimed over in some of the best restaurants in every part of the country. Don't be alarmed at the strange way of putting it together! That uncooked egg blends with the grated cheese and oil to make a smooth coating for each lettuce leaf. This is a wonderful salad to serve at a barbecue supper. Be sure to mix it where everyone can watch the performance.

Several hours before serving time, prepare the garlic-flavored oil this way: chop 3 or 4 peeled cloves of garlic, cover with a cup of olive oil in a bowl, and let stand in the kitchen—not in the refrigerator—until needed. Make the croutons, too: cut thin slices of bread in small cubes and fry in a little oil in a skillet until thoroughly crisp and lightly browned. Have everything else ready, but do not put the salad together until immediately before serving. To serve 6 to 8, you will need to have ready:

3 to 4 heads of crisp, chilled romaine lettuce (about 3 quarts)

1/4 cup garlic-flavored olive oil

1/2 cup plain salad oil (peanut, corn, or cottonseed oil)

1 tablespoon Worcestershire sauce

Salt and freshly ground coarse black pepper

3/4 to 1 cup freshly grated Romanello or other dry hard cheese

1 egg, uncooked

Juice and pulp of 3 lemons (about 1/2 cup)

2 cups crisp croutons

Tear lettuce into not-too-small pieces in a big salad bowl. Pour the garlic-flavored and plain oils over it. Sprinkle with Worcestershire sauce, plenty of salt and pepper, and grated cheese. Break the raw egg directly onto the greens—don't beat it! Sprinkle lemon juice and pulp over all, and toss and mix very thoroughly, until no trace of egg is to be seen. Last, dip the crisp croutons into the remaining garlic-flavored oil, add to the salad, toss again lightly, and serve at once, while the croutons are crisp. (If there is any garlic oil left after dipping the croutons, remove the garlic and save the oil to use in making green salad another time.)

RAW BROCCOLI SALAD

Chop fine the tender florets of a well-washed bunch of young, tender, raw broccoli. (You can cook and use the stalks later.) Sprinkle with salt and pepper, add enough salad oil to moisten lightly (about 1/3 cup) and 2 tablespoons lemon juice. Mix well and chill for half an hour. Cut up 4 peeled ripe tomatoes fairly small, squeezing out most of the seeds; add to broccoli. Add 1/3 cup of sour cream blended with a teaspoon of prepared mustard (or sweet cream and mustard with a tablespoon of lemon juice added); mix well; serve in lettuce cups. Serves 4 to 6.

BOUQUET SALAD BOWL

Fill center of a wide, shallow bowl or chop plate with shredded lettuce to make a non-skid foundation. On it place a chilled cooked whole head of cauliflower that has stood in sharp French dressing for several hours. Around it arrange groups of small whole pickled beets (3 beets in each group); heap chilled cooked peas between groups of beets. Tuck frilly lettuce leaves around edge, and fill in between vegetables and lettuce with rather coarsely shredded raw carrots. Pass French dressing or mayonnaise or Thousand Island dressing separately. This salad can be made small or huge, serving anywhere from 6 to 12. It's an especially pretty one to serve at table.

CHINESE SALAD

2 cups canned or cooked
   bean sprouts
1 cup thinly sliced celery
1 cup thinly sliced radishes
1 cup thinly sliced unpeeled
   cucumber
1 green pepper, thinly
   sliced
1 raw carrot, thinly sliced
3 green onions, thinly
   sliced
French dressing
Soy sauce

Combine the vegetables in a salad bowl, moisten with French dressing, then add soy sauce to suit your taste. Toss until well mixed. Tuck a few lettuce frills around the edge of the salad, and serve. Serves 6.

TOMATO BOWL

1/4 cup finely chopped
   parsley
1/4 cup chopped shallots,
   or green onions, tops
   and all
A few tender leaves of
   fresh thyme or
   marjoram
6 tablespoons salad oil
2 tablespoons wine vinegar
   (preferably tarragon
   flavored)
4 to 6 large ripe tomatoes
Salt and coarse black
   pepper

Mix the chopped green things with oil and vinegar. Peel and slice tomatoes, sprinkle with salt and pepper, and arrange in layers in a shallow bowl, spreading some of the dressing over each layer. Chill. Serve with chunks of hot French bread. Serves 4.

MIXING THE CABBAGE SALAD BOWL

Closely related to the lettuce bowl is that good old standby, cabbage salad. Simplest, and hard to beat, is old-time cole slaw with cream-and-sugar-and-vinegar dressing. The thicker the cream (sweet or sour), the better the slaw; in fact, whipped cream makes it best! To the amount of cream you think you will need, add about 1/3 as much sugar, then stir in just enough cider vinegar to make it sweet-sour in flavor. Stir until sugar is dissolved, pour over crisp, freshly cut cabbage, add salt and pepper to taste, and mix. If it needs more dressing, or more vinegar, or more sugar, add it. You can't go wrong if you follow your sense of taste!

Or you may prefer your cabbage mixed with mayonnaise, or with cooked salad dressing. If so, try blending a good spoonful each of prepared mustard and lemon juice with the dressing. If you want to give the cabbage a personal touch, add any one of these: chopped onion; sliced celery; shredded carrots; strips of green or sweet red pepper; chopped pickled beets; diced oranges; diced pineapple; coarsely chopped walnuts or salted peanuts; raisins, plumped in hot water.

RAW RELISH PLATES

You might call them "salads without dressing"—those colorful arrangements of strips and slices of raw vegetables with pickles and olives, to be eaten out of hand. They are especially practical for buffet supper use, for they offer no hazards in serving or eating.

Any assortment of the following will make a good-looking, good-eating display: carrot and celery sticks; strips or slices of tender turnips; young green onions, or thin slices of sweet big ones; radish roses (leave a little tuft of green on each one); small florets of raw cauliflower; wedges of raw apples or pears, dipped in orange or lemon juice to keep them white; orange sections; pickles; ripe and green olives; pickled beet

Have the raw vegetables washed and crisped, but wait until just before serving to cut them. Don't have the strips awkwardly long or thick. Do group them in piles on the plates with "studied carelessness," making 2 or 3 repeats of some of them in order to balance colors and tie the whole arrangement together.

For a party touch, make your relishes dramatic with an ice ring: pack finely crushed ice into a ring mold, cover with waxed paper, and fasten with cord or rubber band. Bury in 3 parts crushed ice to 1 part coarse salt for half an hour. Dip quickly in warm water, turn out on big plate, and garnish with chicory or parsley. Fill center of ring with celery curls and carrot sticks; arrange olives, radish roses, and pickles around it.

SALSA—FAVORITE AT BARBECUES

3 ripe tomatoes	1 teaspoon salt
1 medium-sized onion	1/2 teaspoon dry mustard
1 green pepper, or 1 or 2	1/4 teaspoon celery seed
canned green chile	2 tablespoons vinegar
peppers	

Chop the tomatoes, onion, and pepper fine, drain slightly, then add seasonings and vinegar. Add also, if you wish, 2 tablespoons salad oil. Mix well and let stand in refrigerator a few hours to blend flavors. Makes a little over a pint. Serve in individual sauce dishes with the meat. Serves 3 or 4.

CELERY VICTOR

Wash small heads or hearts of celery without separating the stalks; cut lengthwise into 2 or 4 pieces, depending on size. Cut off most of the fringy tops. Cook till tender in boiling soup stock, or water with bouillon cubes and a few slices of onion. When done, lift out carefully into a shallow dish and pour well-seasoned French dressing over the pieces. Let cool, turning occasionally in the dressing.

Chill, arrange on water cress or shredded lettuce, and sprinkle liberally with coarse black pepper and chopped parsley. Lay a few thin strips of anchovy over each piece of celery, and garnish the plate with quartered tomato and ripe olives. For *Asparagus Victor,* cook stalks of green asparagus in soup stock until barely tender, then proceed as directed for Celery Victor.

MOCK SEA-FOOD SALAD

2 large, or 5 or 6 small, raw parsnips
3 tablespoons lemon juice
1 medium-sized onion, chopped
1 cup thinly sliced celery
12 stuffed olives, sliced, or 1 pimiento and 2 or 3 pickles, diced
2 hard-cooked eggs, chopped
Salt and pepper to taste
Mayonnaise or Thousand Island dressing

Wash and scrape parsnips, and grind or shred coarsely. Add other ingredients, using enough mayonnaise to moisten well. Serve in lettuce cups. Or, for fun, pack firmly into a fish-shaped mold and chill for a short time, then turn out on a platter and garnish with lettuce and tomato wedges. Serves 6.

RAW BEET AND PEANUT SALAD

2 cups coarsely ground or shredded raw beets
1 cup coarsely ground or chopped salted peanuts
2 tablespoons mayonnaise
4 tablespoons French dressing
1 teaspoon lemon juice
Salt and pepper

Pare raw beets and grind or shred. Mix with peanuts. Blend dressings with lemon juice, add and mix well. Season to taste.

Serve in lettuce cups, garnishing tops with more mayonnaise. Serves 6.

MEXICAN STRING BEAN SALAD

Split green beans lengthwise and cook until tender in boiling salted water. Drain. When cool, add oil, vinegar, minced onion, salt and pepper and grated cheese to taste. Mix well and serve on lettuce. A few mashed or minced anchovies make a flavorful addition to this salad.

HOME CHEF'S SALAD

Rub a large salad bowl with a cut clove of garlic, then put in 3 tablespoons lemon juice or wine vinegar and 1/2 cup salad oil. Beat well. Tear a small head of lettuce, a bunch of water cress, and the heart of a head of chicory in pieces, put into the bowl, and toss until all the leaves are coated. Add 1 cup diced cooked ham, corned beef, or tongue, 1 cup sliced celery, 3 or 4 peeled and quartered tomatoes, and 3 or 4 chopped green onions. Sprinkle with salt and coarse black pepper, and toss again until well mixed. Chop 4 hard-cooked eggs coarsely, season with salt and pepper, mix with 1/2 cup chopped parsley, and sprinkle over the salad. This whole-meal-in-a-bowl salad tastes extra-good served with rye bread and coffee.

CRAB LOUIS—A GOOD LUNCHEON SALAD

Allow half a good-sized cooked crab per serving. (West Coast crabs are big fellows.) Flake the meat in as big pieces as possible, removing all bits of shell and cartilage. On each individual plate put a bed of shredded lettuce, and on it a mound of the crab, topped with big pieces from the legs. Around the crab arrange a ring of finely chopped hard-cooked eggs. Top with a few slices of egg and a sprinkling of chopped chives. Pass the following dressing separately:

1 cup mayonnaise
1/4 cup French dressing
(made with tarragon
wine vinegar)
1/4 cup chili sauce or
catsup
2 tablespoons chopped
chives

1 teaspoon horseradish
1 teaspoon Worcestershire
sauce
Salt and coarse black
pepper

Mix and chill well. Some cooks add chopped pimiento or chopped pickle relish to the dressing; some, chopped ripe or stuffed olives. Follow your own wishes. If served as a first-course salad at dinner, make the serving portions much smaller than for lunch.

HOLLYWOOD SALAD BOWL

1 grapefruit
1 avocado
1 can (7 ounces) crab meat,
or 1/2 pound fresh crab

1 small head of lettuce,
shredded
1/4 cup mayonnaise
1/4 cup chili sauce

Pare grapefruit and separate into segments. Cut avocado in half, peel, cube, and combine immediately with grapefruit to prevent discoloring. Flake the crab meat coarsely, removing all sharp pieces. Combine all these with shredded lettuce in a bowl, and salt and pepper lightly. Dress with the mayonnaise and chili sauce which have been blended together. Serves 6 to 8 as a first-course salad; 4 or 5 as a main dish for luncheon or supper.

AVOCADOS FOR SALADS

Avocados combine well with fruit, vegetables, or sea food in salads or cocktails. When you buy, ask the market man to pick out one that is "just right for tonight," or for tomorrow, or whenever you plan to use it. Don't poke and pinch the avocados on display!

The fruit is ready to use when it feels soft yet firm when held gently between your hands. If you buy a firm one, let it stand at room temperature until soft. Or, if you wish to hold it several days, put it in the least-cold part of the refrigerator; then bring it out and let it soften before using.

Always cut an avocado in half before peeling it. (If you peel it whole, you'll mash the soft flesh while trying to separate the halves.) Cut it lengthwise, twist to separate the halves, remove the big seed, then tear off the peeling and slice the avocado crosswise or lengthwise. (If you want rings of avocado, cut the fruit in half crosswise, remove seed, then peel and slice; or, better yet, cut in slices before removing the peeling.) Dip cut pieces in lemon juice to prevent darkening.

AVOCADOS ON THE HALF SHELL

Try serving avocados on the half shell, filled with a non-oily cocktail sauce and accompanied by salted crackers or potato chips. (Avocados are rather rich in fat, you know.) Or hollow out the center slightly, to make a larger cavity, and fill with small raw oysters, or tiny cooked California shrimp, or big pieces of crab meat mixed with the pieces of avocado and plenty of cocktail sauce. Almost too filling to be served as a first course, but wonderful as a snack with hot buttered toast and coffee.

GUACAMOLE (MEXICAN AVOCADO SALAD)

This Mexican avocado mixture (pronounced wah-ka-MO-leh) is, strictly speaking, not a salad but a dressing or spread. It is sometimes served heaped in a bowl, to be spooned over sliced tomatoes or vegetables or sea-food salad. Sometimes it is spread roughly over a chilled cooked whole head of cauliflower, and decorated with radish roses on toothpicks, stuck into the cauliflower, pincushion fashion. Often at cocktail parties it is served in a bowl set on a big plate, with potato chips, tortilla chips, crackers, short lengths of celery, and thin long carrot slices arranged on the plate, to be dunked in the Guacamole, and eaten out of hand. To make the mixture, you'll need:

1 fresh ripe tomato	Salt and pepper to taste
2 ripe avocados	Chopped canned green
1 small onion, minced	chile peppers, ad lib.
1 tablespoon wine vinegar	

Peel and dice tomato; peel and mash avocados—not too smooth! Mix, add other ingredients. Taste; add more vinegar as needed. If it must stand awhile put the avocado seeds on top; they help to keep it from darkening! Serves 6 to 8.

Some hostesses like to mash a small (3-ounce) cake of cream cheese and mix it with the Guacamole—makes a mighty good addition, especially when used for dunking.

TO FIX ARTICHOKES FOR SALADS

Cook artichokes as directed in the chapter on Vegetables (see Index); drain and cool. If they are to be served as is, chill, trim off stems, stand artichoke on plate, and serve with small nut cup or lettuce cup of French dressing, or of mayonnaise thinned with lemon juice and mixed with prepared mustard to taste.

If artichokes are to be stuffed with sea-food or chicken salad, pull the leaves apart to make a cup or rosette; remove the fuzzy choke, using a spoon; then fill with salad. It's a good idea to roll the whole artichoke in French dressing before stuffing with the salad.

To prepare artichoke bottoms, which are used as the foundation of some fancy salads, pull all the leaves off the bottom of cooked artichoke, cut out choke, and trim bottom neatly. Marinate in French dressing before using.

CITRUS FRUITS IN SALADS

Oranges and grapefruit fit into dozens of salads, not merely fruit combinations, but sea-food, meat, and vegetable mixtures too. And lemon juice is just what many a salad mixture or dressing needs to make it come to life.

It's really easy to fix beautiful membrane-free segments of grapefruit or orange when you have the "know-how." First, with a sharp knife (a saw-tooth edge works fine) pare the fruit as you would an apple, cutting off every bit of the outer membrane. (Hold the fruit over a bowl while you're doing this, so you won't waste any of the juice.) Now, slide the knife blade down beside one of those dividing walls of membrane and push the segment out, whole. Continue on around the fruit in the same way. That's all there is to it!

FRUIT SALAD OR COCKTAIL

2 grapefruit
2 oranges
1/4 cup pineapple syrup

1/4 cup honey
2 slices pineapple
1 pomegranate

Pare the grapefruit and oranges as described above, remove sections, add pineapple syrup mixed with honey, and chill several hours. Drain. Cut pineapple slices in pieces and arrange with grapefruit or orange sections in lettuce cups, or in fruit cocktail glasses. Dot with rosy pomegranate seeds. If served as salad, dress with French dressing, and top with a fluff of cream cheese whipped smooth with a little milk. If served as cocktail, simply pour some of the honey-and-fruit juice over each serving. Makes 6 salads or 10 to 12 cocktails.

USING STRANGE FRUITS IN SALADS

In warm pockets or thermal belts throughout Southern California, many subtropical fruits are grown, largely as ornamentals. While most of these are used locally, some reach the markets in other parts of the state, and some are even shipped East.

Among those occasionally seen in the fruit markets are the mango, the papaya, and the cherimoya. All of these are good to use in salads or as appetizers in one form or another.

Mango. This fruit, which ranges in size from a few ounces up to 3 or 4 pounds, must be thoroughly chilled before serving, as it has a turpentine-like flavor when warm. Cut the chilled fruit in half, freeing it from its big seed, then peel and slice or dice and use in salad or fruit cup as you would use fresh peaches.

From a friend who lives in the Philippines, I learned an unusual way of serving the smaller—say avocado-size—mangos. Slice the halves off the seed and peel as directed. Then place a half, cut-side down, on a salad plate, and cut diagonally into squares. Slip the knife blade under the center squares to raise them, so that they separate slightly. Put a sprig of mint at each end of the fruit, and serve very cold as an appetizing first course.

Cherimoya. Sometimes called custard apple, or sweetsop, or sherbet fruit. In size this fruit runs about like the avocado, but its light green skin is marked off in a flat design which looks vaguely like that of an artichoke. The smooth, custard-like, somewhat perfumy-flavored flesh is dotted indiscriminately with hard black seeds, which make its use in salads somewhat difficult. It is, however, sometimes seeded and added to fruit salads or fruit cup mixtures.

Papaya, or melon pawpaw. This fruit, which is shaped something like a pear but has the flavor and texture and interior arrangement of a melon, grows on a tree that has leaves like those of a fig tree. In spite of seeming not to be able to make up its mind about itself, the fruit is excellent to eat as an appetizer, or in salad, or as a breakfast or dessert fruit.

The papaya varies in size from that of an avocado to that

of a melon, sometimes measuring as much as 20 inches in length. It is ready to eat when the green rind has turned yellow, and when it is soft to the touch. To serve: chill, then cut in half if small, or in good-sized wedges, and remove the seeds as you do cantaloupe. (In the Islands, it is the custom to leave in a few of the round black seeds and eat them for the sake of their concentrated pepsin.) Serve with quarters or halves of lemon or lime to squeeze over them.

For cocktail use, the papaya is cut into balls or cubes and mixed with other fruits; or it may be served by itself, dressed with lemon or lime juice, or with a tomato cocktail sauce, which makes an exceptionally good appetizer. For salads, it is used just as melons are.

Guava. Several varieties of guavas are grown ornamentally in Southern California, the yellow lemon guava and the red strawberry guava being most common. (The so-called pineapple guava is not really a guava, but a feijoa; see below.)

The guava may range in size from that of a walnut to that of an apple, and in color from white to deep pink. Inside the waxy skin is a firm layer of flesh, around a seedy pulpy center. For salad use, the chilled fruit is peeled and the pulpy center scooped out, then the flesh is sliced in strips or rings and combined with bananas, oranges, tangerines, late pears, or other fruits, and used with or without cottage cheese. Sweet dressings, mayonnaise, or French dressing may be used. For directions for using guavas for dessert and for making jam and jelly, see Index.

Feijoa. Peel and slice pineapple guavas without seeding them. Slice thin, and use the circles as a delicately flavored and attractive garnish for fruit salads. Or combine sliced guavas with thinly sliced radishes and shredded lettuce, and dress with French dressing or with mayonnaise thinned with grapefruit juice.

Passion Fruit. Add a small amount of the richly flavored golden pulp or juice of this small dark purple fruit of the ornamental passion vine to fruit salads or cocktails and you turn ordinary good food into something quite exotic.

White Sapota. Called "peach of the tropics," this large, greenish yellow fruit is used as peaches are in salads and desserts.

Kumquat. This tiny golden-orange citrus fruit, about the size of a large walnut, is much used as an edible decoration for fruit salads, either sliced thin or cut in quarters. The rind is sweet, the juice acid, and so the entire fruit is eaten. The kumquat is also popular for marmalade making. (See Chapter Ten, "Relishes and Treats Typical of the Golden State.")

Loquat. Related to the kumquat only in similarity of names is this yellow-to-orange fruit which has a smooth, thin skin covering juicy flesh that has somewhat the texture and juiciness of a cherry, but that contains four or five large brown seeds. Whole or halved small loquats are sometimes used to garnish fruit salads. Simply wipe the downy fuzz off the skin and cut up or leave whole. They are also used to some extent in pies, jellies, and preserves, but are more often eaten out of hand.

Pomegranate. Cut the rose-red pomegranate in half and pull out the beautiful red arils (flesh-covered seeds) with a spoon. Dot them over any fruit salad for color and flavor accent. They do a lot for any too-white salad combination.

PERSIMMON SALAD

3 ripe persimmons   **1/4 teaspoon salt**
1/2 cup whipped cream   **Paprika**
1 tablespoon horseradish

Cut chilled soft-ripe persimmons in halves, crosswise, and place halves in lettuce cups on individual salad plates. Whip cream, add horseradish and salt, heap on persimmons, and dash with paprika. Provide both spoon and fork for eating this salad, which may be either a first course or a dessert salad. Serves 6.

JELLIED TOMATO SALAD

Dissolve a package of salad aspic in 1 1/2 cups hot tomato juice. Add 1 tablespoon each of horseradish and lemon juice or vinegar, and cool until beginning to thicken. Fold in 1 cup thinly sliced celery or shredded cabbage, 1 tablespoon minced onion, 2 tablespoons chopped pickle relish, and salt and pepper to taste. Chill in a small (1-quart) ring or other mold, or in 4 to 6 individual molds. Turn out, garnish with lettuce, heap center with chive cottage cheese or with mixed vegetable salad. Serves 4 to 6.

JELLIED APPLE-WALNUT SALAD

1 package lemon-flavored gelatin
1 1/2 cups hot water
1 1/2 cups diced unpeeled red apple
2 tablespoons lemon juice
2 tablespoons sugar
1/2 cup diced sweet pickle or sweet pickle relish
1 cup coarsely diced celery
1/2 cup coarsely chopped walnuts

Dissolve gelatin in hot water; cool until beginning to jell. While it cools, dice apples, at once add lemon juice and sugar, and toss well to prevent darkening. Add other ingredients. Fold into thickened gelatin, pour into a 1 1/2-quart mold, or 6 individual ones, and chill until firm. Serve on lettuce, garnished with slices of unpeeled red apple, and mayonnaise and walnut halves. Excellent with meat or fish dishes. Serves 6.

JELLIED CUCUMBER SALAD

1 package lime-flavored gelatin
1 cup hot water
2 tablespoons vinegar
1 tablespoon grated onion
1 cup shredded or finely chopped cucumber
1/4 teaspoon salt
1/2 cup mayonnaise

Dissolve gelatin in hot water; add vinegar, and cool until

slightly thickened. While it cools, grate onion and peeled raw cucumber; add salt, mix well, then drain off excess juice. Beat thickened gelatin with rotary beater till fluffy; fold in cucumber and onion mixture and mayonnaise, mix well, and pour into 6 individual molds, or into a 1-quart mold. Chill. Turn out and serve on lettuce; garnish with tomato wedges or with strips of pimiento. Serves 6.

JELLIED CRANBERRY RELISH RING

Dissolve 2 packages of raspberry or cherry-flavored gelatin (or 1 of each) in 2 1/2 cups hot water. Cool until slightly thickened, then fold in 2 cups raw cranberry relish (made by grinding 2 cups raw cranberries with 1 small orange and 1 apple, and stirring in 3/4 cup sugar). Chill in a ring mold or flat pan. Serve with turkey or chicken salad.

At a holiday get-together in Berkeley, a salad similar to this was the feature of the buffet. It was made by dissolving raspberry-flavored gelatin in hot crushed pineapple, then folding in ground raw cranberries and chopped almonds. After chilling, the ring mold of salad was turned out on a huge blue-green pottery plate, and surrounded with sliced turkey and sliced whole oranges, arranged in groups. The center was filled with pineapple chunks. Fluffy fruit dressing and mayonnaise were passed separately. Hot baked ham and hot spoonbread with butter completed the menu.

ROQUEFORT SALAD RING

2 teaspoons plain gelatin
3 tablespoons cold water
1/4 pound soft Roquefort
    cheese
1 pint creamed cottage
    cheese
1 teaspoon Worcestershire
    sauce

Dash of cayenne or
    Tabasco sauce
Salt to taste
1/2 cup mayonnaise
1/2 cup heavy cream,
    whipped

Add gelatin to cold water and let stand 5 minutes, then melt over hot water. Mash Roquefort cheese and gradually add cottage cheese, mashing and blending well. Add seasonings, then stir in melted gelatin. Fold in mayonnaise and whipped cream, pour into a small (6-inch) ring mold, and chill. Unmold and garnish with lettuce, tomato and ripe olives. Serve with French dressing. Serves 6.

JELLIED CHEESE RING

2 tablespoons plain gelatin
1/3 cup cold water
1 cup chili sauce
2 cups cottage cheese
1 cup diced celery

1 cup mayonnaise
1/2 cup sliced stuffed olives
1/2 cup sweet pickle relish
1/4 teaspoon salt

Add gelatin to cold water and let soften while you heat chili sauce just to boiling. Remove from heat, add softened gelatin, and stir until dissolved. Let cool until beginning to thicken. Combine the remaining ingredients, fold into the chili gelatin, pour into a ring mold that holds 1 1/2 to 2 quarts, and chill until firm. Turn out on a plate, garnish with lettuce, and heap any sea-food or vegetable salad in the center. Serves 8 to 10.

FROZEN FRUIT AND CHEESE SALAD

1 No. 2 1/2 can apricot halves
1/2 cup mayonnaise
1/4 teaspoon salt
1/4 teaspoon prepared mustard
1/2 cup coarsely chopped walnuts

1/3 cup Maraschino cherries, sliced
1 tablespoon syrup from the cherries
1 pint creamed cottage cheese

Open can of apricots with can opener that leaves a smooth rim; save the can. Drain apricots, save 6 or 8 halves for garnishing, then cut the rest into quarters and mix with all other ingredients in order given. Put into the apricot can, tie 3 or 4 layers of waxed paper over top, and put can into freezing unit of refrigerator, set at coldest temperature, for about 6 hours or until frozen. At serving time, cut bottom out of can and push out the cylinder of frozen salad. Slice and serve on lettuce garnished with fluffy dressing and apricot halves. Serves 6 to 8. Good to serve with dainty sandwiches for a "ladies' luncheon," or for refreshments.

FROZEN FRUIT SALAD

2 small (3-ounce size) cakes cream cheese
2 tablespoons lemon juice
1/3 cup mayonnaise
1/2 cup diced pineapple, or pitted fresh, canned or frozen sweet cherries

1 cup diced orange segments
1/2 cup chopped walnuts or toasted almonds
2 teaspoons chopped candied ginger
1 cup heavy cream, whipped

Blend cheese smooth with lemon juice and mayonnaise. Fold in other ingredients in order given. Freeze in refrigerator trays 2 to 3 hours, or until firm. Serve on lettuce with fruit dressing. Serves 6 to 8. With toasted crackers and hot tea or coffee, this makes a summer luncheon de luxe.

LUNCHEON SALAD PLATES

On my first visit to California, a friend in Pasadena served a salad luncheon which I've remembered ever since. It was a fruit salad plate accompanied by warm orange rolls dripping with orange butter icing, and hot coffee. (You'll find the recipe for those very rolls in the chapter on Breads.)

On each plate were grouped 4 crisp, cup-shaped lettuce leaves. One cup contained 3 halves of fresh apricots; one a mound of perfect red raspberries; one, 5 or 6 membrane-free segments of orange and grapefruit; one, 10 or 12 pitted dark red Bing cherries. These were firmly established on a bed of shredded outer leaves of lettuce. Between the cups were arranged strips of banana rolled in chopped nuts, and short lengths of celery stuffed with Roquefort cheese mashed with cream cheese. French dressing and fluffy fruit dressing were passed separately.

Since then, I have eaten and have served many a salad plate luncheon. Some of the most satisfactory to serve and satisfying to eat are described below. All of them, of course, are easily changed to suit your own ideas and to make use of what you have on hand.

Tropical Fruit Plate. An individual mold of grapefruit sections in lime gelatin, surrounded with strips or sections of avocado, orange, pear, and persimmon, and accented with a couple of cheese-stuffed dates. Served with hot cinnamon buns and hot tea or coffee.

Fruit Bouquet. On a dinner-size plate, preferably of sparkling glass, arrange with an eye for color contrasts and repeats, any or all of these: quarters of peaches or nectarines and unpeeled pears; chunks of banana; segments of grapefruit, orange and tangerine; quarter slices of pineapple; little bunches of Tokay and Thompson seedless grapes on their stems; halves of fresh prunes or peeled fresh figs. In the center of this abundant display fit a small glass or fluted paper cup of pineapple ice, and tuck two or three buttered crescents of brown bread in amongst the fruits. Pass French and fluffy fruit dressings, and hot muffins or cheese-frosted biscuits or popovers.

Heartier Fruit Plate. Arrange big pieces of fresh and canned fruits on lettuce on each dinner plate, leaving space at one side for a mound of cottage cheese dashed with paprika, a spoonful of salted almonds, and two sandwiches of sliced chicken on whole-wheat bread.

Hot-and-Cold Plate. Arrange any combination of fruit in lettuce cups on a dinner plate. At the last minute, add triangles of toasted open-face cheese sandwiches.

Men Like This. On each plate is a ring of tomato aspic on lettuce, heaped with chived cottage cheese mixed with coarsely chopped walnuts. Beside this on the plate go generous sandwiches of hot baked ham. For dessert, ice cream with chocolate sauce. Coffee, of course.

Autumn Fruit Plate. On large plates arrange banana or guava sections, quartered persimmons (don't try to peel them), strips of ripe pear and peeled Persian melon, groups of yellow-green Thompson seedless or muscat and purple Isabella or Ribier grapes, around a mound of fruited cottage cheese—that is, plain cottage cheese mixed with coarsely chopped dates and nuts. Pomegranate seeds may be tucked in here and there for added color, or may replace some of the fruits mentioned.

Winter Salad Luncheon. On lettuce heap a mound of chicken salad with plenty of walnuts or almonds in it. Garnish the plate with spiced prunes and cheese-stuffed celery. (Blend one of the meat-flavored powders or extracts with cream cheese for this.) Serve with hot rolls and hot tea or coffee. For dessert, pumpkin or lemon chiffon pie.

Mission Inn Specials. Lunching in the umbrella-shaded patio of Mission Inn, at Riverside, we were served a positively spectacular-looking salad—a large ring mold of lemon gelatin with peeled whole persimmons glowing through it. Another time, sliced persimmons combined with balls of honeydew melon and cubes of fresh pineapple were served in hollowed-out pineapple halves. Both salads were fully as good as they were good-looking!

USING DRIED FRUITS IN SALADS

California dried prunes, figs, raisins, and other dried fruits are justly popular for use in salads. Their flavors and textures make a pleasant contrast to those of fresh and canned fruits, and their dark rich colors add accent to any combination.

Dried Prunes. Cook gently until tender—about 40 minutes—before using in salads. Since it is so easy to slip out their stones after cooking, they are usually pitted for salad use, and often stuffed with walnuts or cheese or candied citrus peel or candied ginger.

Dried Figs. Cover with hot water and let stand 10 to 20 minutes, or until soft but not completely cooked. They, too, may be slit or halved, and stuffed.

Seedless Raisins. Plump them by pouring boiling water over them and letting stand about 5 minutes; then drain, cool, and use in almost any fruit or fruit-and-cheese salad. (Especially good with grated raw carrot.)

Dates. California dates are really fresh fruit rather than dried, being kept in cold storage. They need no preparation except pitting, and stuffing if and as desired.

Dried Apricots, Peaches, and Pears. These fruits, simply steamed over boiling water until tender, or treated in the same way as figs, but not stuffed, are interesting when cut in strips with scissors, and used as garnishes for fruit salads. Or mix any one of these fruits, chopped, and a few chopped dates and nuts with cottage cheese, and serve on pineapple slices or other canned or fresh fruit.

WHAT ABOUT HEARTY SALADS?

To round out the buffet or barbecue menu, or to serve as the main course at a home lunch or supper, a hearty, filling salad is a great help. Strictly speaking, these should perhaps be included in the chapter of "Hearty Dishes with Little or No Meat," but since we call them salads, here they are.

LIMA BEAN SALAD

6 cups cooked dried lima
    beans (2 1/2 cups
    uncooked)
1 clove garlic
1/2 teaspoon salt
1/4 teaspoon black pepper

2 tablespoons sugar
1/4 cup finely minced red
    onion
1/4 cup chopped parsley
1/3 cup wine vinegar
2/3 cup bean liquid

Drain the hot beans, saving their liquid. (Beans should be tender but not mushy.) Crush garlic thoroughly with salt in a bowl, add remaining ingredients, mix well, add to beans, toss, and let stand several hours in refrigerator before serving. Serves 6 to 8.

CHOP SUEY SALAD

Combine diced roast turkey, chicken, veal or pork with celery, walnuts, chopped hard-cooked eggs, onion, and pickles; moisten well with mayonnaise thinned slightly with lemon juice or wine vinegar; chill. Serve in individual bowls, garnished with 2 crisp stalks of celery placed like chopsticks on top of each salad. Cubes of avocado tucked into the salad make it even better, and prettier, too.

CRUNCHY SALMON SALAD

2 cups (1 pound) canned red salmon
1/2 cup thinly sliced celery
2 tablespoons capers or diced sweet pickles
2 teaspoons grated onion

2 cups crushed potato chips (1 medium-sized bag)
3/4 cup mayonnaise blended with 2 tablespoons lemon juice

Have everything chilled. Flake salmon coarsely. Add other ingredients, toss quickly together, heap in a loaf-shaped or fish-shaped mound on a platter, garnish with lettuce and quartered tomatoes, and serve at once before potato chips soften. Serves 4 to 6. Canned tuna may be used in this same way.

FRESH SALMON SALAD

Simmer 4 medium-thick salmon steaks or fillets in salted water about 10 minutes, or until fish will flake easily. Cool in broth.

Remove skin and bones and break fish into not-too-small pieces.
Cover with a mixture of:

1 cup white table wine   1/2 teaspoon salt
3 tablespoons oil   1/4 teaspoon black pepper
2 tablespoons lemon juice

Let stand 2 or 3 hours, covered, in refrigerator. Serve cold on
lettuce with plenty of well-seasoned mayonnaise or Thousand
Island dressing. Serves 5 or 6.

PICKLED TUNA OR SALMON

Flake canned tuna or salmon in fairly large pieces. Sprinkle
generously with chopped green onion and coarse black pepper,
and add 1 or 2 chili tepines (little dry hot red peppers, the
kind you find in mixed pickling spices); then add wine vinegar almost to cover. Cover and keep in refrigerator 24 hours
or longer. Serve in small amounts as a cocktail, salad, or relish.

WALNUT-MACARONI SALAD

1 1/2 cups (6 ounces) un-   1/2 cup chopped onion
   cooked short-length   Salt and pepper
   macaroni   1/2 cup mayonnaise
2 cups thinly sliced celery   1 tablespoon prepared
3/4 cup coarsely chopped   mustard
   walnuts   2 tablespoons lemon juice
1/2 cup diced sweet pickle

Cook macaroni tender in plenty of salted boiling water; drain,
run cold water through it, drain again, and add remaining ingredients, mixing the mayonnaise with mustard and lemon
juice before adding. Chill and serve in lettuce-lined bowl,
garnished with pimiento strips and walnut halves. Serves 5
or 6.

PICNIC POTATO SALAD

6 potatoes, boiled in their
    jackets, or 4 cups diced
    cooked potatoes
1/2 teaspoon celery seed
1 teaspoon salt
Pepper
1/2 cup chopped onion
    (green, if possible, tops
    included)
1 1/2 cups thinly sliced
    celery

1/2 cup sweet pickle relish
3 or 4 hard-cooked eggs
Mayonnaise and cooked
    salad dressing, mixed
    half-and-half
2 to 3 teaspoons prepared
    mustard
2 to 4 tablespoons vinegar
    (preferably from sweet
    pickles)

Peel and dice cold potatoes, add seasonings, onion, relish, celery, and 2 or 3 diced hard-cooked eggs. Blend about 1 cup of the mixed salad dressings with mustard and sweet pickle vinegar to taste. Add to potatoes, toss lightly until everything is well coated. Taste, and add more seasonings if necessary. Cover and chill thoroughly. Add more dressing (salad should be quite moist) and toss again. Heap in a wooden salad bowl, tuck lettuce frills around edge, decorate top with quartered hard-cooked eggs, radish roses and strips of pickle or pimiento. Or pack firmly into a melon mold or a tube cake pan, chill, then turn out and "frost" with mayonnaise; decorate the plate with lettuce, tomato wedges, and olives or pickles. Serves 6 to 8 generously.

One friend who makes outstandingly good potato salad generously gives away these "secrets": have the cooked potatoes good and cold before you dice them; use about half as many hard-cooked eggs as potatoes; use plenty of sweet pickle relish, plenty of onion, plenty of salad dressing; use crisp shredded cabbage instead of celery.

CHOOSE THE RIGHT SALAD DRESSING

French dressing and similar light, thin dressings are always suitable for use on green salads and other simple salads that accompany the main course of a meal. Mayonnaise and other rich, thick dressings belong primarily with hearty luncheon or supper salads and dessert salads. The best rule is to consider the menu as a whole, and decide for yourself whether a certain dressing on a certain salad is a good choice or not so good.

SIMPLEST FRENCH DRESSING

Mix together 1/2 teaspoon each of salt, sugar, paprika, and dry mustard and a good dash of pepper. Stir in 1/2 cup of salad oil, then add 1 to 2 teaspoons grated onion, and 2 to 3 tablespoons vinegar (preferably wine vinegar). Beat or shake well before pouring over salad greens. Makes about 1/2 cup. A peeled clove of garlic may be dropped into the bottle or jar of dressing and let stand a few hours. Remove the garlic before serving.

TOMATO JUICE FRENCH DRESSING

Especially good with avocado is this thin, not-too-rich dressing.

1 tablespoon sugar
3/4 teaspoon salt
3/4 teaspoon dry mustard
3/4 teaspoon paprika
1/4 teaspoon coarse black pepper
2 teaspoons Worcestershire sauce

2 tablespoons grated onion
6 tablespoons salad oil
1/2 cup vinegar
1 cup tomato juice
1 peeled clove of garlic, if desired

Mix dry ingredients in a quart jar; add remaining ingredients, cover jar, and shake thoroughly. Dressing may be kept in refrigerator indefinitely, but clove of garlic should be removed after 24 hours or so. Makes 1 pint.

HAWAIIAN FRENCH DRESSING

1/4 cup sugar
1 1/2 tablespoons corn-
    starch
1 teaspoon salt
1 teaspoon paprika
1/2 teaspoon dry mustard

Dash of cayenne
1/2 cup syrup drained from
    canned pineapple
1/4 cup vinegar
1/2 cup salad oil

Mix dry ingredients in top of double boiler, stir in liquid ingredients, and cook over boiling water, beating slowly with rotary beater, until thickened and clear. Chill. Beat again before serving. Makes a little over 1 cup dressing. Delicious on fruits, cottage cheese, or greens. Keeps well.

SHERRY DRESSING

Especially good with chilled melon balls, alone or combined with pineapple, strawberries, or other fruits, is this oil-less dressing.

1/3 cup sugar
1/3 cup lemon juice

1/3 cup sherry
Dash of salt

Stir together until sugar is dissolved. Chill. Pass in a small pitcher or bowl, to be spooned over individual servings of the fruit on plates or in cocktail glasses. Serves 3 or 4. If you wish, add 1/4 cup finely chopped fresh mint leaves to the dressing before chilling it.

LORENZO SALAD DRESSING

1 teaspoon salt
1 teaspoon dry mustard
1 teaspoon paprika
2 teaspoons grated onion

1/3 cup vinegar
2/3 cup olive oil
1 cup chili sauce
1 cup chopped water cress

Mix dry seasonings with onion and vinegar, then add remaining ingredients and mix well. Chill. Makes about a pint. Pour required amount over shredded lettuce and water cress, toss until well mixed, and serve. Sliced fresh pears are a good addition to this salad bowl.

MAGEE FRENCH DRESSING

A friend from Sacramento worked out this dressing. Since she is allergic to all dairy products, she uses it on baked potatoes, hot cooked vegetables, and other foods on which one would ordinarily use butter. It tastes mighty good on them, too, as well as on greens, avocados, tomatoes, and other salad combinations. Make it at least a day ahead of using, by combining in a quart jar:

1 clove garlic, crushed
2 tablespoons grated onion
1 1/2 teaspoons salt
1 teaspoon paprika
Pepper
1/3 cup sugar

1/3 cup cider or wine
   vinegar
1 cup salad oil
1 cup catsup or tomato
   sauce

Cover jar, shake thoroughly, then let stand in refrigerator. Keeps well. If you use tomato sauce instead of catsup, you may like to add a touch of cinnamon and cloves to make up for the spiciness of catsup, or add your favorite seasoning salt to taste. Makes about 2 1/2 cups.

ITALIAN DRESSING

1/4 cup sugar
1 1/2 teaspoons salt
1 teaspoon mustard
1 teaspoon paprika
1 teaspoon Worcestershire
   sauce

1 cup catsup
1 cup salad oil
1/2 cup wine vinegar
1 clove garlic, sliced
1 medium onion, chopped

Measure ingredients into a quart jar, cover tightly, and shake until well mixed. Let stand half an hour or longer, then strain. Makes 2 1/2 cups dressing which keeps well in the refrigerator.

For an unusual, and unusually good, green salad, add 1 teaspoon grated orange peel and 2 tablespoons grated carrots to enough mixed greens to serve 4; moisten with Italian Dressing, toss, and serve.

PEANUT CREAM DRESSING

Blend equal parts of peanut butter, evaporated milk, and lemon juice smooth; add honey and salt to taste. Serve over orange and banana or apple salad.

ORANGE PECAN SALAD DRESSING

1/3 cup lemon juice	2 tablespoons sugar
1/2 cup orange juice	12 large pecan halves

Combine juices and sugar; stir until sugar is dissolved. Chop pecans very fine, then, adding a few drops of juice at a time, mash the chopped nuts thoroughly with the juice. Blend thoroughly. This will keep its fresh flavor several weeks when stored in the refrigerator. Pass in a bowl or sauceboat at table. Excellent with lettuce as well as with fruit salads.

AUTHORITATIVE SALAD DRESSING

1 cup mayonnaise	1/4 teaspoon pepper
2 tablespoons prepared mustard	1 to 3 cloves garlic, grated
4 tablespoons catsup	1 to 2 tablespoons chopped parsley
3 to 4 tablespoons vinegar	2 hard-cooked eggs, chopped fine
1/2 teaspoon salt	
1 teaspoon paprika	

Combine ingredients, mix well, and chill. Toss with salad greens, or use in or on fish or meat salads. Makes 2 cups.

ROQUEFORT CHEESE DRESSING

With a fork, mash about 1/3 cup of Roquefort or "blue" cheese in a bowl. Work in 1/3 cup salad oil. Add 3 to 5 tablespoons vinegar (preferably wine vinegar) a little at a time, beating until smooth. Best way to tell how much vinegar to use is to taste the mixture. Add salt, pepper, and celery salt to taste, also a dash of cayenne. Makes about 1 cup of dressing. Serves 6 to 8. Good on lettuce, or on mixed vegetable or fruit salads.

MUSTARD CREAM DRESSING

2 teaspoons prepared
    mustard
1/4 teaspoon coarse black
    pepper
1/2 teaspoon salt

2 tablespoons lemon juice
Dash of cayenne or
    Tabasco sauce
1 cup sweet or freshly
    soured cream

Mix ingredients in round bowl suitable for whipping cream, and chill thoroughly in the refrigerator. Whip until fairly thick, then mix well with 3 to 4 cups of shredded cabbage and celery. Add more seasonings if needed, and serve at once. Mighty good also used in potato salad.

FRENCH CREAMY DRESSING

Stir 2 or 3 tablespoons mayonnaise into 1/2 cup French dressing; blend well and toss with greens or other salad mixtures.

To Step Up Chicken Salad. Butter-toasted walnut kernels make an excellent addition to chicken or tuna salad. Melt 2 tablespoons butter in a small skillet, add a cup of walnuts, and heat, stirring, until crisp. Let cool, then break into coarse pieces and mix with the other ingredients.

BOHEMIAN CLUB FAVORITE

1 hard-cooked egg
1/4 teaspoon dry mustard
1/4 teaspoon coarse black
  pepper
1/2 teaspoon paprika
3/4 teaspoon salt
1/2 teaspoon Worcester-
  shire sauce
2 1/2 tablespoons tarragon
  vinegar

6 tablespoons oil
2 tablespoons chopped
  parsley
4 tablespoons finely
  chopped green onions
1 large head lettuce, or its
  equivalent in mixed
  salad greens

Rub a small bowl with a cut clove of garlic and in it rub the
egg yolk smooth with seasonings. Gradually stir in vinegar
and oil. Chop egg white fine and add with chopped parsley
and onion. Tear lettuce or mixed greens into bite-size pieces
into a large bowl rubbed with garlic. Shake or beat the dressing thoroughly, pour over greens, and toss until well mixed.
Serves 4.

"BIG" THOUSAND ISLAND DRESSING

1/2 cup mayonnaise
2 tablespoons chili sauce
  or catsup
6 or 8 stuffed olives,
  coarsely chopped
1/4 of a green pepper, cut
  into thin strips

2 green onions, sliced
1 teaspoon minced parsley
1 or 2 hard-cooked eggs,
  coarsely cut
1/4 cup heavy cream,
  whipped
Salt, pepper, and paprika

Combine ingredients, folding in whipped cream last. Season to
taste. Serve on lettuce or on vegetable or sea-food salads.
Makes about 1 1/2 cups. A few coarsely chopped walnuts or
other nuts add to the goodness of this dressing.

MAYONNAISE SPECIALS

Celery Root Dressing. Peel and slice hot, cooked celery root;
at once add a little lemon juice and mix well, to prevent

darkening. Cool, then force through ricer or food mill. Mix about half and half with mayonnaise, adding finely minced onion and salt and pepper to taste. Served on vegetable or sea-food salads, this is really wonderful.

Waldorf Mayonnaise. Mix diced unpeeled red apple, chopped celery and nuts, ad lib., with mayonnaise, and serve on gelatin fruit salads.

Cucumber Mayonnaise. Pare and discard seeds of a crisp cucumber; grate or chop it fine and mix with 1 cup mayonnaise. Season with salt, pepper and a dash of lemon juice, and a little minced onion, if you like. Serve with cold boiled fish.

Green Mayonnaise. Chop water cress fine, mix with an equal amount of mayonnaise, and serve with vegetable salads, or with fruit and cottage cheese.

Russian Dressing. Blend 1/2 cup chili sauce with 1/2 cup mayonnaise, and add 1 to 2 tablespoons each of finely chopped onion and green pepper, and a chopped pimiento. If you want to go really Russian, add also a tablespoon of caviar, a finely chopped hard-cooked egg, and lemon juice to taste.

GREEN GODDESS DRESSING

This is my version of one of the most famous and popular salads served at the Palace Hotel in San Francisco. It was named in honor of George Arliss when he was appearing in the play, *The Green Goddess.*

1 clove garlic, grated
3 tablespoons finely
    chopped anchovies, or
    anchovy paste
3 tablespoons finely
    chopped chives or
    green onions
1 tablespoon lemon juice
3 tablespoons tarragon wine
    vinegar

1/2 cup heavy cream
    (preferably soured)
1 cup mayonnaise
1/3 cup finely chopped
    parsley
Salt and coarse black
    pepper

Combine ingredients in order given. Chill, then pour liberally over coarsely torn mixed greens—romaine, chicory, and escarole, or head lettuce and leaf lettuce. Toss until well coated, adding more salt and pepper as needed. Serve in individual plates or bowls, to accompany the main course. You'll mop up your salad plate with French bread when you finish! Makes about a pint.

OLD-FASHIONED COOKED DRESSING

3/4 cup vinegar
1 tablespoon butter
1/3 to 1/2 cup sugar
2 tablespoons flour
3/4 teaspoon salt
1 teaspoon dry mustard

1 teaspoon celery seed, or
   1/2 teaspoon celery salt
1 whole egg, or 2 yolks,
   beaten with
1/4 cup water

Heat the vinegar and butter in upper part of double boiler. (If you have some spiced vinegar from pickled fruits or other sweet pickles, use it, and use the smaller amount of sugar.) Mix dry ingredients with egg and water, stir into hot vinegar, and cook over boiling water, stirring constantly until smoothly thickened. Store in covered jar in refrigerator until ready to use. Makes about 1 1/4 cups. Keeps well.

For potato salad, mix with mayonnaise, half and half.

For fruit salad, fold into whipped cream in proportions to suit taste.

For cabbage salad, thin with cream or fruit juice, to suit taste.

WOMAN'S CLUB FRUIT DRESSING

1/2 cup currant jelly
Grated peel and juice of 2
   lemons
3/4 cup sugar

2 eggs, separated
Dash of salt
Whipped cream

Put currant jelly to melt over hot water, stirring occasionally. Combine lemon peel and juice, 1/2 cup sugar, and beaten egg yolks in double boiler and cook over hot water, stirring, until thick. Beat egg whites with salt; when stiff, gradually beat in remaining 1/4 cup sugar. Fold into hot mixture with melted jelly and continue cooking about 15 minutes, stirring often. Cool and chill. At serving time, blend dressing with whipped cream to suit taste. Serve with fruit or fruit-and-cottage-cheese salads. Salted nuts go with this to perfection.

SALAD SERVING WAYS

California hostesses often depart from the conventional ways of serving salads. Some of the interesting ideas I've encountered are these: French endive served in those little oval ramekins, with an olive oil dressing greened with lots of finely minced parsley and other fresh herbs. . . . Fish or sea-food salad served in baking shells; also in crisp cabbage leaves which give the effect of shells. (In either case, use shredded lettuce under the shell to make it stay in position on the plate.) . . . "Hot broccoli salad": a platter heaped with freshly cooked, piping-hot, bright-green broccoli served instead of a salad as a separate first course; mustard mayonnaise and sharp French dressing passed separately.

VEGETABLE SALAD TRICKS THAT ARE DIFFERENT

Anchovy Radishes. Mash a small can of anchovies, oil and all. To this add 1 tablespoon salad oil, 3 tablespoons wine vinegar, and salt and coarse black pepper to taste. On each individual salad plate set a small glass of well-seasoned chilled tomato juice; beside it place a spoonful of the anchovy dip, with 5 or 6 crisp red radishes on their green stems at one side, and a few potato chips on the other side.

Butter-Bowl Salad. Into a salad bowl shred half a head of

lettuce; add 2 peeled and quartered tomatoes, membrane-free segments of 1 grapefruit, 1 peeled and cubed avocado. Sprinkle with salt, pepper, chopped chives or green onions, and 2 table-spoons lemon juice. Heat 1/3 cup butter until foamy and golden brown, pour immediately over salad, toss, and serve at once. Serves 4.

Artist's Special. To serve 3 or 4, allow a pint of cottage cheese. Mix it with 1/4 cup mayonnaise or other salad dress-ing, add 2 or 3 tablespoons of horseradish, 2 or 3 chopped green onions, and salt and pepper to taste. Add to a bowl of shredded lettuce or cabbage, mix, and serve as a lunch or sup-per main dish.

Club-House Fix-Your-Own. (An idea featured at the Wom-en's Club House on Treasure Island during the "Fair.") Heap one low bowl with chilled. peeled, whole red tomatoes—the small red-plum type—with their green stems left on. Heap a matching bowl with chilled, shelled hard-cooked eggs. Have another bowl or two filled with crisp mixed salad greens; close by have an assortment of salad dressings, so each guest may assemble his own salad.

Jack-O'-Lantern Salad. For a birthday party for little young-sters, cut jack-o'-lantern faces in half-shells of large oranges; fill shells with shredded carrot and raisin salad, then turn up-side down on lettuce and serve on the plate along with the creamed-tuna-on-rice or whatever simple food you are serving for the main course. Show them how to lift Mr. Jack-o'-Lan-tern off, to eat the salad. They'll love it!

Cabbage Nest. Spoon cabbage salad onto a big plate to form a nest-shaped ring. Fill center with deviled eggs put together in pairs. Garnish discreetly with parsley.

"14-Carrot" Gold Ring. Shape shredded raw carrots roughly into a ring on a big plate. Fill center with apple salad. Garnish with walnut halves.

Tomato Ways. Arrange sliced tomatoes overlapping in rows on platter. Sprinkle lightly with salt, coarse black pepper, and chopped chives or green onions, or a few chopped green herbs.

Serve with whipped cream, mayonnaise, and horseradish, blended together to taste just right.

FRUIT SALAD IDEAS

Good Luncheon Salad. Remove pits carefully from cooked prunes, and stuff each with a stuffed olive. On shredded lettuce on each salad plate group 5 or 6 membrane-free grapefruit segments and 3 stuffed prunes; center with a dot of mayonnaise or Thousand Island dressing and a stuffed olive.

Fruit Compote Salads. Arrange sliced pears and oranges and walnut-stuffed prunes in shallow bowls without lettuce, or on shredded lettuce on salad plates; serve with cooked salad dressing blended with whipped cream, and sprinkle grated orange peel on top. Or heap balls or cubes of honeydew melon and cantaloupe in peeled rings of melon on pretty plates; serve with dressing just described.

Cherrytime Salad. Combine pitted fresh or canned Bing or other dark red cherries with white Royal Annes. Heap on lettuce. Sprinkle with coarsely chopped nuts. Serve with lemon French dressing or with fluffy salad dressing. (See section of this chapter devoted to dressings.)

Stuffed Fig Salad. Split fresh, canned, or cooked figs, arrange on shredded lettuce, and heap each half with cottage cheese mixed with chopped nuts and chopped candied ginger. Serve with mayonnaise or fruit dressing.

Grapefruit Combinations. Arrange grapefruit segments around halves of peeled ripe persimmons on lettuce, or alternate the segments with avocado slices or sections of peeled ripe pear; serve with Roquefort cheese dressing.

Fruit Salad Appetizer. Dice 3 oranges, add 2 cups orange juice, and freeze in ice trays until fairly firm but slushy. Scoop out into crisp lettuce cups and serve—quick!—with French dressing.

Salad Dessert. Cut chilled cantaloupe or honeyball melons in halves, scoop out part of meat with measuring teaspoon or ball cutter. Put a scoop of lemon or orange sherbet in the shell and decorate with the melon balls and fresh strawberries, raspberries, youngberries, or white or Tokay grapes. Serve a half to each person.

Apple Salad Notes. Add pineapple cubes or orange sections to apple salad (helps to keep apples from darkening); when a zippy apple salad is wanted, add chopped dill pickle; when a fancy one is called for, heap apple mixture into a ring of jellied cranberry salad. That boiled dressing given earlier in this chapter is just right for apple salad combinations.

Fruit Salad in Melon Bowl. Cut a large watermelon lengthwise, dividing it so that one piece is larger than the other. Remove the red part from both pieces, cutting it in good-sized cubes or rounded chunks. In the big bowl thus made of the larger part, arrange a variety of fresh or canned fruits in large pieces (fresh peach sections add a delicious touch) mixed with the watermelon cubes or chunks. Serve on a leaf-decorated tray; pass French and fluffy fruit dressings separately.

WAYS WITH JELLIED SALADS

Reminder. Always add a dash of salt to gelatin mixtures. It not only brings out flavors, but helps set the gelatin.

Buffet Salad Plate. Mold jellied beet salad in individual molds. Arrange them on lettuce, around the edge of a big chop plate or platter, and heap center with shredded red and white cabbage dressed with French dressing. Serve mayonnaise separately.

Layered Fruit Salad. Arrange orange slices and banana slices in alternate layers in a loaf pan. Fill with enough orange gelatin to hold the fruit together. Chill until firm. Serve in slices with whipped cream dressing.

Jellied Persimmon Salad. Peel 3 large, very ripe persimmons and mash thoroughly. Add 1 cup drained crushed pineapple. To pineapple syrup add water to make 1 1/2 cups; heat and use to dissolve 1 package lemon-flavored gelatin. Cool until slightly thickened, then fold in fruit and dash of salt. Chill in mold. Serve on lettuce with garnish of grapefruit or pineapple. Pass fluffy fruit dressing.

When you make Jellied Grapefruit Salad. Add 1/2 teaspoon onion juice or scraped onion; it really does something to and for that salad.

GARNISHES FOR SALADS

To Garnish Vegetable Salads. Use radish roses; red or green pepper rings or strips; thin slices of unpeeled cucumber, or of peeled cucumbers that have been marked lengthwise with fork tines before slicing; slices, halves, or quarters of hard-cooked egg; lemon wedges.

To Garnish Fruit Salads. Pomegranate seeds; sprigs of mint; strawberries with stems left on; bunches of fresh cherries; dried figs, prunes, or dates stuffed with cream cheese blended with chopped candied ginger or nuts.

To Garnish Hearty Bowl Salads (such as potato and macaroni). Heap salad in lettuce-lined bowl; over top arrange rings of green and red pepper, or slices of hard-cooked eggs, or quarters of tomato.

To Garnish Relish Plates. String pitted ripe olives or green olives on edible "skewers"—thin sticks of celery and carrot. You can buy ripe olives already pitted. For the green olives, just "unstuff" stuffed ones.

SEA-FOOD, VEGETABLE AND FRUIT COCKTAILS

Interchangeable with first-course salads are the cocktails of sea food, vegetable, or fruit. Since their purpose is to sharpen, not dull, the appetite, the portions should be small (about 1/4 cup per person), and the sauce snappy. Combinations of raw and cooked foods are especially appealing. So are chilled juices of fruits, vegetables, or sea-food, or a mixture of the last two. Serve generous wedges of lemon with all first-course cocktails.

COCKTAIL SAUCE

3/4 cup catsup
1/4 cup chili sauce
2 tablespoons finely chopped
    celery
1 tablespoon finely chopped
    onion
1 to 2 tablespoons horse-
    radish

2 tablespoons lemon juice
    or tarragon wine vine-
    gar
1 teaspoon Worcestershire
    sauce
Dash of Tabasco sauce
Salt to taste

Combine and chill. Mix with sea food or coarsely chopped vegetables. (Diced cooked carrots, sliced celery, chopped cucumber and avocado make a good combination.) Makes 6 to 8 servings.

CREAMY COCKTAIL SAUCE

Richer than the sauce just given, but appropriate to use in some menus for diced avocado, or avocado-and-vegetable, or sea-food cocktails, is this smooth sauce.

1/4 cup chili sauce
1/4 cup catsup
1/4 cup mayonnaise
1 teaspoon Worcestershire
    or A-1 sauce
1 teaspoon horseradish

1 teaspoon grated onion
2 teaspoons tarragon wine
    vinegar
1/4 cup heavy cream,
    whipped

Combine ingredients, folding in whipped cream last. Pour over mixture in cocktail glasses, sprinkle with chopped parsley, and serve very cold. Serves 6 to 8.

Holiday Appetizer. Cut unpeeled ripe avocado into inch-thick rings and place on beds of water cress. Fill with highly seasoned tomato juice that has been frozen to a mush.

SHERRIED SHRIMP COCKTAIL

2 cups cooked or canned
   shrimp
1 cup diced celery
Salt and pepper
1 tablespoon chopped green
   pepper

1 teaspoon horseradish
1/2 cup catsup
1/4 cup chili sauce
1/4 cup vinegar
1/2 cup sherry

Remove black veins from shrimp; mix shrimp with celery, season to taste, and heap in 8 or 10 individual serving glasses. Mix remaining ingredients, pour over shrimp, chill, and serve. Flaked crab or mixed sea food may replace shrimp in this recipe.

ABALONE COCKTAIL

Use canned abalone, or simmer fresh abalone in small amount of lightly salted water until tender. Dice the meat. To abalone liquid add plenty of lemon juice. If you like things hot, add Tabasco sauce to taste, or a little of the juice from canned green chiles or Jalapeños peppers. Go easy!

TOMATO COCKTAIL SAUCE

6 large ripe tomatoes,
   peeled and chopped
3 green onions, chopped
   fine
Salt and black pepper

1/3 cup mayonnaise
3 tablespoons chopped
   parsley
3/4 teaspoon curry powder

Mix tomatoes, onions, and salt and pepper to taste; chill thoroughly in freezing tray of refrigerator but do not freeze. Serve in small bowls or little cups, topped with mayonnaise blended with parsley and curry.

FRUIT CUPS

Heap chilled and lightly sugared melon balls, diced fresh or canned fruits, or any fruit cocktail mixture, in sherbet glasses. Over the fruit pour (1) chilled orange, grapefruit, grape, or other fruit juice; or (2) chilled ginger ale; or (3) chilled white table wine (sauterne, Chablis, or the like), or sherry, or a little brandy. Sprinkle with finely chopped mint, or garnish with small sprigs of it, or tuck in a tiny lettuce leaf for its color and perkiness. Or top with a small ball or a spoonful of lemon, lime, pineapple, or orange sherbet. Serve as first course or as dessert. If red berries are to be used with wine or brandy, add them shortly before serving, or their bright colors are likely to fade.

FRUIT COCKTAIL IDEAS

Add pineapple cubes or grapefruit sections to glasses of chilled loganberry or grape juice, or to cranberry juice cocktail. . . . Add diced fresh pears to glasses of chilled orange juice. . . . Cut out cores and loosen sections of grapefruit halves; fill with sherry or rum, sprinkle with sugar if you like, and chill 2 to 3 hours. Serve for first or last course. . . . Mix diced fruits (canned or fresh) with seedless grapes, top with small scoops or spoonfuls of lemon, lime, pineapple, or orange ice. . . . Wash red apples, shred fairly fine, mix at once with an equal amount of orange juice; chill, and serve in cocktail glasses or sherbet cups for first course. . . . Dice ripe bananas, mix with cocktail sauce made with chili sauce base. Unbelievably good!

SERVING CUPS FOR COCKTAILS

It's smart to serve that vegetable or fish salad in a hollowed out tomato or green pepper or avocado shell. Fruit cocktails go equally well in orange, grapefruit, or avocado shells. I say "smart" for such service gives a bright touch to the first-course salad, and saves dish washing, too! One such set-up you'll like to serve is this: Select medium-sized well-ripened tomatoes of uniform size. Chill. Skin, cut a slice off top of each, and spoon out part of pulp. To this pulp add Tabasco sauce, lemon juice, and salt and pepper to make a highly seasoned cocktail sauce. In it, marinate small Olympia oysters, allowing 5 or 6 oysters to each serving. At serving time, put oysters into tomatoes, add sauce, and serve icy cold.

CRANBERRY JUICE COCKTAIL

2 cups cranberries   1/2 cup sugar
3 cups water   2 tablespoons lemon juice

Simmer cranberries with water, covered, about 5 minutes, until all have popped. Drain through cheesecloth. Add sugar to juice and stir until dissolved. Chill. At serving time, add lemon juice (also 1/2 cup to 1 cup orange, grapefruit, or pineapple juice, if you wish). Makes 6 to 8 small servings.

TOMATO JUICE COCKTAIL

To 5 cups tomato juice add 2 tablespoons each of sugar, lemon juice and grated onion; 1 tablespoon each of Worcestershire sauce and horseradish; add also, if in season, 1/3 cup grated raw cucumber. Salt to taste. Chill several hours in covered jars. Serve in small glasses, as an appetizer.

OTHER "LIQUID SALADS" OR COCKTAILS

Mix in any desired proportions, chill thoroughly, and serve in small glasses: pineapple and orange juice; pineapple and grapefruit juice; pineapple and loganberry juice; prune and orange juice; grapefruit and orange juice; sauerkraut and tomato juice; clam and tomato juice.

By-laws
for Soup Making and Serving

1. Make the soup balance with the rest of the meal. That is, serve a light, thin soup as an appetizer for a formal or informal dinner; serve a hearty, thick soup or chowder as a first course for a slim dinner, or as a main course dish (with salad and bread) for lunch or supper.

2. Always serve hot soups as hot as they can be; cold soups as cold as they can be.

3. Serve clear soups in bouillon cups for luncheon or informal dinners, in shallow soup plates for formal dinners; jellied bouillon in bouillon cups. Serve thin cream soups in cream soup dishes, large cups, or shallow soup plates for informal dinners. (Cream soups are not served at strictly formal dinners.) Serve thick cream soups or chowders in cream soup dishes, large cups, soup plates, or pottery bowls for lunch or supper main dish.

4. In planning how much soup to make, allow about ¾ cup of thin first-course soup per person; 1 to 2 cups, or more, of hearty main-course soup per person depending upon the person, the occasion, and the rest of the menu.

5. Dramatize your soup service. Give it an unusual garnish. Serve an out-of-the-ordinary accompaniment. Try a different way of serving. For example, at a barbecue pour hot bouillon from a big pottery pitcher into cups and let the people drink it while standing around waiting for the steaks.

6. When soup and salad make the main course for supper, have something substantial and outstanding for dessert—something as different as possible from soft hot soup. Apple pie and cheese are one good example.

Chapter 2

Soups and Chowders That Are Really Different

CASUAL living means easy, pleasant living. That includes the enjoyment of good food served with a certain style. No wonder, then, that soup so often appears as the main dish of a casual yet delightful lunch or supper. It may be a canned or dehydrated or frozen soup, or an old-fashioned home-made one. It may take minutes or hours to prepare. But whatever its type or nationality, it is certain to be good eating. For example:

GOLDEN WEST VEGETABLE SOUP

Don't be alarmed at the butter called for in this big recipe. The soup is worth it—and besides, no meat is used.

1/2 cup butter
2 large onions, chopped
1 large green pepper,
    chopped
6 stalks celery, chopped
2 or 3 sprigs parsley,
    chopped
2 large potatoes, diced

4 large tomatoes, chopped
4 to 6 cups boiling water
1 teaspoon meat-flavored
    extract
1 tablespoon catsup
1 tablespoon Worcester-
    shire sauce
Salt and pepper to taste

Melt butter in kettle, add chopped vegetables, cover, and simmer slowly 30 minutes, stirring occasionally. Add water and seasonings, cover, and simmer 1 hour longer. Makes about 2 quarts, or 6 to 8 large servings.

VITAMIN-SAVING TOMATO SOUP

This is old-fashioned unstrained tomato soup, made the new-fashioned way, without soda. Just stir *cold* canned tomatoes (or chopped fresh ones) into *cold* milk, heat slowly just to boiling, but do not let it boil, season with salt and pepper, serve. Use about one-third as much tomato as milk.

QUICK POTATO SOUP

Why anyone should start with cream sauce in making potato soup is a mystery, when it is easier, quicker, and better, I think, made this way. Exact amounts are unimportant.

To serve 2, pare and slice or dice 2 or 3 medium-sized potatoes, add a slice or 2 of onion, barely cover with boiling water, add a little salt, cover, and boil until potatoes are very tender. Don't drain. Mash part of the potatoes with a fork, in the liquid, for thickening. Add milk to make the amount of soup you want, season to taste, heat, and serve sprinkled with parsley. If you have a carrot on hand, dice it fine and cook with the potato, and you'll have a beautiful and good golden chowder.

LEEK AND POTATO CHOWDER

6 leeks
4 tablespoons butter or margarine
3 tablespoons chopped parsley
3 or 4 peeled potatoes, sliced
2 cans condensed consommé
1 can water
2 cups top milk
Celery salt and pepper
2 hard-cooked eggs, chopped fine
3 strips crisp bacon, chopped

Slice the leeks (including part of their green tops) thin, and cook in butter very slowly, covered, until tender. Add parsley, potatoes, consommé, and water, and cook until potatoes are soft. Mash them slightly in soup. Add milk, season to taste, heat just to boiling, and serve, sprinkling chopped egg and bacon over each serving. Makes about 1 1/2 quarts.

CRÈME VICHYSSOISE

Have you eaten frosty-cold Vichyssoise at the Ambassador in Los Angeles, or in some other excellent dining room? The soup looks and tastes as if it would be difficult to make, but really it is quite simple. One of its advantages is that you make it 24 hours before serving. You'll need:

6 leeks, or 8 or 10 green onions
1/4 cup butter
4 cups chicken broth or consommé
4 medium-sized potatoes, diced
1 cup heavy cream
Salt and white pepper
Chopped chives

Mince the leeks or green onions fine and simmer in the butter about 5 minutes—don't let them brown. Add the chicken broth (diluted canned consommé can be used very nicely), heat to boiling, add potatoes and cook until they are very tender. Force potatoes, leeks, and all through a wire strainer, add cream, season to taste, and reheat. (This seems to help to keep the potatoes from sinking later.) Pour into small serving cups and chill thoroughly. Serve icy cold, with a good sprinkling of chopped chives on each serving. A little grated raw carrot is pretty with the chives, too, if you feel inspired to add it. Serves 6.

FRENCH ONION SOUP

6 medium-sized onions,
   sliced
4 tablespoons butter (or
   butter and oil)
1/4 teaspoon pepper
5 cups bouillon, or water
   and 6 bouillon cubes

1/2 cup sherry, if desired
1 teaspoon Worcestershire
   sauce
Salt to taste
6 slices French bread,
   toasted and buttered
Grated Parmesan cheese

Cook onions gently in butter until golden, sprinkling with pepper while cooking. Add bouillon, sherry, Worcestershire, and salt if necessary, cover, and simmer 20 to 30 minutes, until onions are very tender. Pour into a large casserole, float the slices of toast on top, sprinkle them thickly with cheese, and bake in the top of a hot oven (450° F.) about 10 minutes, until cheese browns slightly. Serves 4 to 6.

CREAMY ONION SOUP, BAKED

Though you start this soup about 5 hours before it is to be served, you need pay very little attention to it while it bakes.

1/2 cup (1 cube) butter
5 medium-sized onions,
   sliced
1 can (10 1/2 ounces) condensed consommé

1 quart rich milk
Salt and pepper
Grated Parmesan cheese

Melt butter in a big (2-quart) deep pottery or oven-glass casserole, add sliced onions, cover, and bake in a very slow oven (275° F.) for 3 to 3 1/2 hours. Add consommé, cover, and bake

1 hour. Add milk, cover, and bake 30 minutes. Taste before adding salt and pepper. Serve with grated Parmesan cheese and hot or toasted French bread. Makes about 2 quarts, usually serves 4 to 6.

This, like most other soup recipes, is quite flexible. You can use a cup of strong bouillon (made with 2 or 3 cubes) in place of the consommé. And you can cheat a little on the butter if you wish and still have wonderfully good soup.

SPLIT PEA SOUP WITH HERBS

Travelers along El Camino Real (The King's Highway, or Highway 101) like to stop at Buellton to enjoy this famous soup. Its originators, the Andersens, generously pass along the recipe, so you can duplicate it wherever you are. Surprisingly, it calls for no meat.

2 quarts soft water	1/4 teaspoon dried thyme
2 cups green split peas	1/4 teaspoon dried
1 or 2 outer stalks of celery,	marjoram
chopped	Dash of cayenne
1 or 2 carrots, chopped	1 bay leaf
1 onion, chopped	Salt and pepper to taste

Combine ingredients, rubbing the thyme and marjoram between the hands before adding to the soup. Cover, and boil for 20 minutes. Then reduce heat and simmer about 30 minutes longer, until very soft. Force through colander or coarse wire strainer. Serve in bowls, with rye bread and butter and a green salad. Makes 8 servings.

LIMA BEAN CHOWDER

Wash 1 1/2 cups dried limas, and soak 4 to 6 hours, or overnight, in 1 quart cold water. Put on to cook in same water, skimming when the beans reach boiling. Add a small onion, diced, and 1 1/2 teaspoons salt, cover, and cook gently about an hour, until tender and broken. Mash thoroughly, or force through a coarse wire strainer. Add 2 to 3 cups rich milk, heat just to boiling, and serve sprinkled with minced parsley or chopped crisp bacon. Serves 4 to 6.

SIMPLEST CLAM CHOWDER

2 slices salt pork or bacon
1 pint milk
1 onion, chopped
3 or 4 potatoes, pared and
    diced

Water
1 to 2 cups fresh clams, or
    a 7-ounce can of
    minced clams
Salt and pepper

In a heavy kettle fry the salt pork or bacon. Put milk to heat in double boiler. When pork is browned, remove and set aside. To the fat in the kettle add the onion and let simmer until soft, then dice the pork or bacon and add with the diced potatoes, barely cover with water, cover kettle, and cook until tender. If you are using fresh clams, grind them coarsely in the food chopper, or cut them up with scissors; whether fresh or canned, add the clams with their liquor to the milk and let heat. When the potatoes are tender, add the hot milk and clams, season to taste, heat just to boiling and serve. Serves 2 or 3.

PISMO BEACH CLAM CHOWDER

If you like your clam chowder made with tomato, you'll like this one especially well.

1/4 cup diced salt pork or
    bacon
1/4 cup chopped onion
2 cans (10 1/2-ounce size)
    condensed consommé
2 cups diced raw potatoes
1/2 cup diced raw celery

1 1/2 cup canned tomatoes
1 1/2 cups chopped clams
    and their liquid (fresh
    or canned)
Salt and pepper
1/2 teaspoon minced fresh
    thyme

Heat the salt pork or bacon gently in a large kettle, add onion, and cook a few minutes until soft. Add consommé and heat to boiling. Add potatoes and celery, cover, and cook 15 to 20 minutes, until vegetables are tender. Add remaining ingredients, season to taste, and simmer 15 minutes longer. Serve with minced parsley sprinkled over the chowder. Makes about 2 quarts.

QUICK CRAB CHOWDER

1 can (10 1/2 ounces) condensed tomato soup
1 can (10 1/2 ounces) condensed pea soup
1 can (10 1/2 ounces)
bouillon or consommé
1 can water

1 cup flaked crab meat
1 cup finely diced raw
celery
1 cup thin cream
Salt and pepper
Sherry

Combine the soups and heat to boiling. Add crab, celery, cream, and salt and pepper to taste, heat again just to boiling. (No, the celery is not supposed to be cooked—just heated through. It should still be crunchy.) Serve in hot bowls, adding 1 to 2 tablespoons sherry to each serving if you wish. Serves 8 to 10 as a first-course soup; 4 or 5 as a hearty main-course soup.

MUSSEL CHOWDER

3 pounds mussels in their
shells
2 cups water
1/2 cup (1 cube) butter
2 medium-sized onions,
chopped
1 tablespoon chopped
parsley
1 green pepper, chopped
2 medium-sized potatoes,
chopped

1 teaspoon meat-flavored
extract
1 tablespoon Worcester-
shire sauce
1 tablespoon chili sauce
1 quart milk
3 slices bacon, fried crisp
and chopped

Wash mussels, add water, cover and steam 10 to 15 minutes, until shells open. Remove from shells, trim off and discard their horny "beards" and set mussels aside. Strain liquid through cheesecloth. Melt butter, add vegetables, meat extract, Worcestershire and chili sauce, and 1 cup mussel liquid. Cover, and simmer 1 hour. Add milk and mussels and heat gently. Serve sprinkled with chopped bacon. Makes 1 1/2 to 2 quarts, serving 4 to 6 as a main dish. (Serve remaining mussel broth later, hot or chilled.)

BASIC SOUP STOCK

Most soups are greatly improved when at least some meat stock or chicken broth is used in their preparation. Vegetable soups particularly need this added richness of flavor; otherwise they are likely to "taste pretty strong of water," as the Richardson family expresses it.

To make really good soup stock, you need a good big soup bone. For beef stock (bouillon) a meaty beef shank weighing 3 to 4 pounds, sawed into short lengths, is a good choice. If you want the stock brown, cut off part of the meat and brown it in the soup kettle in a little marrow from the bones. For white stock, use a knuckle of veal instead of beef shank, and don't brown it. For consommé, use half beef, half veal, plus uncooked chicken necks and wing tips, or bones from cooked chicken. Chicken broth, of course, is usually arrived at by cooking a fowl for salad or other purpose.

Whatever the kind of meat, cover the bones with cold water (about 3 quarts). Slice and add a small onion, a carrot, and an outer stalk of celery or a handful of leafy tops. Add also a few sprigs of parsley, 1 or 2 bay leaves, 8 or 10 peppercorns, and 2 teaspoons salt. Heat to boiling, skim, then turn heat low and simmer, loosely covered, for 3 hours or longer. Strain, let cool uncovered. (Soup, like beans, is likely to sour if the cover is left on while cooling.) Chill, then lift off the cake of hard fat. This makes about 2 quarts of broth, which you can season further and serve hot as plain broth, or use as the foundation of vegetable soup, minestrone, onion soup, or other soup.

MINESTRONE

There are surely as many versions of this full-meal-in-a-soup-plate as there are Italian restaurants that make it superlatively. Points which all minestrones have in common are: lots of vegetables, long cooking, complete satisfaction! Minestrone may be made with or without meat, with or without dried beans, with or without spaghetti or other paste. Don't hesitate to adapt this recipe to suit your own convictions in these respects. And you don't need to be too exact about the amount of vegetable of each variety. The proportions I use are these:

1/2 cup dried lima or kidney beans, or 1 cup fresh shell beans
2 quarts soup stock
1/2 cup diced salt pork, bacon, or smoked ham with fat
1 small clove garlic, minced
1/2 cup minced onion or leeks
1/4 cup minced parsley
1/2 cup diced celery
1 cup diced carrots
1 potato, diced
1 cup chopped fresh or solid-pack canned tomatoes

1 teaspoon minced basilica, if available
2 cups shredded cabbage (curly green savoy if possible)
1 cup diced turnips or other vegetables (green beans, sliced zucchini, shredded spinach, etc.) if desired
1/2 cup vermicelli, spaghetti, or other Italian paste
Salt and pepper to taste
Grated Parmesan cheese

If dried beans are used, soak them several hours in water to cover, drain, then add to boiling soup stock and simmer about an hour before adding any other ingredients. Fry diced salt pork, bacon, or ham with minced garlic until lightly browned, add onion, parsley, celery, carrots and potato, and cook 10 minutes, stirring, then add to soup stock. (If fresh shelled beans are used, add them at this time.) Add tomatoes and basilica and simmer about 30 minutes. Add cabbage, other vegetables, and vermicelli, season well, and cook 30 minutes. Serve in big soup plates or bowls, with grated cheese to sprinkle over it at table, and hot French bread to eat with it. Makes about 2 1/2 quarts, or about 10 servings. (Note that I do not say, "Serves 10." Better count on its serving 5 or 6.) It's even better when reheated.

To be just right, minestrone should always have a touch of fresh basilica added at the last. Traditional way is to chop basilica leaves very fine, mix with a few drops of olive oil, shape into balls about the size of small marbles, and drop one into each soup plate of minestrone.

If you haven't meat stock on hand, you can use 2 quarts water with 8 bouillon cubes dissolved in it, or with meat-flavored extract added to make a rich broth. Or begin by simmering a large cracked soup bone in 2 1/2 quarts water for 2 hours or longer, cooking the soaked dried beans along with it. Remove bone and proceed as directed.

RUSSIAN HILL BORSCH

There are even more ways of making Borsch than there are ways of spelling it! Most Russian cook books seem to spell it as given above, but their ways of making it are anything but simple. Here on Russian Hill we like to make this fairly quick and easy version:

1 quart basic soup stock or
    bouillon
1 medium onion, chopped
3 medium-sized raw beets,
    peeled and chopped or
    shredded

1 cup shredded cabbage
1 tablespoon lemon juice
    or vinegar
Salt
Freshly ground black
    pepper

If you haven't basic soup stock in the refrigerator and don't wish to make it, use 2 cans (10 1/2-ounce size) of condensed bouillon or consommé plus water to make a quart, or dissolve bouillon cubes or meat-flavored extract in a quart of hot water to make a strong broth. Heat it to boiling, add the chopped onion and beets, cover, and simmer 20 to 30 minutes, until beets are tender. Add cabbage and cook 10 minutes. Add lemon juice or vinegar, salt (very little, if any) and pepper to taste, reheat and serve with a spoonful of sour cream floating on top. Serves 3 or 4. Good with Russian rye bread, cheese, dill pickles, and potato chips.

Some good cooks like to add another grated raw beet just before the final reheating, to intensify the deep red of this savory soup. Some substitute chopped canned beets (about 2 cups) for the fresh ones, and use the beet juice to dilute the condensed bouillon. Some cook a small amount of diced raw potato, turnip, and carrot with the beets and onion. It is still Borsch!

CALIFORNIA CHICKEN GUMBO

This recipe, which came from the kitchens of the University of California Hospital in San Francisco, makes one of the best soups ever.

4 tablespoons butter
1/4 cup diced smoked ham
1/2 cup diced celery
1 green pepper, chopped
1 large onion, chopped
1/4 cup raw rice
1 tablespoon flour
2 quarts strong chicken
    broth
1 cup sliced okra (fresh or
    canned)

1 cup chopped fresh or
    solid-pack canned
    tomatoes
2 tablespoons chopped
    pimiento
1/2 cup coarsely diced
    cooked or canned
    chicken

Fry the ham, celery, green pepper, and onion in the butter until soft. Add rice and cook, stirring, 5 minutes. Add flour, blend, then stir in broth and heat. Add remaining ingredients, season to taste with salt and pepper, cover, and let simmer 40 minutes. Makes about 2 1/2 quarts, or 10 generous servings.

TRICKS WITH CANNED SOUPS

Make jellied consommé by leaving cans of consommé in refrigerator for several hours. Open can, pour out the jellied contents, stir lightly with a fork to break it up and make it sparkle, and serve in cups with lemon wedges.

MEAL-IN-A-BOWL SOUP

Make this soup early in the day, so it can stand long enough to let the flavors blend.

2 quarts rich beef broth
3 or 4 small carrots, sliced
1 package frozen green beans, or 1/2 pound fresh ones, cut short
2 or 3 ears of corn, cut in 1 1/2-inch lengths
2 or 3 zucchini, cut in chunks
Salt and pepper

To make the stock, buy 2 pounds beef shank and a good marrow bone. Simmer about 3 hours in 3 quarts water with 2 cloves garlic, a sliced onion, and 6 or 8 peppercorns. When meat is tender, take it out and strain the broth. There should be about 2 quarts left.

Heat broth to boiling. Add carrots and beans; cook 20 minutes. Add cut-up corn and zucchini; cook 10 minutes. Cut meat from bones, dice and add. Taste; add salt and pepper as needed. Remove kettle of soup from heat, tilt lid, and let stand 2 or 3 hours or longer. Reheat and serve. Makes about 3 quarts, or enough for 4 to 6 as the main dish. (You pick up the corn in your fingers, of course.) With garlic French bread, crisp celery, and perhaps lemon meringue pie—wonderful!

Try various combinations: a can of cream of pea soup with a can of cream of tomato; a can of clam chowder with a can of vegetable soup; and so on. Makes for variety, new taste touches.

Make Clamato Broth by combining 1 cup clam juice with 3 cups tomato juice, and heat, seasoning with butter and minced parsley.

Add dry sherry or white table wine to taste to any clear light soup or fish chowder, just before serving. Add sherry to black bean soup. Add red or white table wine to tomato broth. About 1 to 2 tablespoons wine to a serving of soup is usually right.

Add extra tomato to clam chowder, if you're a family of tomato eaters. Changes the flavor decidedly.

Add herbs or herb seasonings ad lib. to any canned cream soups; add extra vegetables, too.

Look over the soup shelf at your grocer's. Try some of the kinds you haven't been in the habit of using. You're almost sure to discover what will eventually become a great family favorite.

SOUP GARNISHES AND ADDITIONS

Grated Parmesan cheese. Good sprinkled over almost any soup. A "must add" for onion soup or minestrone.

Chopped parsley, chives, or green onion tops. Especially right floating on "white soups" such as cream of celery.

Thin slices of stuffed olives or finely diced carrots. Try one or the other on split pea soup—it needs a bright bit of color. A dash of paprika helps here, too.

Thin slices of pickle on soups that lack decided flavor. Or on vegetable soups where the texture of chopped vegetables becomes monotonous.

Finely chopped salted peanuts or almonds, or crumbled cooked bacon on cream soups or meatless soups.

Small cubes or balls of avocado, dropped into the cups of hot bouillon.

Marble-sized meat balls that have been dipped in flour, then fried in hot fat, added hot to hot soup. A Mexican touch.

Thin slices of lemon. A "must" for bean soups, especially black bean soup. (Some of those canned black bean soups are wonderful!) Mix chopped hard-cooked egg with a little chopped parsley and sprinkle over the soup along with the lemon.

Puffs of salted whipped cream on top of cream of tomato. Good on many others, too.

Custard cubes. Combine beaten egg with chicken broth or bouillon (3 tablespoons broth for each egg used), season with paprika, salt, pepper, and herb seasoning. Bake slowly in a thin layer in greased shallow pan until firm. Cool. Cut into tiny cubes, drop into hot clear soups at last minute.

Croutons, of course. Cut bread into small cubes and brown crisply with a little melted butter or margarine in the oven or in a skillet. For garlic croutons, so good with peasant soups, drop a peeled clove of garlic in with the butter and bread cubes.

TO GO WITH SOUP

Crackers, crisp, of course; preferably heated and possibly dusted with paprika. Cheesed crackers, too.

Crisp toast, cut in strips or triangles, lightly buttered, and sprinkled with seasoning salt.

Tortilla chips; toasted French bread; bread sticks. Potato chips, too.

Squares of onion fuggaccio, heated. This flat bread can usually be bought in Italian bakeries.

Toasted minced ham sandwiches; especially good with bean soup for lunch.

Griddle-toasted cheese sandwiches; just right with potato soup or clam chowder.

Crisp pickles, slightly on the sour side. Remember, soup tastes better when there's something crunchy and tasty to go with it—something to hold in the hand!

OUR FAVORITE SOUP AND SALAD SUPPER
Special Black Bean Soup
Grilled Cheese Sandwiches   Celery   Carrots   Pickles
Baked Apples   Crisp Oatmeal Cookies
Coffee

SPECIAL BLACK BEAN SOUP

2 cans condensed black
   bean soup
1 can condensed bouillon
1/2 cup water
1/2 cup Burgundy wine

Small piece of bay leaf
3/4 cup diced garlic salami
Salt and coarse black pepper to taste

Empty the black bean soup into a saucepan, and gradually stir in the bouillon, otherwise it's inclined to be lumpy. Add rest of ingredients and heat thoroughly, stirring. Serve with paper-thin slices of lemon floating on top—also a little finely chopped hard-cooked egg, if convenient. Makes about 5 cups, or enough for 3 or 4 big servings. Good with toast or crackers.

By-laws of Fish Cookery

1. When you buy fish, fresh or frozen, allow 1/2 to 3/4 pound of whole fish or about 1/3 pound of fish fillets or steaks per person.

2. Use fresh fish and sea food while they are really fresh—within 24 hours after purchase. Remember, there is practically no odor to really fresh fish. Cook frozen fish while it is still frozen, or when only partly thawed. Never refreeze it after thawing has begun.

3. Wash fish quickly—don't let it soak in water. Wipe dry with paper towels before frying or broiling.

4. Loosely wrap or cover uncooked or cooked fish or other sea food, and keep in the coldest part of refrigerator. Treat canned fish, after opening, the same way. Kippered and smoked or jerked fish are only lightly cured, and so should be kept in the refrigerator and used within a relatively short time. Dried salt fish need not be refrigerated.

5. Cook fish and other sea food only a short time. Overcooking spoils its flavor and texture. Test with a fork— when flesh separates easily from the bone, the fish is done.

6. If you're catching your own, be sure to observe strictly all local fish and game regulations. Not only do these laws protect the next generations of sea food, but they protect you, too. For example, quarantines are placed on mussels and clams during summer months because at this season those bivalves feed on a poisonous type of algae and are extremely dangerous to eat. Take no chances.

Chapter 3

Recipes Featuring
Western Fish and Sea Food

WHICH way is best to cook a certain variety of fish depends chiefly on whether that particular fish is fat and oily, or lean and dry. *Fat fish* are usually best broiled or baked. Salmon, mackerel, halibut, rock cod and other rock fishes; tuna, albacore, barracuda, and yellowtail; pilchard and other herrings—all these are classed as fat fish. *Lean fish* are usually best fried, or "poached" in water or other liquid and served with a sauce. Sole, flounder, and other flat fish; hake, trout and steelhead (ocean-going trout); swordfish—these are classed as lean fish. *Shellfish* of all kinds are rich in flavor, and are usually prepared in some way which does not obscure their own character, but which does stretch a small amount of sea food to make a reasonable number of servings.

The following general directions apply to fresh and quick-frozen fish, from either salt water or fresh water. Ways of preparing shellfish and canned fish and sea food are given later in this chapter.

TO BROIL FISH

Split medium-sized fish lengthwise and remove bones; wipe dry with paper towels. Leave small fish whole; leave heads and tails on or remove as you like, but do not cut off the fins. Cut large fish crosswise into sections (steaks), or lengthwise into boneless strips (fillets). Whatever the size or shape, brush both sides with oil or melted butter or margarine, sprinkle generously with salt and pepper, also with paprika if you like. Lay fish on kitchen foil in a pan. (I don't use the rack—it's too hard to remove the fish afterward without breaking.) Broil until lightly browned. It is not necessary to turn fish while broiling, no matter how thick or thin the pieces. If thin, the fish will be completely cooked by the time it is browned on top. If thick, simply reduce the heat and place the pan farther down until the fish flakes easily when tested with a fork. Baste frequently with the juices in the pan, to keep the surface of the fish from drying out. Serve at once, sprinkled with chopped parsley. And don't forget big wedges of lemon; lemon slices are inadequate for squeezing over fish.

TO BAKE FISH WHOLE

Leave head and tail on, or cut them off if you prefer. Sprinkle fish inside and out with salt and pepper, fill cavity with well-seasoned poultry stuffing (oyster stuffing is especially good), then sew or skewer and lace the opening shut. (See chapter on Poultry for recipes for stuffing.) Lay fish in a greased shallow baking pan; brush with oil, bacon drippings, butter, or margarine, or lay slices of bacon over it. Bake uncovered in a hot oven (450° F.) until tender and well browned, allowing about 10 minutes to the pound.

While baking, you may like to baste the fish with white

table wine mixed with finely chopped parsley and green onions, or you may decide to pour over and around it a well-
seasoned tomato sauce, or chili sauce slightly diluted with
water.

A sheet of heavy kitchen foil under the fish will help
later in transferring it from baking pan to platter. A bed of
finely chopped celery, parsley, and onion under the fish adds
flavor and helps to prevent sticking. If fish is lean, gash the
skin in a few places to keep it from bursting.

TO BAKE FISH SLICES OR FILLETS

Place the slices in a greased shallow pan, brush with oil, melted
butter or bacon drippings, sprinkle with salt, pepper, and
paprika, and lay a thin slice or 2 of lemon on each piece. Bake
uncovered in a hot oven (450° F.) until well browned and tender. Sprinkle with chopped parsley. Serve with lemon wedges.

TO OVEN-FRY FISH

This is one of my favorite ways of doing fish, because there's
little or no odor while cooking. Dip fillets of sole or other fish
in well-salted milk (1 tablespoon salt to 1 cup milk), then roll
the pieces in sifted fine dry bread crumbs. Place in oiled shallow pan, sprinkle lightly with oil or melted butter, and bake
in a very hot oven (500° F.) for 10 to 15 minutes, until well
browned and done. Serve at once with tartare sauce. Creamed
potatoes with chopped green onions added go well with these.

TO PAN-FRY FISH

Sprinkle fish fillets or slices, or small whole fish, with salt and
pepper, then roll them in flour or in flour and corn meal mixed
half and half. Brown in a small amount of hot bacon drippings or oil or shortening in a skillet, turning once. Serve immediately, with lemon and parsley.

CAMPFIRE FISH

Every western fisherman has his own way of cooking fresh-caught fish over the open fire. Some experts insist on rolling the fish in corn meal—stone-ground meal if it is to be had. One fisherman recommends dipping the trout into undiluted evaporated milk, then rolling them in a half-and-half mixture of prepared pancake flour and fine bread crumbs, with plenty of salt and pepper added. Fry in the bacon skillet, and serve with crisp bacon. Still another sportsman insists that trout be grilled, not fried. He wraps each fish in strips of bacon, fastens ends with skewers, then grills them over a bed of coals. When the bacon is done on both sides, the fish is ready to eat.

Whatever the rites of the individual fisherman, these are basic rules: Wipe fish dry after cleaning and washing quickly. When frying, have pan good and hot before putting in fish. Use just enough bacon fat to keep fish from sticking. Turn carefully. If possible, baste with lemon juice and butter as the trout cooks.

TO POACH OR "BOIL" FISH

Actually, fish should never be boiled, but simmered gently until tender. For a large chunk, easiest way to manage is to tie it loosely in cheesecloth and lower into a kettle of boiling water. For slices or fillets, it is more convenient to poach them as you do eggs, in a skillet, in enough water barely to cover the fish. In either case, do add seasonings to the water. Salt, a piece of bay leaf, a few peppercorns, and 2 or 3 tablespoons of vinegar or lemon juice are needed, or 1/2 cup of white table wine. (The use of one of these last 3 ingredients helps to keep the fish firm, and white fish white.)

In addition, a few tablespoons each of chopped onion, carrot, and celery, a few sprigs of parsley, and a tiny sprig of fresh thyme or basilica will help. Fish slices will be tender in about 10 minutes. For a larger piece, allow 10 to 12 minutes per pound. Lift out, and serve at once with any of the fish sauces given later in this chapter. Or chill and serve with mayonnaise or tartare sauce.

SANDDABS MEUNIERE

Sanddabs, those delicate little flat fish of the flounder family, are a San Francisco institution. They are at their best, we think, when prepared simply, as follows:

Skin the fish, sprinkle with salt and pepper, roll in flour, and brown quickly in butter. Take up on a hot platter. Add a little more butter to the skillet and heat to a golden brown. At once add (for 4 to 6 servings) the juice of 1 lemon and 1 tablespoon chopped parsley, pour over the fish, and serve. Sole and flounder may be done the same way.

WHEN CLEANING FISH

When cleaning fish, dip your damp fingers in dry salt and you can get a firmer grip on the slippery fish. . . . To get rid of fishy odors from your hands and cooking utensils, wash them thoroughly in hot strong salt water—about a tablespoon of salt to a pint of water—before using soap.

BAKED ROCK COD STEAKS

Sprinkle 4 steaks of rock cod with salt and pepper, and place in an oiled shallow pan. On each steak put a thin slice of lemon and a slice of onion. Drizzle 3 or 4 tablespoons oil over the fish. Season 3 cups puréed solid-pack tomatoes with salt, pepper, and (if available) 1 teaspoon dried oregano rubbed between the hands. Pour this sauce over and around the fish (it should be about half the depth of the slices), and bake uncovered in a fairly hot oven (375° F.) from 45 to 60 minutes, until well done. Serves 4. Striped bass is excellent prepared this same way. Oregano (pronounced o-REGG-an-o) is a Mexican herb, much used in Mexico and California for flavoring sauces, fish and meats.

BAKED BASS

Wash and dry a medium-sized bass or similar fish. Rub outside with oil, sprinkle inside and out with salt and pepper. Into the cavity put 2 or 3 chopped green onions (or 1 small dry onion, chopped) mixed with a chopped stalk of celery, add a few dots of butter or margarine. Place in a baking pan, pour 1 cup white table wine around it, and bake in a moderate oven (350° F.) 30 to 40 minutes, or until done, basting occasionally with the wine.

BAKED SEA BASS WITH MUSHROOM SAUCE

Have sea bass sliced 2 to 3 inches thick. Place in a shallow pan, pour any good commercial or homemade mushroom spaghetti sauce over the fish and bake 20 to 30 minutes in a moderate oven (350° F.). Superb!

HALIBUT ROAST

Have a thick slice—about 2 1/2 to 3 pounds—cut from a fairly large halibut. Wipe with paper towel, spread cut surface generously with soft butter, and place in a shallow baking dish. Sprinkle with salt and pepper, and bake in a moderately hot oven (375° F.) for 30 minutes. Pour 1 cup sweet or sour cream over and around the fish, and continue baking about 30 minutes longer, basting occasionally with the cream. Serve in its baking dish, with green rice and scalloped tomatoes. Serves 6. If you like, add a generous sprinkling of chopped green onions with the cream.

BETTER BROILED SALMON STEAKS

Sprinkle salmon steaks generously with lemon juice. (They may be kept overnight or longer in the refrigerator without odor when coated with lemon juice and covered with waxed paper. Or simply cover with dry white table wine in a shallow dish and cover with waxed paper or foil.)

Flour one side only. Place this floured side down in pre-heated broiler pan (not on the rack) containing enough oil to cover bottom of pan. Turn *immediately*. Sprinkle with salt and paprika and broil until well browned without further turning, or about 12 minutes. Serve with lemon halves, and tartare sauce if wished.

SOLE SPECIAL

Pound 4 large fillets of sole lightly with the blade of a knife. Beat 2 eggs, season well with salt and pepper, put in the fillets and let stand 2 hours, turning occasionally. When ready to cook, roll them in fine bread crumbs and brown quickly in olive oil. Pour a little of this oil into another pan, add a table-spoon of butter and 1/4 cup white table wine, season with salt and pepper, put in the browned fish, sprinkle with chopped parsley, and let cook 5 minutes. Serve sprinkled with grated Parmesan cheese and garnished with wedges of lemon.

FILLET OF SOLE IN WHITE WINE SAUCE

Salt and pepper 4 large or 8 medium-sized fillets of sole or flounder. In a large skillet combine the following:

2 tablespoons butter	2 or 3 fresh or canned
1 teaspoon chopped green	mushrooms, chopped
onion	1 stalk celery, chopped
1 teaspoon chopped parsley	

Let cook a few minutes, then add:

1 bay leaf	1/2 cup canned consommé
1 cup white table wine	

Heat to boiling; then lay the fish fillets in this hot liquid, a few at a time, and let simmer 5 to 10 minutes, until cooked-looking and barely tender. (It is easy to lift off the dark skin from the fillets at this stage.) Using a pancake turner, carefully remove fillets to large ovenproof platter or shallow baking dish. Boil down the liquid in which fish was cooked until about 3/4 cup remains. Add 2 tablespoons cream, and strain liquid over fish on platter. Sprinkle thickly with grated Parmesan cheese, and bake in a hot (450° F.) oven about 10 minutes, until lightly browned and bubbling. Serve in the baking dish, garnished with parsley and lemon. Serves 3 or 4. This is a good "company" main dish (especially for Fridays), for you can fix it in advance to go into the oven, and let it stand in the refrigerator until time to bake—that is, about 15 minutes before serving time.

SOLE MIO

6 large fillets of sole
1 tablespoon vinegar
1 cup cream
1 package (3-ounce) pimiento cheese
1 tablespoon cornstarch
1/4 cup milk
50 Olympia oysters, or 1/2 pint small oysters

1/3 pound, or 1 cup, cooked shrimp
1 tablespoon Worcestershire sauce
2 tablespoons lemon juice
Salt and pepper to taste

Wipe the fillets of sole with a damp cloth, place in a frying pan, cover with cold water, add a tablespoon of vinegar, and heat just to boiling. Lift out and arrange on a buttered ovenproof platter. Sprinkle lightly with salt and pepper. Put the cream and pimiento cheese to heat in a double boiler, and add the liquor drained from the oysters. When hot, blend the cornstarch with the cold milk, stir in, and cook until smoothly thickened. Add the oysters, shrimp, and seasonings, and pour over the sole on the platter. Bake in a fairly hot oven (400° F.) just until it bubbles and browns, and crisps slightly along the edges. Serve at once. Serves 6.

HALIBUT CREOLE

Simmer a 3/4-pound slice of halibut in a small amount of salted water with herbs to suit your taste. (See "To Poach or Boil Fish.") When tender, drain and flake the fish, and combine lightly with the following mixture heated in a double boiler:

2 cans condensed chicken gumbo soup	**1 teaspoon curry powder**
1/2 cup cream or undiluted evaporated milk	**Salt and pepper to taste**

Heat thoroughly and serve on steamed rice. Serves 4.

BAKED CANNED SALMON

Drain a 1-pound can of red salmon, break into large pieces, and remove large bones and pieces of skin. Place in baking dish, sprinkle with a tablespoon of lemon juice and a tablespoon of minced onion, and pour 1/2 cup sweet or freshly soured cream over all. Sprinkle lightly with salt, pepper and minced parsley if desired, and dot with butter. Bake uncovered in a hot oven (400° F.) 20 minutes. Serves 4.

Another way. Put hot cooked macaroni or spaghetti in bottom of 1 large or 4 individual casseroles. Top with flaked salmon, then add 1 tablespoon lemon juice and 1/3 cup cream or 4 tablespoons melted butter, and bake as described. Garnish with green pepper rings.

SALMON CHEESE LOAF

2 cups (1 pound) canned salmon	**1/2 teaspoon salt**
	1/2 teaspoon celery salt
1 cup grated American cheese	**Pepper to taste**
	1 egg, beaten
1 cup cracker or bread crumbs	**2/3 cup milk**
	2 tablespoons melted butter
1 tablespoon grated onion	

Flake salmon, add other ingredients, and mix well. Shape by hand into a fish-shaped loaf or oval ring in a greased shallow baking pan, dot with butter and bake in a moderate oven (350° F.) about 30 minutes, until lightly browned. Serve hot, with Olive-Almond Sauce (see Sauces at end of this chapter), and parsley-buttered potatoes. Serves 6.

If you prefer, shape this mixture into 6 croquette-shaped mounds and bake on a greased pan 20 to 25 minutes; or shape into patties and brown in butter or bacon drippings in a skillet.

SALMON DUFF

4 cups (2 pounds) canned salmon
1 tablespoon lemon juice
3 eggs, beaten
1 medium-sized package of potato chips, crushed
Salt and pepper to taste

Flake salmon coarsely, removing pieces of skin and large bones. Add other ingredients and mix well. Pack firmly into a well-buttered ring mold or ovenproof baking bowl, and bake in a hot oven (450° F.) about 20 minutes. Turn out onto a hot platter and arrange hot cooked vegetables around it. Pass highly seasoned cream sauce with the loaf if you wish. Serves 6.

BAKED TUNA PUFF

Actually this is just extra-good creamed tuna with a puffy omelet topping, baked briefly; but it looks and tastes much more dramatic than that sounds!

1 can (7 ounces) tuna
1 can (10 1/2 ounces) condensed cream of mushroom soup
A little chopped green pepper or pimiento, if wished
1/2 cup top milk
4 eggs, separated
Salt and pepper
Tiny bit of soda (about 1/8 teaspoon)

Combine tuna, soup, green pepper or pimiento, and milk in a shallow baking dish (about 1 1/2-quart size) and put into moderate oven (375° F.) to heat while you mix the puffy topping: Add a dash of salt to egg whites and beat stiff. Then, using the same beater, beat yolks light; stir in pepper and soda, then fold yolks into the beaten whites. Pour over the hot tuna, and bake at 375° F. for 20 to 25 minutes. Serve at once in its baking dish. Serves 3 or 4.

ABOUT CALIFORNIA SHELLFISH

In shellfish, as in some other features—temperatures, altitudes, and redwood trees, for example—California rather runs to extremes. Shrimp found in our markets vary from tiny local ones to out-sized, shipped-in prawns. Oysters, too, vary from the infinitesimal 100-or-more-to-the-pint Olympias, through the medium-sized locally cultivated "Eastern" variety, to the huge dozen-to-the-pint kind that are produced along the northwest Pacific coast. Clams run from little butter clams through 1 1/2-pound Pismo clams, to giant 6-pound geoducks (pronounced "gooeyducks"). And then we have that peculiar one-shelled mollusk, the abalone (ab-a-lo-ny) which is neither fish nor clam, but something of both! Our crabs are oversize, our lobsters, which are really crayfish, are undersize by eastern standards.

As with all fish, freshness is the first and most important attribute of shellfish. If bought or caught in the shell, they must give evidence of being alive. Oysters, clams and mussels show this quickly by their shells' being tightly closed, or closing quickly when they are touched. Crabs and lobsters should be either squirmingly alive, or freshly cooked. The shells of crabs and lobsters and the flesh of shrimp change from gray to rosy red when cooked.

If you live in an apartment, you'll probably prefer to buy your crabs precooked at the wharf or market. (Your neighbors are almost certain to prefer that you do so!) If you have an outdoor grill, however, you may like to cook your own and serve a feast of hot or cold cracked crab with mayonnaise and lemon wedges, potato chips, hot French bread, and cold beer. Here's how you proceed.

To Cook Live Crab

Have ready a large kettle of boiling water, with 2 tablespoons salt added for each quart of water. (If you are cooking crabs at the beach, use sea water.) Drop in the live crab, head first. (Kitchen tongs are a help here.) Cover, and boil hard for 5 minutes, then let simmer 10 to 20 minutes longer, depending on its size.

If the crab is to be eaten cold, plunge it immediately into cold water for a few minutes, then drain again, and set it out on a rack, so it will cool quickly.

To serve cracked crab, break the shells and big claws with a wooden mallet or a hammer. Don't remove the meat from the claws—let everyone do his own. Do break off the tail or apron, pull the upper and lower shells of the body apart, and remove and discard the digestive tract. (In the crab markets on Fisherman's Wharf, the pieces of crab are held under running cold water just long enough to wash away this spongy material.) Heap the big pieces in the center of a platter, arrange the brilliant claws around them and serve, with stacks of paper napkins handy. If you are preparing crab meat to use in salads or other dishes, be sure to pick it over carefully, removing all bits of hard shell and cartilage.

To Cook Live Lobster

Follow directions for cooking crab, allowing 20 minutes for boiling. After boiling, split lobster in half and remove digestive tract and liver, then broil or prepare otherwise. If you are serving it in the shell, as Lobster Thermidor, rub a little oil over the shell to brighten it.

To Cook Shrimp or Prawns

Raw shrimp or prawns, gray or pale green in color, are usually sold frozen. Wash them quickly. To cook plain, simply drop into boiling salted water as for crabs, and boil 12 to 15 minutes, or until bright pink in color. Drain, run cold water over them for a few minutes, drain again, and spread out so they will cool quickly.

Some good California cooks, following the example of their Gulf Coast neighbors, like to add a couple of pods of cayenne pepper to water in which shrimp are boiled. Some throw in black pepper, celery salt, bay leaf, garlic, onion, sliced lemon —any or all of these, in generous measure—along with the cayenne.

After cooling, peel off the shells and with the tip of a knife remove the black vein that runs down the back. Serve as is, or fry, or use in any one of dozens of other ways.

To Cook Clams

Scrub the tightly closed shells of the clams with a stiff brush under running cold water. To steam them, put them into a large kettle with about 1/4 cup boiling water for 2 quarts of clams. Cover tightly, and steam 8 to 12 minutes. Heap the opened clams in soup dishes, allowing 15 to 20 small clams per person. Strain the hot broth in the kettle through doubled cheesecloth and serve a small cup of it to each person with a thin slice of lemon floating in it. Provide also small dishes of melted butter into which to dip clams.

To Open Clams. Easiest way is to pour boiling water over clams and let them stand a few minutes, or spread in a pan and place in a moderate oven for several minutes, until shells open. Remove from shells at once and chill in refrigerator until used. If clams are large, cut off their siphons or necks, peel off skin, and grind tough muscle; also remove and discard the dark portions.

To Cook Mussels

Mussels, which are between clams and oysters in flavor and appearance, may be used in practically any recipe calling for either of these shellfish. Steam as you do clams. Cut off and discard the tough "beard" before serving or using.

To Cook Oysters

Oysters should be cooked as briefly as possible, just enough to heat them through and make them plump. Allow not more than 5 to 10 minutes for broiling or frying. For oyster stew, drop oysters into hot milk and heat just until they plump up and their edges frill. In scallops, stuffings, and made dishes, the most important rule is to be sure to use enough oysters!

FRIED ABALONE

Pound slices of abalone vigorously with a wooden mallet or the flat side of a cleaver. (Otherwise it is extremely tough.) Wipe it dry, sprinkle with salt and pepper, dip into well-beaten egg and then into fine cracker crumbs. Brown quickly —but don't let it scorch—in plenty of olive oil or butter and shortening mixed, allowing not more than 1 1/2 to 2 minutes to each side. Serve immediately. No sauce is needed.

SEA FOOD NEWBURGH

To 1/2 pound flaked crab meat, or lobster, or shrimp (with black veins removed), or a mixture of all these, add about 1/3 cup dry sherry and let stand 2 hours in the refrigerator. Make a rich cream sauce, using 4 tablespoons butter, 3 table-spoons flour, 2 cups top milk. When smooth, add the sherried crab (or combination), season to taste with salt, pepper, cayenne, and a dash of nutmeg, and heat thoroughly. Shortly before serving, carefully stir in 2 beaten egg yolks and cook, stirring, 1 minute. For a grand finale, add 2 tablespoons brandy, and serve piping-hot on toast or crisp crackers, or in pastry shells. Serves 3 or 4. Baked potatoes are fine with this.

CURRIED SEA FOOD

2 tablespoons butter
2 green onions, chopped, or
    1 tablespoon minced
    onion
1 small clove garlic, peeled
1 1/2 tablespoons flour
2 teaspoons curry powder
1/2 cup canned consommé
    (or chicken broth, or
    milk)

1 cup cream
1 tablespoon chutney
2 tablespoons lemon juice
Meat of 1 large crab, or
    about 1 cup fresh
    cooked or canned crab
    meat
1 1/2 cups fresh cooked or
    canned shrimps

In top part of double boiler, over direct heat, cook onion and garlic gently in butter 5 minutes. (Don't let them brown.) Discard garlic, and to onion and butter add flour and curry powder, blend smooth, then stir in consommé and cream. Cook, stirring, until smoothly thickened. Cool, and let stand in refrigerator until shortly before serving. (This improves curry, always.) Then add chutney, lemon juice, crab, and shrimp (remove their black veins first). Heat thoroughly over hot water, season to taste and serve with plain hot cooked rice and the usual accompaniments. These include chutney, always, plus any or all of the following: chopped walnuts, peanuts, or almonds; crumbled crisp bacon; finely chopped hard-cooked egg; shredded fresh coconut; tiny pickled onions; chopped preserved ginger. Serves 4 or 5.

Lobster may be used in place of the crab or shrimp; or oysters may replace one of these. The exact amount of each kind of sea food is not vital. In general, you'll want 2 to 2 1/2 cups of sea food altogether for this quantity of sauce.

FRIED SHRIMP

Wash raw jumbo shrimp and peel off thin shells. Remove dark veins. Rinse, then sprinkle with salt, roll in flour, dip in well-beaten egg, roll in fine bread crumbs, and brown in butter in a skillet. Cooked or canned shrimp may be used in the same way; so may the meat of big crab legs.

FRIED SHRIMP ANOTHER WAY

Either shucked raw prawns or large shrimp, or cooked or canned shrimp may be dipped in an egg batter and browned in fairly deep hot shortening or oil. For raw shrimp a thin batter works best. For cooked or canned shrimp you may prefer a fluffy batter, and so I am giving recipes for both kinds. Be sure to sprinkle shucked raw shrimp with salt and let stand while you are mixing the batter; canned ones are salty enough without this treatment.

THIN EGG BATTER

1/2 cup flour	1 egg, slightly beaten
1/2 teaspoon salt	1/4 cup milk
1/4 teaspoon baking powder	1/4 cup water

Sift flour with salt and baking powder. Combine egg, milk and water, and stir into dry ingredients, mixing only until smooth. Drop in a few of the shrimp at a time, lift out with a fork (so that they won't be too heavily coated with batter), and place in hot fat (390° F. to 400° F.), and cook until well browned all over, turning as necessary. Large raw shrimp will require several minutes' cooking to turn them "shrimp pink" inside and golden brown outside. Cooked or canned ones will take only a few minutes. This amount of batter will be enough for serving 4 or more.

FLUFFY EGG BATTER

This is an excellent batter for dipping cooked shrimp, crab legs, boned chicken, and other cooked foods before frying.

3 tablespoons flour   1/4 cup milk
1/2 teaspoon salt   2 eggs, separated
Dash of pepper

Sift flour, salt and pepper. Stir in milk and slightly beaten egg yolks. Just before using, fold in stiffly beaten whites. Dip shrimp in this fluffy batter and fry in deep or semi-deep fat (390° F.) until golden brown; turn immediately after dropping into hot fat.

SHRIMP SAVORY

5 tablespoons butter or   2 1/2 cups milk
   margarine   1/2 cup mayonnaise
5 tablespoons flour   2 cups cooked shrimp
1 teaspoon salt   3 tablespoons lemon juice
1/4 teaspoon pepper

Melt butter, stir in flour, salt and pepper, then add milk and cook, stirring, until smoothly thickened. Add mayonnaise and shrimp and heat thoroughly. Last, stir in lemon juice and serve on toast. Serves 6.

SHRIMP AND RICE, LAGUNA BEACH STYLE

A big kettle of this savory mixture, plus a bowl salad of mixed greens with chunks of avocado, and a basket of piping-hot cheese-toasted rolls, make a dinner that any kitchen artist may proudly serve. Start it about an hour before time to serve.

2 cups uncooked rice
1/2 cup oil or bacon drippings
1 or 2 cloves garlic, minced
1 large onion, sliced
1 green pepper, cut in strips
1 cup diced raw or solid-pack canned tomatoes
1 cup diced smoked ham
2 cups cooked or canned shrimp
2 cups water
1 tiny sprig fresh thyme or marjoram
1 small piece of bay leaf
Salt, pepper, and cayenne

Wash rice if necessary; drain and dry well between towels. Brown dry rice slowly in oil or drippings, stirring frequently. Add garlic and onion, and cook a few minutes longer, then add remaining ingredients, with seasonings to taste. Cover and let simmer slowly about 45 minutes. If it should cook dry, add a little hot water. For extra color and goodness, add 1 to 2 cups cooked peas just before serving. Serves 6.

CRAB CURRY CREOLE

2 cans (10 1/2-ounce size) condensed chicken gumbo soup
1/2 cup cream or undiluted evaporated milk
3/4 to 1 teaspoon curry powder
1/2 pound crab meat
Salt and pepper to taste

Heat soup with cream and curry in double boiler. Flake crab in good-sized pieces, combine lightly with soup, and heat thoroughly. Season, and serve over hot steamed rice. Walnuts or peanuts, crisp bacon, and green onions, chopped and served separately in little dishes to sprinkle over curry, make an excellent addition. Canned crab, tuna, or chicken may be used instead of fresh crab. Serves 4.

CREAMED CRAB IN AVOCADO

This is a mighty rich dish, so keep everything else in the menu as simple as you can.

1/2 pound coarsely flaked crab meat, or a 7-ounce can
1 1/4 cups milk
3 tablespoons flour
4 tablespoons soft butter
Salt, pepper, and cayenne
2 large or 3 medium-sized ripe avocados
3 tablespoons grated American cheese

Heat crab meat and milk in double boiler. Blend flour and butter smooth, drop into the hot milk, and stir quickly and thoroughly until smooth and thick. Season to taste. Cut avocados in halves, peel, and place in shallow pan. Heap with the thick creamed crab and sprinkle with grated cheese. Pour hot water around avocados, just enough to cover the bottom of the pan, and bake, uncovered, in a moderate oven (375° F.) 15 minutes. (Some cooks prefer to cover the pan so the avocados will keep their color better.) Serves 4 or 6. With a fruity gelatin salad and hot toast strips this makes a good "fancy" lunch.

DEVILED CRAB

2 tablespoons butter
1 tablespoon minced onion
2 tablespoons flour
1/2 teaspoon dry mustard
1/2 teaspoon salt
1 cup rich milk
1 teaspoon Worcestershire sauce
2 teaspoons lemon juice
Dash of Tabasco sauce
1/2 cup thinly sliced celery
2 pimientos, chopped
1 tablespoon chopped parsley
2 hard-cooked eggs, chopped fine
2 cups flaked crab meat
1/2 cup buttered crumbs

Melt butter, add onion, and cook a minute. Stir in flour, mustard, and salt, and cook until it froths, then add milk and cook, stirring, until thick and smooth. Add remaining ingredients, except crumbs. Put into buttered crab shells, ramekins, or baking shells. Cover with buttered crumbs, and bake in a fairly hot oven (400° F.) about 20 minutes, until browned. Serves 6.

DEVILED CRAB DIFFERENT

3 tablespoons butter or oil
1 large onion, minced
1 clove garlic, minced
1 green pepper, minced
2 tablespoons minced
    parsley
1 teaspoon sugar
1/2 teaspoon salt
Pepper to taste

1 teaspoon Worcestershire
    sauce
1 tablespoon chili sauce
1 tablespoon catsup
2 to 3 cups flaked crab meat
3 tablespoons cracker
    crumbs
1 cup grated cheese

Cook minced onion, garlic, green pepper, and parsley gently
in butter or oil until soft. Add sugar, salt, pepper, Worcestershire sauce, chili sauce, and catsup and let simmer 15 minutes. Add flaked crab meat, plus just enough cracker crumbs
to hold mixture together. Let stand an hour or so, then put
into crab shells or baking shells, sprinkle with cheese, and
bake in a moderate oven (350° F.) 15 to 20 minutes. Serves
6 or 7.

CALIFORNIA CRAB CAKES

2 cups flaked crab meat
1 tablespoon lemon juice
1 tablespoon minced parsley

1 egg, beaten
1 cup bread crumbs
Salt and pepper

Mix ingredients thoroughly. If mixture is too dry to hold
together, add a little water to moisten the crumbs. Shape into
small patties, dip in fine corn meal or crumbs, and brown
lightly in a mixture of butter and oil. Serves 3.

SAN FRANCISCO OYSTER LOAF

Cut top off a round or oval loaf of French milk bread, hollow
out loaf, then brush loaf and lid lightly inside and out with
melted butter. Bake in a hot oven (400° F.) until very hot
and slightly toasted.

While loaf is heating, fix regulation Fried Oysters. (Roll medium-sized fresh or thawed frozen oysters in fine dry bread crumbs, then in slightly beaten egg, then again in crumbs, and brown in a small amount of butter in a skillet, seasoning as they cook. Do not overcook them. They need only 4 or 5 minutes for browning.) Fill the hot loaf with hot oysters, pour a little butter over them, cover with thin slices of lemon, put on lid, and loaf is ready to eat. It may be kept hot in a slow oven until wanted, or it may be wrapped in waxed paper and newspapers and taken along for picnic eating. Some people like to mix lemon juice and catsup, and pour it over the fried oysters in the loaf. Others—of which I am one—prefer to have catsup or chili sauce served separately. Pickles are an important adjunct to oyster loaf.

Long French rolls, hard or soft, may be made into individual oyster loaves, following the procedure given above. Serve very hot.

How to eat an oyster loaf is something of a problem to the uninitiated. Usually, someone "carves" the loaf into chunks and serves it. Then everyone follows his own idea, using his fingers for the toasty bread, his fork for the oysters.

HANGTOWN FRY

From Placerville—the Hangtown of Gold Rush days—has been handed down this way of fixing oysters with eggs. To serve 2, allow

6 to 8 medium-sized oysters   2 tablespoons milk
3 or 4 eggs   Salt and pepper

Season the drained oysters, roll them in flour, then in beaten egg (the flour keeps the egg from sliding off), then in fine dry bread crumbs, and brown on one side in a little hot butter in a skillet. Turn them. Add eggs beaten with milk and seasonings, and cook as you do a French omelet, lifting cooked portion of egg to let uncooked part run down onto hot skillet.

When lightly browned underneath, fold and serve with bacon or sausages.

OYSTERS WITH MACARONI

1 cup broken uncooked
   macaroni
2 cups small oysters,
   uncooked
Salt, pepper, and paprika
1 cup grated American
   cheese

2 tablespoons butter or
   margarine
1/2 cup fluffy bread crumbs,
   buttered

Cook macaroni tender in boiling salted water, drain, rinse with hot water, drain again. In a buttered baking dish put half the macaroni, then half the oysters. Sprinkle with salt, pepper, paprika, and about a third of the grated cheese, dot with butter. Repeat. Top with buttered crumbs mixed with remaining cheese. Bake in a fairly hot oven (400° F.) about 20 minutes, until well heated through and lightly browned. Serves 4 to 6. Other sea food may be substituted or mixed with oysters in this dish.

CLAMS FRICASSEE

This is an especially good way with fresh clams. The recipe is Belgian in origin.

2 slices bacon
1 tablespoon bacon
   drippings
1 tablespoon butter
1 clove garlic, minced
2 tablespoons minced onion
2 tablespoons minced
   parsley
1 tablespoon minced celery

3 tablespoons flour
1 1/2 cups hot clam juice,
   or clam juice and milk
1 teaspoon Worcestershire
   sauce
1 teaspoon lemon juice
Salt, pepper, and paprika
1 to 1 1/2 cups small clams

Cook bacon lightly in a heavy saucepan, then cut it up and set aside. Pour off all but 1 tablespoon of the drippings from the pan, then add butter, garlic, onion, parsley, and celery, and cook, stirring, until golden brown. Stir in flour, then add clam juice, and cook, stirring, until thickened. Add seasonings, clams, and bacon. Cook a few minutes, and serve with toast or hard rolls. Serves 4 or 5. Coarsely chopped large clams may be used instead of whole small clams in this recipe.

MINCED CLAM AND EGGPLANT CASSEROLE

"There are some who think they don't like eggplant, others who think they don't like clams—but whatever they think, I find that they like this combination," says the Hollywood radio home economist who gave me this recipe.

1 large or 2 small eggplants
1 small onion, minced
3 tablespoons butter or
   margarine

2 cans (7-ounce size)
   minced clams
2 cups bread crumbs
Salt and pepper

Wash and dice unpeeled eggplant, cover with boiling salted water, and boil 10 minutes, then drain. Fry minced onion in butter until soft. Drain clams, saving liquid, mix cooked onion with clams. Now in a greased casserole put a thin layer of crumbs, then a layer of eggplant, then one of clams and onion, seasoning each layer lightly with salt and pepper. Repeat, finishing with a layer of crumbs. Over all pour the clam liquid. Dot top with a little more butter or margarine, and bake in a moderate oven (350° F.) about 45 minutes. Serves 6.

CIOPPINO

This dish (pronounced cho-PEEN-o), a specialty of San Francisco's Fisherman's Wharf, is rather messy to eat, but worth it! It is a sort of fish stew in tomato sauce. Whether it is made with crab only, or with a variety of fish and sea food, depends on where your recipe came from. Here are two general favorites.

CRAB CIOPPINO

Use uncooked crabs if possible. Have crabs split and cleaned and the claws cracked, but do not remove meat from shells. Put into a big kettle. For 3 crabs (serving 4 to 6), add 1 cup each chopped onion and parsley, and almost a cup of olive oil. Sprinkle lightly with salt and pepper. Cover, and simmer 20 to 30 minutes. Heat 3 cups canned tomatoes with 1 small can (1 cup) tomato sauce and plenty of chopped basilica. Pour boiling hot over the crab, cover, and simmer 30 minutes longer. Serve heaped in soup plates, with plenty of sauce. Bibs and paper napkins are necessities with this dish. Garlic French bread, hot, and green salad are just right with it.

MIXED CIOPPINO

To serve 4 to 6, allow 1 or 2 large crabs (preferably uncooked) prepared as directed above; 1 pound large shrimp or prawns (preferably uncooked); and 2 pounds uncooked sea bass, rock cod, or halibut, cut in about 2-inch pieces. About 1 pound well-washed clams in their shells may be tucked in, too. Put all these into a big kettle with onion, parsley and oil as for Crab Cioppino, sprinkle with salt and pepper, and simmer about 30 minutes. Add boiling tomato with basilica, simmer 30 minutes longer, and serve as you do Crab Cioppino.

SAUCES FOR FISH OR SEA FOOD

Quick Tartare Sauce: Chop 6 green olives, 1 sweet pickle, 1 tablespoon capers, 1 tablespoon parsley, 1 tablespoon chives. Mix with 1 cup mayonnaise, and add lemon juice and Tabasco sauce to taste. Serve with cold boiled fish, crab, or lobster.

Mustard Butter Sauce: Heat 4 tablespoons butter until golden brown, stir in 1 teaspoon prepared mustard and 1 teaspoon lemon juice, and serve with boiled or broiled fish.

Catsup and Mustard Sauce for Fried Prawns: Mix stout dry

mustard to a paste with cold water, let stand about 20 minutes. Pour catsup into a little bowl, then pour mustard into center of catsup. Don't stir. Serve with hot fried prawns or large shrimp. A favorite at best Chinese restaurants.

Parsley Butter: Blend 1 tablespoon soft butter with 1/2 teaspoon salt, 1/2 teaspoon paprika, 1/2 tablespoon lemon juice, 2 tablespoons minced parsley. Spread or dot over broiled or fried fish.

Mornay Sauce, Simplified: Mix 1/3 cup grated Swiss or Parmesan cheese with 1 cup hot well-seasoned cream sauce. Stir in a beaten egg yolk and a tablespoon of butter, then fold in 1/2 cup whipped cream. Spread over poached fish on flameproof platter, and brown lightly under broiler.

OLIVE-ALMOND SAUCE FOR FISH LOAF

This sauce really does something for salmon or tuna fish loaf.

1 cup hot medium-thick white sauce

1/4 cup stuffed olives, sliced

1/4 cup toasted almonds, cut in strips

1/4 cup mayonnaise

Add olives and almonds to white sauce and heat in double boiler. Just before serving, stir in mayonnaise, add more seasonings if needed, and serve at once. Serves 3 or 4.

WHITE WINE SAUCE

2 tablespoons butter or margarine

2 tablespoons flour

1 cup consommé, or 1 cup water and 2 bouillon cubes

2 cloves

1 small bay leaf

1/2 cup white table wine (sauterne, Chablis or Riesling)

Salt and pepper

1/4 cup finely diced celery, or 1 tablespoon minced parsley

Melt butter, stir in flour, add consommé and cook, stirring, until smooth. Add cloves and bay leaf and simmer 10 minutes. Strain, add wine, season to taste, and reheat. Just before serving, stir in raw celery or parsley. (Don't cook it; it should stay crisp and crunchy.) Serves 4. Especially good with baked, broiled, or boiled fish.

EGG SAUCE FOR BOILED FISH

3/4 cup mayonnaise	Salt and pepper to taste
1/2 cup milk	Dash of cayenne
2 hard-cooked eggs, chopped	

Stir milk into mayonnaise in top of cold double boiler. When smoothly mixed, add eggs and seasonings, place over hot water, and cook 5 minutes, stirring constantly. Serve with boiled fish or any fish loaf. Serves 4 or 5. A chopped sweet pickle or a little sweet pickle relish may be added to this sauce to its advantage.

BE SURE TO TRY THESE

Midnight Supper Dish: Fry chopped onion in butter, add drained canned mussels mixed with slightly beaten eggs, scramble, and serve immediately, with bacon.

Hearty Casserole: Half-fill a casserole with steamed rice. Over it pour a can of mussels and their liquid. Over all, pour well-seasoned tomato sauce (made with plenty of onion, parsley, and celery), dot with butter, cover, and bake until bubbly. A little grated cheese scattered over all before baking makes it even better.

Toast Topper: Cook short-length asparagus, drain if necessary, then add coarsely flaked crab, and mix with hot cream sauce. Heat thoroughly, and serve on toast.

Sunday Supper Oysters: Fry a tablespoon of minced onion

in a tablespoon of butter a few minutes, add a can of condensed tomato soup. When boiling, add 1/2 pint oysters (picked over first, of course, to remove bits of shell). Season well, and heat until their edges curl. Serve at once on hot buttered toast. Serves 3.

Quick Creamed Tuna: Heat 1 can condensed cream of mushroom soup with 1/4 cup top milk in double boiler. Add coarsely flaked tuna (a 7-ounce can), or 1 to 1 1/2 cups canned shrimp (black veins removed). Heat thoroughly, and serve on waffles or toast. Serves 3.

Baked Tuna: Mix tuna and cream of mushroom soup (as directed in previous paragraph), pour half of it into a baking dish, cover with crushed potato chips, add remaining tuna mixture and more potato chips, and bake 20 minutes in a fairly hot oven (400° F.). Or pour all the tuna-mushroom mixture into a baking dish, top with corn flakes, dot with butter, and bake as described. Serves 3 or 4.

Herb Touch: Favorite fresh herbs to use in fish sauces or stuffings are parsley, chives, fennel, basilica or sweet basil, and thyme. A bay leaf is a good addition when poaching or boiling fish.

Pickled Tuna with Sour Cream: Empty a 6 1/2 or 7-ounce can of tuna, oil and all, into a bowl; flake into large-sized pieces. Cover with thin slices of Bermuda or red onion and thin slices of lemon. (You'll need 1 large onion and 1/2 a lemon for this.) In a sauce-pan simmer together for about 5 minutes 3 tablespoons wine vinegar, 2 tablespoons water, 1 bay leaf, and 1 teaspoon pickling spices, slightly crushed. Pour over tuna and mix lightly. Stir in 1/2 cup sour cream. Chill thoroughly. (Even better if made several days before using and refrigerated.) Serve on rye wafers, or rye or pumpernickel bread. Makes about 2 cups.

By-laws of Meat Preparation

1. When buying meat, allow 1/4 to 1/3 pound boneless or ground meat per person; at least 1/2 pound if it has considerable bone or fat.

2. To keep uncooked meat safely, unwrap it, place on plate or pan, cover loosely with waxed paper, and set in the coldest part of the refrigerator. Meat in large pieces—roasts, thick steaks, et cetera—keeps best; may be held up to 3 days if very cold. Ground meat, liver, kidneys, et cetera, spoil quickly; use them within 24 hours after buying, or freeze them in ice trays. Use your eyes and nose to detect signs of spoilage.

3. Keep frozen meats in freezing unit, frozen solid, until time to use. For commercially frozen meats, follow directions on package for thawing and cooking. Otherwise, thaw on refrigerator shelf, allowing 3 to 5 hours per pound; or thaw smaller pieces in kitchen, allowing 1 to 2 hours per pound. (Using an electric fan will speed up thawing.) Cook at once. *Never refreeze meat after thawing.*

4. Store all cured meats—such as bacon, ham, et cetera—covered in refrigerator. Use shortly after buying—sliced ham within 3 days; bacon, and larger pieces of ham, within a week.

5. Except for pan-broiling or frying, cook meats at fairly low temperature. Broiling as well as roasting is now being done with moderate heat. See roasting chart later in chapter.

6. To store cooked meats safely, leave in large pieces. Cover loosely. Keep very cold. Chop or grind just before using.

Chapter 4

Best Ways to Cook Meats
on Range or Garden Grill

How do California ways with meats differ from those followed in other parts of the country? Not drastically, perhaps. We do, however, use considerably more lamb than most other states do. Influenced by good cooks of other races, we use more garlic and herbs and more wine in preparing meats. And we make more of a specialty of outdoor cooking of meats on garden grills and over mountain and beach campfires.

It is hard, of course, to improve on good roasts, well-broiled steaks and chops, really good pot roasts and stews. And so, since all the other ways of fixing meats, indoors and out, are in

93

reality just different twists on those fundamental methods, we'll include here up-to-date directions for broiling, roasting, and the like, as well as specific recipes.

TO BROIL STEAKS OR CHOPS

Have tender steaks or lamb chops cut 1 to 2 inches thick. (Thin steaks should be pan-broiled.) If convenient, take thick steaks out of refrigerator about 30 minutes before cooking, so that they can come to room temperature. Trim off excess fat, slash edges to prevent curling. Place on greased broiler rack with surface of meat 2 to 5 inches from heating unit. Follow range manufacturer's directions as to pre-heating, and whether to keep oven door closed or partially open during broiling. Broil until brown as you like on top side, season with salt and pepper, turn, broil other side, season, serve at once on hot plates. A 1-inch-thick steak will take 10 to 16 minutes altogether for rare to well done; a 2-inch steak will require about 3 times as long, or 30 to 45 minutes altogether. Lamb chops should be cooked medium or well done. Allow 12 to 16 minutes altogether for chops 1 inch thick; up to 25 to 30 minutes for chops 2 inches thick.

Veal and fresh pork are not ordinarily broiled, as the long cooking required for these meats is likely to dry them out too much. If you do wish to broil them, have meat cut thin and broil it slowly. Brush veal liberally with melted fat while cooking.

To broil calf or baby beef liver, have slices cut 1/2 inch thick. Brush with melted butter. Broil 3 inches from heat; allow 8 to 10 minutes altogether. (For directions for broiling chicken, see Chapter Five; for fish, see Chapter Three.)

TO BROIL OR ROAST OUT OF DOORS

To broil steaks or chops successfully over an outdoor grill, the first and most important rule is to have a good thick bed of red coals. How deep it should be will depend on the thickness of the meat. Charcoal makes an especially steady, even fire, ideal for broiling. It is best used in a special grate. The charcoal should be lighted about an hour before grilling is to begin. If wood is to be used, it should be hardwood, except perhaps for thin hamburgers or wieners. The fire should be started 1 to 2 hours before cooking is to begin. Trim off all but a minimum of fat from the meat, for the dripping fat is bound to blaze up and set fire to the steak itself. A folding wire toaster is a great help in broiling steaks, chops, and hamburgers; it keeps these flat, simplifies turning—and if the steak should catch fire, you can snatch it off and blow out the flame.

For roasting over an outdoor grill, follow the same rules. A long, rather slender roast, such as a rack of lamb, is more easily and successfully roasted than a thick chunky one. Have an extra-deep bed of coals. Turn the meat frequently while roasting.

Whether or not to use a barbecue sauce on steaks, chops, or roasts is a matter of personal preference—and I prefer to omit it, ordinarily. I do like occasionally to let the meat stand for several hours in a simple wine-and-herb sauce or marinade before broiling or roasting. You'll find directions for such sauces later in this chapter.

GRILLED STEAKS, HOLLYWOOD

Since some like them rare and some demand them well done, the simplest way is to serve individual steaks rather than to broil the meat all in one piece. Have steaks cut at least 1 inch thick (club steaks arrange to advantage on the open grill); remove from refrigerator long enough in advance for meat to lose its chill before broiling; trim off most of fat. Let fire of hardwood or charcoal burn down to a good thick bed of live red coals. Set grill 3 to 5 inches above coals; rub hot grill with pieces of suet to keep meat from sticking. Sear steaks quickly on both sides, then finish cooking, turning only as necessary, using tongs. While meat is broiling, peel several cloves of garlic and place them in a garlic press. After the second turn-ing, sprinkle steaks generously with salt and coarse black pep-per, and squeeze garlic juice ad lib. over all. When steaks are done on both sides, flop onto hot plates, give the new-browned side the salt, pepper, and garlic treatment, and rush to table. Do lamb chops the same way.

BROILED STEAKS ON STICKS

Have the meat man cut thick round steak into inch cubes. On skewers (or ends of sturdy green sticks) arrange alternately steak cubes and peeled small white onions, allowing 3 cubes of steak and 2 onions per serving. Brush well with oil or melted margarine. Broil over bed of hot coals, brushing frequently with any well-seasoned barbecue sauce.

BARBECUED STEAK SANDWICHES

Good as these grilled sandwiches are when done in the broiler of the kitchen range, they're even better when browned over the garden barbecue. For 4 sandwiches, have 4 cube steaks (or pieces of pounded round) and 8 slices of bread, and this Bar-becue Sauce:

4 tablespoons catsup
3 tablespoons vinegar
2 tablespoons water
1 1/2 tablespoons melted
    butter or margarine

2 teaspoons Worcestershire
    sauce
1/2 teaspoon salt

Combine everything and heat, not quite to boiling. Pour over steaks and let stand 15 minutes. Lift out steaks and arrange on grill, 2 inches from the hot coals. Broil quickly on one side (about 3 minutes), baste with barbecue sauce, and turn and cook other side. While steaks are broiling, spread bread slices lightly with butter or margarine, adding any barbecue sauce that may be left. Pop the hot steaks between bread slices, and serve pronto.

SAGEBRUSH PORK CHOPS, GRILLED

Because pork must be thoroughly cooked, best system for garden grilling is to select lean loin chops cut rather thin. Allow 2 chops per person. Trim off fat (to keep it from spattering on the fire). Rub dried sage over both sides of chops, patting it gently into the meat. Broil slowly until meat is thoroughly done and well browned on both sides, brush with hot bacon fat as chops cook, and sprinkle well with salt and pepper.

GRILL-TOASTED VEAL CHOPS

Secrets of good campfire veal are to have veal round or chops cut thin and to have the fire burned down to a thick bed of glowing embers. Place veal slices in an old-fashioned wire bread toaster (to keep them from curling) and broil very slowly, turning frequently. Season to taste with salt and pepper while cooking, and brush frequently with melted butter.

PICNIC LAMB CHOPS

Allow 1 medium-thick shoulder chop or 2 or 3 rib chops per capita. Remove all surplus fat and lay chops in bowl. Partially cover with a mixture of 2 parts salad oil and 1 part wine vinegar, and add 2 or 3 peeled cloves of garlic. Let chops soak for 2 or 3 hours (or overnight), turning occasionally. Broil quickly over hot coals, seasoning well with salt and pepper.

TRY THESE ON YOUR GARDEN GRILL

When the fire is a charcoal one, which lacks the fragrance of wood smoke, lay a few twigs of apple wood or shrubby herbs alongside the coals to impart aroma—not eucalyptus, though, for the medicinal odor may penetrate the meat.

If there's barbecue sauce to be applied, swish it on with a branch of garden sage or mint.

For a change from hamburgers, brown thick slices of liverwurst or salami in a little butter in a skillet and pop them into toasted buns.

Instead of putting onions in sandwiches, have a dish of onion slices so that eaters can quota themselves according to taste; if you soak the onion slices an hour or more in water to which a little sugar has been added, they'll be milder and more generally appealing.

SHISH KEBABS

To achieve the most dramatic effect, use those vicious-looking long steel skewers for broiling these Shish Kebabs over the glowing coals of the garden grill. The amounts given here are about right for 4; multiply as necessary for a crowd.

2 pounds lean lamb (leg or shoulder), cut in 1 1/2-inch cubes
2 onions, sliced
2 teaspoons salt
1/2 teaspoon black pepper

1/2 teaspoon dried oregano or rosemary (fresh or dried)
1/2 cup sherry
2 tablespoons salad oil

Mix the cubes of meat, and onions. Sprinkle with salt, pepper, and herbs. (If dried oregano or rosemary is used, crumble it between the hands. If fresh rosemary, chop it coarsely with a knife or scissors.) Pour sherry and oil over all and let stand in refrigerator overnight or for several hours, stirring once or twice. Take out meat, string on metal skewers, and broil over the coals or in the broiling oven until well done.

Capretti, or kid goat, is seen in Italian markets at Eastertime. When well cooked, in the same ways that lamb is done, it is a real delicacy.

LAMB CHOPS SPECIAL

Soak 4 thick kidney lamb chops several hours in this marinade before broiling:

4 tablespoons olive oil	1/2 teaspoon coarsely
1 tablespoon tarragon	ground black pepper
vinegar	1 bay leaf, broken
1 small onion, sliced thin	Few sprigs parsley
1 clove garlic, mashed	Few strips yellow lemon
1 teaspoon salt	peel

Mix well, pour over chops, put into refrigerator. Turn occasionally. Broil as usual in kitchen range or on garden grill.

20-MINUTE DINNER

4 medium-thick loin lamb	4 thick slices unpeeled
chops	orange
4 bananas, peeled	2 tomatoes, cut in halves

Broil meat about 10 minutes on one side, season and turn. Arrange other items on broiler, broil 10 minutes longer, and serve at once with a spoonful of chili sauce on each orange slice if you wish, or a sprinkling of cheese on each tomato, or both. Serves 4.

TO ROAST MEATS

Use tender cuts, weighing at least 3 pounds. Wipe with damp cloth, sprinkle with salt and pepper, and place fat side up in shallow pan (on rack if roast is boneless). Do not add water. Do not cover pan. Roast in moderately slow oven (325° F.). If you have a meat thermometer, insert it in thickest part of meat, not resting on fat or bone, and roast to the proper internal temperature as given below. If you haven't a thermometer, figure as follows, remembering that the smaller the roast, the more minutes per pound you must allow:

TIMETABLE FOR ROASTING MEATS

BEEF—STANDING RIB ROAST *

Oven Temperature	Degree of Doneness	Allow for 3 to 5 pound roast	Allow for 6 to 8 pound roast	Temperature on meat thermometer
325° F.	Rare	26 minutes per pound	22 minutes per pound	140° F.
325° F.	Medium	30 minutes per pound	26 minutes per pound	160° F.
325° F.	Well done	35 minutes per pound	33 minutes per pound	170° F.

LAMB—LEG, CROWN, SHOULDER, RIB AND LOIN *

325° F.	Medium	35 to 40 minutes per pound	30 minutes per pound	175° F.
325° F.	Well done	40 to 45 minutes per pound	35 minutes per pound	182° F.

VEAL —LEG, LOIN, OR SHOULDER *

325° F.	Well done	35 to 45 minutes per pound	30 to 40 minutes per pound	180° F.

PORK—LEG, LOIN, OR SHOULDER *

325° F.	Well done	45 to 60 minutes per pound	35 to 40 minutes per pound	185° F.

* For all boned and rolled roasts, add 5 to 10 minutes per pound.

ROAST LEG OF LAMB, THREE WAYS

1. Wipe leg of lamb with damp cloth. Don't remove the "fell" (the thin skin that covers it). Rub with salt and pepper and powdered rosemary or thyme. Stab meat in several places near bone with a pointed knife, and insert slivers of garlic. Place it, fat side up, skin side down in a shallow pan, and roast uncovered in very moderate oven (325° F.) about 3 to 3 1/2 hours. (See "To Roast Meats" for number of minutes per pound.) Make brown gravy in pan.

2. Follow directions above, but baste the lamb frequently while roasting, using 1 cup red or white table wine mixed with about 1/4 cup oil. Make gravy in the pan, adding a little more wine.

3. Follow directions given under 1, but glaze the surface this way: About 20 minutes before the end of roasting time, mix 2 tablespoons currant jelly, 2 tablespoons brown sugar, 1 tablespoon vinegar, and spread over the meat. Finish roasting as usual.

Note: For a summer dinner, roast a leg of lamb the day before, but don't cut into it while it is hot. Then, when you slice it cold, you'll find the meat pink and juicy, far different from mere leftover roast lamb. Serve with boiled potatoes and hot brown gravy made in the roasting pan; or with potato salad, a hot green vegetable, relish plate, and hot rolls.

BAKED CORNED PORK

Not everyone seems to be acquainted with corned or pickled pork, which seems a shame, because it is so very good. It is easy to do, too. (By the way, pickled means lightly corned.)

Cover a corned or pickled pork shoulder or leg with cold water, heat to boiling, skim, then turn heat low and simmer, covered, 2 1/2 to 3 1/2 hours, until tender. Let cool in cooking water. Take out meat, pull off the skin and trim off excess fat. With a knife mark surface of fat on meat into squares, stick with cloves, place in a baking pan, pour 2 cups claret or other red table wine over the meat, and bake in moderately hot oven (375° F.) about 40 minutes, basting often with wine in pan. Then spread fat with 1/2 cup brown sugar mixed with 1 tablespoon cornstarch. (The cornstarch helps to make a beautiful glaze.) Bake about 20 minutes longer, basting occasionally with liquid in pan, until browned and glazed. Serve hot or cold. If it is to be served hot, stir a little more wine into the syrup remaining in the pan, add a handful of raisins, too, if you like, heat, and serve as a sauce with the meat.

HAM BAKED WITH BURGUNDY

Bake half a ham cut side down in uncovered pan in very slow oven (275° F.), allowing 30 minutes per pound, or at 325° F., allowing 22 minutes per pound. Remove skin, score fat, stick with cloves, and spread with 1/2 cup brown sugar mixed with 1 tablespoon cornstarch. Pour 1 cup Burgundy wine around the ham, and bake in moderately hot oven (375° F.) about 20 minutes more, basting frequently with wine in pan to glaze it. For a whole ham, allow 20 to 25 minutes per pound at 275° F., or 16 to 22 minutes at 325° F. Place skin side up, and bake as directed.

BARBECUED BREAST OF LAMB

Spread a whole breast of lamb (about 3 pounds) fat side down in a shallow baking pan. Sprinkle with salt and pepper, and bake uncovered in moderately hot oven (400° F.) about 1 1/2 hours, until well browned and tender. Serves 6 to 8.

If preferred, the uncooked lamb breast may be marinated for several hours in barbecue sauce, or in French dressing, or the sherry dressing recommended for Shish Kebabs in this chapter, before roasting as above.

Friends in Palo Alto make a specialty of barbecued riblets cut from lamb breast. They serve them hot with small dishes of barbecue sauce for dunking.

HAIGAGAN KEBAB

The "Armenian Mystery Package," George Mardikian calls this; and guests at his famous Omar Khayyam restaurant in San Francisco make it disappear in a mysteriously amazing way. It is so easy and inexpensive to make at home, so much fun to serve, and so good to eat, I recommend it heartily. To serve 4, you'll need:

4 pieces heavy foil, 18 x 18 inches, or light foil, 12 x 18 inches	2 tomatoes, halved
	1 or 2 onions, quartered
4 round-bone, 1-inch-thick shoulder lamb chops	1 or 2 large potatoes, pared and quartered
2 green bell peppers	Salt and pepper

In the center of each piece of foil put a lamb chop, half a green pepper, half a tomato, and a half or quarter each of onion and potato. Sprinkle with salt and pepper. Wrap up carefully, double-folding edges together to make steam-tight packages; place side by side in an open pan and bake in a moderate oven (350° F.) for 2 1/2 hours. Don't add water, don't cover, don't turn the packages, and don't try to hurry the cooking. Serve the packages on individual plates.

TO POT ROAST OR BRAISE MEATS

Use a good-sized piece—3 to 5 pounds or more—of any of the less tender cuts of beef, veal, or lamb. (Rump, chuck, or shoulder, short ribs, bottom round, are good choices.) Roll meat in flour or not, as you choose. Heat a little suet, shortening, or oil in a Dutch oven or heavy kettle and in it brown meat slowly on all sides. Sprinkle generously with chopped onion, if you wish, and with salt and pepper. (A discreet sprinkle of dried or chopped fresh herbs may be added at this time, too. Fresh basilica, for example, is the making of a veal pot roast.) Add about 1/2 cup hot water—just enough to cover bottom of kettle, to provide steam. Cover, and simmer slowly 3 to 4 hours, until thoroughly tender, turning occasionally and adding a little hot water as needed. If you wish to cook vegetables with the meat, add them about half an hour before serving time. Carrots, celery and potatoes, cut in fairly large pieces, and onions sliced or quartered, are good additions. When meat and vegetables are done, take them up on a hot platter. Make brown gravy in the kettle and serve it separately.

LAMB CHOPS SAN DIEGO

Start these a little more than an hour before serving time. When done they should be richly glazed, tender enough to cut with a fork, completely delicious. To serve 4, you will need:

4 shoulder lamb chops
1 peeled clove garlic
3 tablespoons oil
Salt and pepper
1 medium onion, chopped

1 can (10 1/2 ounces) condensed consommé
3/4 cup white table wine (dry sauterne, Chablis, or the like)

Cut each chop into 2 or 3 pieces, so they won't curl too much. Heat oil with whole clove of garlic in large skillet with snug-fitting cover. In this brown the pieces of meat, salting and peppering them lightly. When browned, remove garlic and add onion, consommé, and wine. (If you have fresh rosemary or thyme, it's good to drop in a very small sprig to cook with the meat for 10 or 15 minutes, then remove. Beware of overdoing a good thing!) Cover, turn heat low, and simmer for an hour or longer, until the meat is very tender and the liquid has almost completely evaporated.

If you like, you can arrange 4 carrots, scraped and cut in halves lengthwise; 4 turnips, peeled and halved; and 4 small potatoes, pared and halved; over and around the meat about half an hour before serving time. Cover, and let them steam until tender. And if you want more gravy, you can, of course, add a cup or so of hot water to the liquid in the pan after taking up the meat and vegetables, and thicken it slightly with a tablespoon or so of flour shaken up in a covered jar with about 1/4 cup warm water.

LAMB SHANKS CHABLIS

Insert slivers of garlic near bone in meaty lamb shanks. Brown on all sides in a little hot oil in a large kettle, seasoning while cooking. When browned, add (for 4 shanks) 1 medium-sized onion, chopped, and 1 cup Chablis or dry sauterne or other white table wine. Cover and simmer slowly 1 1/2 hours or longer, until meat is very tender. Take up shanks and arrange on platter with vegetables. Make gravy in kettle, adding water (or wine and water mixed half-and-half) to make the amount needed, serve separately.

Sometimes I brown the shanks in a skillet, then transfer them to a large casserole, add onion and wine, cover, and bake in moderate oven (350° F.) for 2 hours or longer, until very tender. Diced or whole raw vegetables (carrots, small onions, green beans, and celery) may be put into the casserole with the shanks for the last 40 minutes or so of baking. Or 1 to 2 cups of dried limas, soaked overnight, then heated to boiling in their soaking water, may be poured into the casserole with the browned shanks, and the whole thing baked until both shanks and beans are completely tender and most of the liquid has been absorbed. Season the beans with salt to taste while they are baking. Serves 4. (In this recipe, you may substitute water for white wine, if you wish, but you'll be missing something good if you do!)

LAMB SHANK DRUMSTICKS

Insert garlic slivers in 4 lamb shanks, season, roll in flour, and brown slowly in 4 tablespoons oil in a big, heavy kettle. Add a bay leaf, 2 tablespoons grated lemon peel, and 1/2 cup lemon juice, cover, and simmer about 1 1/2 hours, until tender, adding a little water if necessary. Take up shanks and make gravy in kettle. Serves 4.

TO COOK VENISON

The method of cooking venison and other 4-footed wild game, and the eating quality of the meat, depend upon the age and tenderness of the animal more than the amateur hunter or cook is likely to realize.

Venison is much like beef—like utility beef usually—for deer are certainly "range-fed," with lots of exercise thrown in, and so their meat is very lean. After butchering, venison must be hung for at least 6 to 10 days for development of tenderness and flavor. After that, the various cuts may be cooked as corresponding cuts of beef are cooked, basting with additional fat when roasting or broiling the more tender cuts, and braising, pot-roasting, or stewing the less tender ones. Basting with a barbecue sauce during cooking definitely improves venison in the opinion of many persons.

VENISON STEAKS BORDELAISE

Cut tender, well-aged venison steaks about an inch thick. Sprinkle with salt and pepper. Fry until well browned in half olive oil, half butter, then cover and cook slowly until well done and tender. Take up steaks. Add more butter to the skillet, also 2 or 3 finely chopped cloves of garlic, and about 1/4 cup red table wine. Let boil up, stirring and scraping pan, strain over steaks, sprinkle generously with chopped parsley, and serve immediately.

SMOKE-BARBECUED SPARERIBS

Have 3 to 4 pounds spareribs sawed into 3- or 4-inch lengths, then cut apart into serving-sized pieces. Spread, meaty side up, in a single layer in a large shallow pan, sprinkle lightly with smoke-salt and curry powder, and roast in hot oven (450° F.) 30 minutes. While they roast, make this sauce:

Barbecue Sauce

1 cup catsup
1 cup claret or Burgundy
wine
1/4 cup vinegar
1/2 cup water
2 tablespoons brown sugar
2 tablespoons Worcester-
shire sauce

1/2 teaspoon salt
1 teaspoon dry mustard
1 teaspoon chili powder
(may be omitted)
Generous dashes of
cayenne or Tabasco
sauce
1 onion, grated

Combine ingredients and pour over ribs. Reduce heat to 350° F. and bake 45 minutes, basting occasionally. Then sprinkle with more smoke-salt and with 1 teaspoon celery seed, and bake 15 minutes longer, or until well done. Serves 4 as a main dish.

To serve with drinks (preferably out of doors), place the cooked ribs on a rack in an open pan and heat slowly in the oven or over the grill until hot and fairly dry. Cut ribs apart and serve with plenty of paper napkins. Serves 8 to 10.

CHINATOWN SPARERIBS

These sweet-sour spareribs are simple to make, when you know how! Have your meat man chop the ribs into 2-inch lengths. To serve 4, you'll need:

2 pounds spareribs
1 tablespoon peanut oil or
pork fat
2 tablespoons brown sugar
2 tablespoons cornstarch
1/2 teaspoon salt
1/4 cup vinegar
1/4 cup cold water

1 cup pineapple juice
1 tablespoon soy sauce
1 bouillon cube
1/4 cup boiling water
1/4 cup diced onions
3/4 cup diced pineapple
3/4 cup diced carrot
3/4 cup diced green pepper

Separate ribs, cover with boiling salted water, cover kettle, and simmer 1 hour, or until tender. Drain. Brown ribs slowly in oil. Mix sugar, cornstarch, salt; stir in vinegar, cold water, pineapple juice, soy sauce; add bouillon cube dissolved in boiling water. Add this mixture to ribs and cook, stirring constantly, until the sauce is transparent. Add onion, pineapple, carrot, and green pepper, and cook until vegetables are tender but still crisp. Serve with rice or fried noodles.

SPARERIBS SAN JOAQUIN

Have spareribs cut in pieces about 4 or 5 inches long and 2 or 3 ribs wide. Mix a marinade in these proportions:

2 tablespoons dry mustard	1/2 teaspoon Tabasco sauce
2 tablespoons Worcester- shire sauce	1 cup catsup
2 tablespoons oil	Salt and black pepper

Roll ribs in this mixture and let stand an hour or longer, turning occasionally. Grill slowly over hot coals or in broiling oven, basting frequently with the sauce while grilling.

DUDE RANCH PORK CHOPS

Brown thick pork chops, spread in a shallow baking dish, cover with sliced onions, pour bottled chili sauce generously over all, cover, and bake slowly (at 300° F.) for 2 hours.

VEAL SCALLOPINI SAUTERNE

1 pound veal round, sliced 1/4 inch thick	3 tablespoons butter or oil
Salt and pepper	1 clove garlic, crushed
Flour	1/2 cup sauterne
	1/2 cup water

Cut veal in small pieces, sprinkle with salt and pepper, roll in flour, and brown in butter or oil in a skillet, with garlic. Remove garlic, add wine and water, cover, and simmer about 30 minutes, until the meat is tender. A pinch of marjoram or thyme may be added while cooking. Serves 4. Good with rice or noodles.

BAKED VEAL SCALLOPINI

Buy a thin slice of veal round—about a pound. Cut it into small pieces, and brown delicately in oil with a peeled clove of garlic in the skillet. Wash but do not peel 2 or 3 medium-sized tomatoes, cut them into thick slices, and put in with the veal. Add also 1 cup drained canned mushrooms (or dried mushrooms that have been soaked half an hour in hot water to cover). Stir 1/2 cup dry white table wine (sauterne, Chablis, or the like) into 1/2 cup grated Parmesan cheese, pour over all, and put into fairly hot oven (400° F.) for 20 to 30 minutes, until everything is bubbling hot and the cheese tinged with brown. Serves 4.

VEAL CHOPS IN WINE

4 double-thick veal chops, with kidneys
Salt and pepper
3 tablespoons flour
4 tablespoons butter

1/4 pound (1 cup) fresh mushrooms, sliced
1 small onion, minced fine
1 cup sauterne or other white table wine

Season chops, roll in flour, and brown lightly in 3 tablespoons of the butter. Remove to a casserole. To the skillet add the rest of the butter, and in it cook sliced mushrooms and onion gently for 5 minutes. Add to the chops. Heat wine in the same skillet, pour around chops, cover casserole tightly, and bake in moderate oven (350° F.) about 45 minutes. Serves 4.

This may all be done in the skillet on top of the stove if more convenient. Also, if you prefer, you may substitute 1/3 cup sherry and 2/3 cup water for the sauterne in this recipe. Either way the chops are excellent.

TO MAKE A GOOD STEW

Use neck, chuck, or other less tender cut of beef or veal, cut in about 1 1/2-inch cubes. Roll the cubes in flour if you wish and brown slowly on all sides in a little suet, shortening, or oil, in a heavy kettle. Add salt, pepper, a bay leaf; chopped onion, celery and parsley as desired; and boiling water almost to cover meat. Cover and simmer about 2 hours. Add small onions, pared and quartered potatoes, and scraped carrots; cover, and simmer 1 hour longer. Thicken the liquid for gravy as directed below, add more seasonings if necessary and serve.

For Savory Oxtail Stew for 4 use 2 oxtails disjointed, 1 cup claret or Burgundy wine, plus water to cover meat. Proceed as directed above, simmering 3 to 4 hours before adding vegetables.

For Irish Stew use lamb stew meat and don't bother to brown it. For something special use 1 cup white table wine in place of that much water in making stew for 4.

TO MAKE REALLY GOOD GRAVY

Whether made in the roasting pan or in the skillet in which meat has been fried, the same general directions and cautions apply. First, pour off excess fat, leaving about 1 1/2 to 2 tablespoons for each cup of gravy wanted. Second, add the same amount of flour as you are using of fat, and stir over direct heat until it is lightly browned. Third, rapidly stir in cold or lukewarm water (or milk, or meat stock) to make gravy a little thinner than you want it, season to taste just right, and let cook 10 to 15 minutes, so that flour is completely cooked and gravy is the right consistency. Don't strain it. Serve boiling hot.

To make gravy for stews and the like, allow 1 1/2 to 2 tablespoons flour for each cup of gravy to be made. Mix flour with enough warm water to make a thin, smooth paste. (Easiest way is to shake them together in a covered jar.) Add slowly to the boiling liquid, stirring fast with wire whip. Cook 10 to 15 minutes. If it isn't as brown as you like it, add 1 or 2 bouillon cubes or some meat-flavored extract, or a little Kitchen Bouquet. Season just right before serving.

FOUR WAYS TO COOK BACON

To Fry. Spread slices in cold skillet and cook slowly, turning frequently, until crisp as you like it. Pour off fat as it accumulates.

To Broil. Spread on cold broiling rack, place 4 to 5 inches below heating unit and broil, turning once or twice, until done.

To Oven-Cook. Spread slices on rack in shallow pan. Bake in moderately hot oven (375° F. to 400° F.) until crisp. Need not be turned.

To Grill Out of Doors. Buy bacon in the piece—a pound slab to serve 6 is about right. Have rind removed and bacon sliced about twice as thick as ordinarily. Put slices back together in slab form, set in big pan, and heat slowly in a 250° F. oven in order to melt out much of the fat. Separate the partially cooked slices, lay in cold skillets or on the grill, and cook quickly. Doing this way keeps surplus fat in kitchen for future use; lessens chances of the bacon's being burned in cooking.

LIVER AND ONIONS, ITALIAN STYLE

Pour 1/2 cup claret or Burgundy wine over 8 thin slices calf or lamb liver, and let stand in refrigerator half an hour or longer. Drain, saving the wine. Slice and fry 4 onions in bacon drippings, remove and keep hot while you season and flour the liver slices and brown quickly in the same skillet, adding more fat if needed. Take up. Stir a teaspoon of flour into the fat in skillet, brown lightly, add wine drained from liver, and cook, stirring, until smooth. Season well, and pour over liver and onions on hot platter. Serves 3 or 4.

DEER LIVER AND BACON

To be at its best, deer liver must be cooked in camp, old-timers say. Slice liver 1/4 inch thick, cover with cold water, and let stand 5 minutes, drain. To a quart of boiling water add 1/4 cup vinegar, pour over liver, and let stand a few minutes. Drain, and roll slices in flour. Set aside while you fry a skillet or two of bacon. Take up bacon and in the hot fat brown liver quickly, seasoning it well with salt and pepper. When well browned, call in the crowd.

It's a good idea to rub the skillet with a cut clove of garlic before frying liver or kidneys. Rolls, split, buttered, sprinkled with onion salt, then toasted, go well under or with these meats.

KIDNEY SAUTÉ

To serve 2 or 3, buy about 1 pound kidneys—2 veal, 3 pork, or 5 or 6 lamb. Slice them, cutting out white tubes. Soak in cold salted water 15 to 30 minutes, drain. Fry a chopped onion in 3 tablespoons butter until soft, add kidneys and brown well. Season, stir in 2 tablespoons flour, and brown lightly, stirring. Add 1/2 cup claret or Burgundy and 1/2 cup consommé or water. Cook, stirring, until smooth, then cover and simmer 10 to 15 minutes, until tender. A beef kidney may be used in this recipe, but it will need to simmer about 45 minutes, with a little more water added to keep it from cooking dry.

KIDNEYS ON SKEWERS

2 veal or 5 lamb kidneys	1 small onion, grated
4 strips bacon, cut in squares	1 teaspoon salt
1/2 cup claret or other red table wine	1/2 teaspoon coarsely ground black pepper
1/4 cup salad oil	1/2 teaspoon dry mustard
	Dash of cayenne

Cut kidneys in about inch cubes, removing all membranes, soak in cold salted water 15 to 30 minutes. Drain and arrange on skewers, alternating cubes of kidney with squares of bacon. Mix rest of ingredients in shallow dish, lay the skewered kidneys in it, and let stand half an hour or longer, turning occasionally. Remove from sauce and broil slowly until browned, turning and basting frequently with the remaining sauce. Serves 4. This wine marinade is equally good to use for chops or steaks.

THREE WAYS TO COOK SAUSAGE

To Cook Sausage Patties. Place patties in cold skillet and cook slowly on top of stove or in moderate oven (350° F.) until well browned and thoroughly done.

To Fry Link Sausage. Place links in skillet, add a little water, cover, and steam 5 minutes. Drain off water and finish cooking slowly, turning often, until well browned. Don't prick the links.

To Bake Link Sausage. When a pound or more of sausage is to be cooked, spread links in shallow pan and bake uncovered in fairly hot oven (425° F.), turning to brown evenly.

SOUTH-OF-THE-BORDER CHILI

1/2 pound suet, chopped	1 tablespoon salt
3 cloves garlic, minced	1 teaspoon cumin seed
2 pounds ground beef	1/2 teaspoon pepper
3 tablespoons chili powder	2 chili tepines, crushed
1 1/2 tablespoons paprika	3 cups water

Fry out suet in a heavy kettle. Add garlic, meat, and seasonings, cover, and cook very slowly for 4 hours, stirring occasionally. Add water and cook about 1 hour longer, stirring occasionally. Serve hot, separately, or mixed with cooked pink beans. Serves 6, plain; more if mixed with beans.

MARVELOUS MEAT BALLS

Serve these once, and you'll find them a "request number" from then on. They're as satisfactory from the standpoint of the hostess as of the guests, for they are actually improved by being made a day in advance and heated up at serving time. And 1 pound ground beef actually makes 40 to 42 balls, serving 5 or 6 generously!

1 **pound lean beef, ground 2 or 3 times**	1/4 **teaspoon pepper**
4 **Holland rusks, crushed, or 1 cup fine dry bread crumbs**	**Dash of allspice**
	1 **egg, beaten**
	1 **cup top milk or cream**
1 **teaspoon cornstarch**	1 **small onion, minced**
1 **teaspoon salt**	1 **tablespoon butter or margarine**

Combine ingredients, frying onion briefly in butter before adding. Shape into 40 or 42 small balls, using a rounded teaspoon for each one. Brown balls lightly all over, not too many at a time, in a little butter and oil in the onion skillet, transferring them to a heavy saucepan as they are browned. Into fat left in skillet stir 3 tablespoons flour, stir in 2 cups water and 1 cup Burgundy or claret (or 3 cups water), add 1 or 2 bouillon cubes, and cook, stirring, until smooth. Season to taste and pour the thin gravy over meat balls. Set aside until half an hour before serving, then reheat thoroughly on top of stove or in the oven. For something really outstanding, serve these with Feathered Rice. (See Index.)

KITCHEN BOUQUET OF HERBS

Tie together a sprig each of fresh parsley, savory and thyme, a leaf of fresh sage and a bay leaf. Drop into simmering soup or stew and leave until liquid is delicately flavored, then remove.

PEPPITIS

Here is a different kind of meat balls, with a Mexican flavor. First makes tomato sauce by simmering together for half an hour:

1 large onion, chopped
1 clove garlic, minced
1/3 teaspoon pepper sauce
1 large can (No. 2 1/2) or 1
    quart canned tomatoes,
    forced through a wire
    strainer

1 teaspoon salt
1/4 teaspoon pepper
1 teaspoon Worcestershire
    sauce
1 teaspoon oregano, rubbed
    between palms of hands

While sauce simmers, make meat balls:

1 small onion, chopped
1 clove garlic, chopped
2 tablespoons oil
1 1/2 pounds ground lean
    pork
2 cups bread crumbs

1/2 cup chopped parsley
2/3 cup grated cheese
1 teaspoon salt
1/4 to 1/2 teaspoon pepper
1/2 teaspoon oregano
2 eggs, beaten

Fry onion and garlic in oil and mix well with meat and other ingredients. Shape into small balls, and fry for about 5 minutes only in a little hot oil. Then add to sauce and let simmer, covered, 2 hours. Serves 6 to 8.

DANISH MEAT BALLS

If they are to be really right, you must use just the mixture of meats called for, says the Danish friend who is responsible for this just-right recipe.

1/2 pound ground round
    steak
1/2 pound ground lean pork
1/2 pound ground veal
3 slices bread

Milk
1 onion, grated
1 1/2 teaspoons salt
Pepper, ad lib.
2 eggs, unbeaten

Ask your meat man to grind the meats together 2 or 3 times, or else regrind them at home. Break up bread, almost cover it with milk, and let soak until it has taken up every bit of milk it can hold. Add to meat with grated onion, salt, and pepper, and mix very thoroughly (with the hands, preferably). Add unbeaten eggs and mix a lot more. Shape into balls with a tablespoon, slapping them against the side of the bowl. (You may be able to do them without slapping them, but no good Danish cook would believe such a thing!) Drop the meat balls into boiling salted water (or broth from meat or vegetables), cover, and simmer slowly about 30 minutes, until done. Take up meat balls and keep hot while you thicken gravy with 2 tablespoons each of butter and flour rubbed together; add a little cream, too, if you like. Serve meat balls in bowl, with gravy poured over. Serves 4 to 6.

For Danish Meat Balls with Celery Root, pare a large celery root, cut in good-sized pieces, and cook tender (30 to 45 minutes) in boiling salted water. Take up celery root and keep it hot while you cook those Danish meat balls in the celery root broth. When done, arrange celery root in center of hot platter with meat balls around it; keep hot. Make gravy as described above and pour over all. Serves 4 to 6.

HAMBURGUNDIES

Shape ground lean beef into patties, 3 to the pound. Place in a shallow pan, sprinkle with sliced onion, and pour in Burgundy wine almost to cover meat. Let stand several hours in refrigerator, turning patties once. Remove, brush with oil or butter, and broil; or fry in part butter, part oil, in skillet. Season while cooking. Make thin pan gravy, using wine in which meat was marinated.

"Size" and "Half-Size"—At Ptomaine Tommy's in Los Angeles, and at some other eating places, too, you find on the menu those peculiar items, "Size" and "Half-Size." Order a "size" and you get a large toasted bun topped with a generous

hamburger, which in turn is topped with chili beans, all served very hot. A "half-size" is, quite naturally, a smaller edition of the structure! Makes a good barbecue specialty; all you need in addition is a salad, maybe pickles, coffee, and dessert.

HAMBURGER FLAPJACKS

Making these on an outdoor grill is almost as much fun as eating them, which is saying a lot. Broil or fry thin hamburger cakes. While they cook, bake flapjacks on a lightly greased griddle. Pop a hamburger between two hot cakes, and eat with or without catsup, mustard, or pickle relish.

Mustard Gravy for Hamburgers. Make a medium-thick cream sauce, season it highly with prepared mustard, and serve very hot in a pitcher, to pour over hamburger patties. (Not intended for 'burgers in buns.)

How Much Salt? To season ground meat—beef, lamb, veal, pork, or a mixture of any of these—a teaspoon of salt to each pound is a good average allowance. If crumbs, egg, or other unsalted materials are added, increase the salt. If you are using part sausage or smoked ham, make allowance for the salt they contain.

BUFFET MEAT LOAF

1 pound beef chuck, ground
1/4 pound bulk sausage
1 1/2 cups fluffy bread
    crumbs
1 egg, beaten
3/4 cup milk
1 small onion, grated

1 teaspoon salt
1/2 teaspoon pepper
1/4 teaspoon powdered sage
1 can (8 ounces) tomato
    sauce
Several sprigs of parsley

Combine all ingredients except parsley and tomato sauce, and mix thoroughly, using the hands. Pack into a lightly greased bread loaf pan. Make a little "trough" down the center of the top, tuck in parsley sprigs, and press them firmly into meat mixture. Bake in moderate oven (350° F.). After 45 minutes, remove from oven, pour off the fat and liquid that have collected around the loaf, pour the tomato sauce over the meat, and put back to bake for 20 to 30 minutes longer. Turn out and serve hot. Serves 6.

BUFFET MENU

Buffet Meat Loaf

Mushroom-Scalloped Potatoes   Browned Carrots

Green Salad Bowl

Lemon Chiffon Pie   Coffee

EXTRA-GOOD VEAL LOAF

3/4 pound ground veal	1 cup soft bread crumbs
1/4 pound ground lean pork	2 tablespoons grated cheese
1 small clove garlic, minced (may be omitted)	1 1/4 teaspoons salt
	1/4 teaspoon pepper
3 tablespoons finely chopped onion	1 egg, beaten
	1/2 cup milk

Combine ingredients in order given, mixing well. Pack firmly into a well-greased loaf pan, and bake in hot oven (400° F.) for 20 minutes, then reduce heat to 350° F. and bake about 45 minutes longer. Serves 5 or 6. The use of that small amount of cheese makes this loaf slice exceptionally well either hot or cold.

DANISH LIVER LOAF

Serve this cold, as a spread for pumpernickel, toast, or crackers for canapés, or as a hearty sandwich filling. The trick in grinding liver is to freeze the slices in the ice trays and grind them while still frozen.

1 pound sliced pork liver,
    frozen
1 small onion
1 egg, beaten
1 teaspoon salt
Pepper

3 tablespoons flour
6 tablespoons bacon or pork
    drippings
1 small can (2/3 cup)
    evaporated milk

Grind liver and onion, add other ingredients, mix well, pour into a greased small loaf pan, place in a pan containing hot water 1/2 inch deep, and bake in moderate oven (350° F.) for 1 1/2 hours. Turn out and cool. Keeps well in refrigerator.

BEST-EVER HAM LOAF

1 pound ground veal
1 pound ground smoked
    ham
4 tablespoons catsup
2 tablespoons minced onion
3 tablespoons chopped
    green pepper

2 eggs, beaten
1 cup dry bread crumbs
1 can condensed cream of
    mushroom soup
1/4 cup water
1/2 teaspoon salt
Dash of pepper

Mix together in order given, pack into greased loaf pan and bake in moderate oven (350° F.) 1 hour. Serves 8. Serve hot or cold, preferably with mustard sauce.

HOT STUFF MUSTARD SAUCE

1 egg, well beaten
1 tablespoon sugar
1/4 teaspoon salt

3 tablespoons dry mustard
1/2 cup white vinegar
1 tablespoon olive oil

Mix egg, sugar, salt, mustard (yes, 3 tablespoons is right!) and vinegar in top of double boiler, and cook, stirring, until thick. Cool, then stir in the oil. Serve cold with cold or hot meats.

PLAIN HOT MUSTARD

Stir into good, full-flavored dry mustard enough cold water to make a smooth paste. Let stand 20 minutes. Serve with hot corned beef, ham loaf, or cold sliced meats.

CREAMY MUSTARD SAUCE

Excellent with baked ham or ham loaf, hot or cold, is this creamy, sweet-sour mustard sauce:

2 cups thin cream	2 tablespoons flour
2 egg yolks	1/2 teaspoon salt
1 cup sugar	3/4 cup vinegar, heated
3 tablespoons dry mustard	

Heat 1 1/2 cups of the cream in a double boiler Beat yolks with remaining cream, add sugar mixed with mustard, flour, and salt, stir into hot cream, and cook, stirring until thick. Stir in hot vinegar and beat well. Cool.

TWO GOOD MINT SAUCES FOR LAMB

Heat 1 cup sugar and 1/2 cup vinegar to boiling. Add 1/2 cup finely chopped fresh mint leaves, remove from heat and let stand an hour or longer. Reheat just before serving. Serves 6.

Stir together 1 cup sugar, 1/2 cup lemon juice, 1/4 cup finely chopped mint. Let stand 1/2 hour. Serves 6.

BÉARNAISE SAUCE

Make Hollandaise sauce by the recipe in the chapter on Vegetables. (See Index.) When done, remove from heat and add a teaspoon each of chopped parsley and grated onion or chopped chives and a tablespoon of tarragon wine vinegar. (Add a teaspoon of finely chopped fresh tarragon leaves, too, if you have the herb available.) Serve with broiled steak.

EASY BÉARNAISE SAUCE

1 cup mayonnaise
1 tablespoon tarragon wine
    vinegar
1/2 tablespoon grated onion

2 tablespoons butter
1 egg yolk, beaten
2 teaspoons finely chopped
    tarragon leaves

Heat mayonnaise in a double boiler. Simmer vinegar and onion gently for a few minutes, then add butter and let it melt. Stir this into hot mayonnaise, add beaten egg yolk and beat well. Add tarragon, and serve with steak. Makes 1 cup, serving 4 to 6.

BARBECUE SAUCE AD LIB.

Add to or subtract from the ingredients in this sauce according to your own ideas and taste. No two "experts" ever yet agreed that any one recipe for barbecue sauce was exactly right!

1/4 cup butter, margarine,
    or oil
1 clove garlic, grated
1 large onion, grated
1 teaspoon sugar
1 teaspoon salt
1 teaspoon dry mustard
1 teaspoon paprika
1 to 2 teaspoons chili
    powder

1/2 teaspoon black pepper
1 tablespoon Worcester-
    shire sauce
2 tablespoons vinegar
1 tablespoon horseradish
1 tablespoon minced fresh
    herbs
2 1/2 cups water

Cook grated garlic and onion in butter, margarine, or oil for a few minutes, stir in blended dry ingredients, then liquids, and simmer about 30 minutes. Marinate meat in this sauce (cooled, of course) before cooking, or brush meat with hot sauce while cooking, or serve separately, hot or cold, with the meat at table. Makes about 2 cups.

MOONLIGHT STEAK FRY

Tomato Juice in Paper Cups

Thin Filet Steaks (fried in butter and olive oil in huge skillet and popped into buttered buns)

Potato Salad   Sliced Tomatoes   Pickles

Coffee   Frosted Cup Cakes   Fresh Apricots, Plums, Figs

Personal Note. Inspiration for this menu came from Sequoia National Park where 20 of us were served such a feast on such a night!

———

BUCK BARBECUE

Cups of Hot, Well-Seasoned Tomato Bouillon

Barbecued Venison Steaks or Chops

Scalloped Potatoes   Garlic Buttered French Bread

Red and White Cabbage Slaw

Old-Fashioned Fruit Gelatin Topped with Cream Cheese

Molasses Cookies   Coffee

Old-West Way: Ask guests to bring sharp pocket knives with which to cut the meat. Even though your venison is cooked to a turn, it may be a bit rugged!

GARNISHES FOR MEATS

For roast lamb, hot or cold, lay sprigs of crisp, tender garden mint or rosemary, or marjoram, on the platter. . . . For hot roast pork, veal or beef, try hot catsup apples; rosy glazed apple quarters or slices; jellied cranberry sauce or raw cranberry relish in small lettuce cups or orange shells; cherry olives; pickled crabapples, peaches, or other fruits; baked orange slices and parsley. (See Chapter Eleven.)

For hearty dishes (casseroles and such) featuring meat, see Chapter Seven.

AFTER THE SYMPHONY

Crème de Menthe Highballs
(Mix Crème de Menthe with sparkling water and plenty of ice)

Cold Roast Lamb   Rye Bread

Salad of Chilled Grapefruit Sections with Roquefort Cheese Dressing

Coffee-Flavored Candies

AFTER-THE-BIG-GAME BUFFET

Baked Corned Shoulder of Pork
(Platter garnished with lightly browned pineapple slices)

Horseradish Sauce   Mustard Sauce

Macaroni-Cheese Casserole   Lettuce Bowl with Shrimp

Hot Rolls   Assorted Relishes

Individual Pumpkin Pies   Coffee

By-laws of Preparing Poultry

1. In buying ready-to-cook fresh or frozen turkey or other poultry, allow 3/4 to 1 pound per person. If you buy a "market dressed" or "New York dressed" turkey (that is, picked but with head, feet, and internal organs still in place), subtract 15 per cent of its weight and you'll have the approximate ready-to-cook weight for figuring how much time to allow for roasting.

2. For broiling, frying, or roasting (that is, cooking with dry heat), buy young birds, less than a year old. Birds over a year old need to be cooked with moist heat; that is, braised, fricasseed, smothered, or stewed.

3. Have your poultry man draw the bird for roasting, or split it for broiling, or disjoint it for frying. When you get it home, pull out any pinfeathers, using paring knife, tweezers, or strawberry huller; singe off any remaining hairs, using gas flame or small paper torch in sink; remove any remaining bits of lungs, windpipe, stringy odds and ends, using a paper towel to grasp the slippery things; cut out oil sac on top of tail. Wash in cold water, pat dry inside and out, and store in coldest part of refrigerator until cooking time.

4. Defrost frozen poultry by letting it stand in refrigerator 24 hours for a small bird, or 2 or 3 days for a large one. To hurry thawing, put bird in its moisture-proof wrapping in pan and run cool water over it 4 to 6 hours or longer. Don't refreeze thawed poultry.

5. Don't stuff turkey until you are ready to cook it. Don't partially-cook turkey one day and finish it the next; do it all at one time. See directions for stuffing and roasting on page 136; timetable for roasting on page 140.

Chapter 5

Indoor and Outdoor Cooking of Poultry and Wild Fowl

CHICKENS and turkeys are among the tremendously **important** products of the state of California. Drive along **any** road near Petaluma and you see batteries of chicken houses that turn out broilers and fryers and roasters on an endless production line. Drive through the San Joaquin or Sacramento Valley and you see vast turkey ranches that keep the market supplied not merely at holiday time, but every month in the year. Not all of these fine-feathered friends are shipped to other parts of the country—not by any means. Millions of pounds of them stay right here each year to be barbecued, roasted, fried, and made into all sorts of delicious dishes, California style.

This chapter is devoted mostly to out-of-the-ordinary ways of cooking poultry and wild fowl as it is done here in California. All of these are, of course, just as usable and just as delightful in Georgia and Oregon and Maine and Missouri, and all the other states.

BROILED CHICKEN WITH WINE AND HERBS

To serve 4, have 2 broiling chickens (about 1 1/2 pounds each) split. Cut off necks, and simmer them (the necks) with giblets and a small sliced onion, a sprig of parsley, a bay leaf and 1 cup water in a covered pan until tender. Strain, add 1 cup Chablis, sauterne or other white table wine, and set aside. (Add also, if you have them, about 1/2 teaspoon each of chopped fresh rosemary and marjoram.) Chop giblets fine, and set aside.

Rub the chickens all over with a cut clove of garlic, sprinkle them with lemon juice, brush with melted butter or oil, sprinkle with salt and pepper and place, skin side down, in a shallow pan—not on a rack. Place low under broiler and broil, turning occasionally, and basting frequently with the wine-herb sauce until well browned and thoroughly done, about 30 to 45 minutes altogether. Remove chickens to a platter and put into the oven to keep hot. Thicken sauce remaining in pan with a tablespoon each of butter and flour rubbed together, add the chopped giblets, season, and heat again. Serve the chicken skin side up, with a little of the sauce poured over each.

From a man who is one of the best cooks I know, I learned this company-dinner trick: arrange browned (but not overdone) broiler halves on a deep bed of cooked wild rice mixed with mushrooms in a big roaster, cover, and place in very slow oven (300° F.). You can ignore them almost indefinitely and know they will be improved rather than spoiled by waiting.

Squabs and young tender quail, grouse, and other wild birds

may be broiled just as chickens are, allowing 15 to 20 minutes for quail, a little longer for the larger birds.

BARBECUED CHICKEN

Have broilers split or, if heavy, quartered. Rub with cut garlic, then with oil, sprinkle with salt, and place on grill about 4 inches above red coals. Cook cut side down until fairly well done inside, then turn and brown the skin side. Brush frequently with melted butter or oil or herb-flavored barbecue sauce while cooking. Sprinkle with salt, pepper, and paprika, and serve with a final dot of butter on each piece.

To barbecue broilers whole, wash and dry them inside and out, then rub them well with oil (garlic-flavored if you wish), salt, pepper, and chopped fresh herbs. Let stand for an hour before cooking, so that the seasonings will permeate the meat. String on a revolving spit or place on the grill and cook, turning frequently, until beautifully browned and really well done. (Test by twisting a broiler leg: if the joint breaks easily, it is done. Underdone chicken is inexcusable!)

WINE BARBECUE SAUCE FOR POULTRY

Though specially designed for chicken or veal, this sauce is equally good made with red table wine and used for steaks or lamb.

1/4 cup salad oil
1/2 cup white table wine
    (Chablis, sauterne,
    et cetera)
1 clove garlic, grated
1 onion, grated
1/2 teaspoon salt
1/2 teaspoon celery salt

1/2 teaspoon coarsely
    ground black pepper
1 teaspoon each chopped
    fresh thyme, marjoram,
    and rosemary; or 1/4
    teaspoon each dried
    herbs

Mix and let stand several hours. Use to baste or brush over

broiling chicken or veal steaks, applying frequently during the cooking. Makes enough for 3 or 4 broilers.

RUSSIAN HILL CHICKEN

Disjoint a good-sized frying or roasting chicken and salt and pepper the pieces, but don't flour them. In a big skillet that has a tight-fitting lid, heat about 2 tablespoons each butter and oil or shortening. Cover bottom of skillet with a thin layer of sliced onions, put in the pieces of chicken, and let cook very gently, turning often until well browned. Now pour over all 1/2 cup brandy. Cover, and let simmer slowly, turning occasionally, until tender. Pour 1/4 cup cream over all, heat a few minutes longer, and serve with the rich skillet-gravy poured over the chicken.

P. S. If you like curry, sprinkle 1/4 teaspoon curry powder over the browned chicken before you add the brandy.

HOW TO FRY CHICKEN TO PERFECTION

Disjoint heavy frying chickens. Coat with heavily salted and peppered flour. (Easy way: shake a few pieces at a time with the flour in a paper bag.) Heat oil or shortening in a heavy skillet—I like to have it about 1/2 inch deep. Put in meaty pieces first and fry, not too fast, to golden brown on all sides. To avoid spattering of hot fat, keep skillet covered with 2 thicknesses of paper toweling. This is a wonderful help. It lets the chicken brown nicely without steaming, yet protects you and the kitchen from spatters. Try it, please. (Of course you'll be careful not to let the paper catch fire.) Kitchen tongs are most convenient for handling and turning the chicken.

As pieces are browned, transfer them to a casserole. When finished, dot with butter if you like (I like to do this, rather than to use part butter in frying), cover, and put into moderate oven (325° F.) to finish cooking and to keep hot. Make gravy in skillet and pour it into a double boiler to keep hot or to reheat. That way, you can have everything ready in advance and the kitchen "neated up" before guests arrive.

Fry young turkey the same way, but allow at least an hour in the oven so it will be thoroughly cooked.

THIS FRIED CHICKEN DINNER IS EASY TO MANAGE FOR COMPANY

Fried Chicken   Cream Gravy
Feathered Rice
Green Peas with Mushrooms
Green Salad Bowl
Peach Halves with Raspberries   White Cup Cakes   Coffee

CHICKEN STEAKS

A friend from Cebu, P.I., first told me about this way of glamorizing chicken, as her Chinese cook used to do. It sounds a bit on the exotic side, but is really quite practical and easy to do.

Bone the legs, thighs, and breasts of tender chickens, cut them in small steaks, then pound these pieces with the edge of a saucer to flatten them. Season the pounded steaks with salt and pepper, roll them in flour, then in a thin egg batter (the one given for Fried Shrimp, on page 80, is good to use), and fry in shallow hot fat (360° F.) until well browned and done. If you want to carry out the Chinese cook's idea completely, chop the leg bones into short lengths and stick a bit of bone into each piece before frying—or, easier, tuck in an inch-long piece of uncooked macaroni!

The bones that are left, of course, you simmer with the necks and backs and giblets for soup.

CHICKEN LIVERS ON SKEWERS

For a garden or indoor breakfast or luncheon, it would be hard to find a greater delicacy than this. You can buy fresh chicken livers in many city markets.

Allow 2 or 3 livers, 1 slice bacon, and 2 fresh or canned mushrooms per person. Cut livers in halves, bacon into inch squares, leave mushrooms whole. On each skewer string first a mushroom cap, then alternate pieces of liver and bacon, and finish with another mushroom. Sprinkle with salt and pepper, dip in melted butter, then in fine cracker crumbs (these may be omitted if you prefer) and broil slowly over coals or under broiling unit, basting with melted butter as they cook. When well browned, serve immediately. These are superb served with baked tomatoes or stuffed peppers, or individual casseroles of scalloped vegetables.

GUERNEVILLE CHICKEN CURRY

Cut up a 5-pound fowl and simmer until tender in 2 1/2 quarts boiling water, adding 2 teaspoons salt while cooking. About 1 1/2 hours before serving time, melt 1/4 cup (1/2 cube) butter. Chop fine and add a carrot, a green apple, a banana, an onion, a small piece of green ginger root, and 2 stalks celery. Cover and simmer until soft and pulpy. Add 2 quarts chicken broth and simmer 1 hour, then force through a wire strainer or food mill. Thicken slightly with 4 tablespoons flour blended with 1 tablespoon curry powder and 4 tablespoons soft butter. (If you like more curry, add more to taste.) Add 1/4 cup hot cream, also 1/4 cup shredded fresh coconut if you like. Arrange the pieces of hot chicken around mounds of flaky hot cooked rice on a large platter, pour the hot curry sauce over chicken, and serve with the usual accompaniments. (See Index.) Serve 6 to 8.

STEWED OR FRICASSEED CHICKEN

Cut up a fricassee hen, cover with boiling water, add a few sprigs of parsley and celery tops, a sliced onion, and a sliced carrot. Cover and simmer slowly 2 to 3 hours or until very tender, adding salt to taste when about half done. Take up chicken, skim fat off broth. Thicken broth with 3 tablespoons flour blended with 3 tablespoons chicken fat for each 2 cups broth. Season to taste. Pour part of gravy over chicken, and serve remainder in sauceboat. Serve with hot biscuits or corn bread.

GOLDEN FRICASSEE OF CHICKEN

1 fricassee hen (4 to 5 pounds)

1 1/2 cups sauterne or other white table wine

1 1/2 cups water

1 1/2 teaspoons salt

3 or 4 slices carrot and onion

Few sprigs parsley and celery tops

Salt and white pepper

3 tablespoons flour

1/2 cup thin cream

2 egg yolks, beaten

Cut up the chicken and place in kettle with wine, water, salt, carrot, onion, parsley, and celery. Cover and simmer slowly 2 hours or longer, until very tender. Take up chicken. Strain broth, skim off excess fat, measure broth and add water and sauterne, half and half, to make 3 cups liquid. Heat to boiling, adding salt and white pepper to taste. Mix flour, cream, and beaten egg yolks, stir into hot broth and cook, stirring constantly, until smoothly thickened. Put the chicken back into this gravy to reheat. Arrange the pieces of chicken on a large platter and surround with a border of green rice—hot steamed rice mixed with enough chopped parsley to give a pretty green-and-white effect. Pour some of the golden gravy over the chicken, serve the rest separately in a sauceboat. Serves 5 or 6.

CHICKEN MONTEREY

1 frying chicken (about 3 pounds), cut up

Flour, salt, and paprika

1 tablespoon grated onion

2 cups sour cream

1/2 pound sliced mushrooms

Roll pieces of chicken in seasoned flour, place in a shallow casserole, add onion, cream, and mushrooms. Cover, and bake slowly (at 300° F.) for 2 1/2 hours or thereabouts.

SPECIAL CHICKEN PIE

A pie without a crust is this savory mixture, excellent to serve as the main dish of a buffet supper in late summer or early fall.

1 tender, meaty chicken (a roaster, preferably)	24 ripe olives
3 tablespoons chicken fat	1 small clove garlic
2 onions, chopped	1 teaspoon salt
2 green peppers, chopped	7 large ears of corn, cut off cob
1 1/2 tablespoons flour	Salt and pepper
5 tomatoes, peeled and cooked	

Cut up chicken, cover with boiling water and simmer, covered, until tender, seasoning to taste while cooking. Drain. (Save the broth for use later.) When chicken is cool enough to handle, remove meat from bones in fairly large pieces. Skim fat from broth. Now, in 3 tablespoons of the fat cook chopped onion and green peppers 5 minutes. Blend in flour, then stir in tomatoes and ripe olives. Chop and mash garlic with salt and add. Grease a large baking pan with chicken fat. In it arrange half the corn, sprinkle with salt and pepper, then add half the chicken, then half the tomato sauce. Repeat. Cover and bake in moderate oven (375° F.) about 45 to 60 minutes. If not brown enough, remove cover and bake 10 to 15 minutes longer. Serves 8. To make this in winter, use canned whole-kernel corn and canned solid-pack tomatoes.

SUNDAY CHICKEN CASSEROLE

If your range has an oven heat regulator (which I hope it has), you can put this casserole to bake and go off to church or out to the garden and let it look after itself. To serve 4 or 5 amply, provide:

1/4 pound salt pork, sliced thin	Flour (about 2/3 cup)
	Seasonings
1 large roaster (4 to 5 pounds)	1 quart skim milk

Fry out the slices of salt pork in a large heavy skillet, take up and set aside. Sprinkle pieces of chicken with very little salt, roll in flour, and brown well on all sides in pork fat. Remove to a large casserole. Into the remaining fat stir about 1/3 cup flour. (Use what is left from flouring the pieces of chicken, of course.) Add milk and cook, stirring, until smooth. The gravy should be quite thin. Season to taste, pour over chicken, put in a couple of slices of cooked salt pork, and bake in very slow oven (250° F.) for 1 1/2 to 2 hours.

FOR SUNDAY DINNER
Sunday Chicken Casserole
Mashed Potatoes   Green Beans
Jellied Grapefruit Salad with Tomato Slices
Heated Rolls   Jam
Warm Apple Pie   Cheese   Coffee

Instead of making milk gravy, you can pour off fat from skillet after frying, then into the skillet empty two 10 1/2-ounce cans of condensed cream of mushroom soup and 1 1/2 cans of milk or water, heat to boiling, pour over chicken in the casserole, and bake as directed.

CHICKEN PANCAKES

Here is something really different and extra-delicious for a luncheon for "the girls"—or, for that matter, for dinner for the family or company any day. It's sort of a French version

of enchiladas. You can get the dish ready for baking hours—
or a day—in advance, and keep in the refrigerator until time
to bake it.

First, simmer a fricassee chicken in a small amount of water,
adding plenty of celery and onion and other seasonings to
taste. When tender, let cool in the broth, then remove meat
from the bones and dice it in not too tiny pieces. Season
chicken well. (To make it even better mix some buttered
cooked mushrooms with the chicken.) Set aside. Strain the
broth, thicken it with a little thin flour-and-water paste, and
add 1/2 cup cream. Set this gravy aside.

Now make these easy French pancakes—really just French
omelets cooked in a very thin layer in the skillet. (These
amounts make 6 to 8 medium-sized pancakes.)

4 eggs	4 teaspoons flour
8 tablespoons milk	1/2 teaspoon salt

Beat eggs with a rotary beater, beat in milk, flour, and salt.
Melt a teaspoon of butter or margarine in a 6- or 7-inch skillet
and spread it around to grease the entire surface. Pour in
about 1/3 cup of the mixture—enough to cover the bottom of
the skillet well. Cook fairly slowly until firm enough to roll.
Don't turn it—just slip the pancake, cooked side down, onto
a large sheet of heavy waxed paper. Bake the rest of the cakes
and slip out the same way. Now on each cake spread a good
big spoonful of the diced chicken, roll up, and place side-by-
side in a shallow oblong baking dish. Pour a little of the
chicken gravy over the rolls, and sprinkle thickly with grated
American cheese. Bake in moderately hot oven (375° F.) about
25 minutes, until the rolls are thoroughly heated and the
cheese melted and lightly browned. Serve at once, passing the
rest of the hot gravy separately. With perhaps buttered green
beans or peas, and jellied grapefruit salad with avocados or
tomatoes, you'll have something really special in the way of
a luncheon.

LEFTOVER CHICKEN DE LUXE

When you have a few spoonfuls of gravy and just a little chicken left over from Sunday's dinner, do this: dilute the gravy with milk or canned consommé or water, season with curry, and cook noodles in it. Add the chopped chicken, season to taste, heat, and serve topped with plenty of chopped parsley.

Or plan in advance to have some chicken left over. Cook the giblets separately in seasoned water to cover. When tender, take them out, and cook rice or noodles in their broth. Chop the cooked giblets and any leftover chicken and add to the rice mixture, plus chopped parsley and coarsely shredded almonds to suit your taste. Serve with grated Parmesan cheese to sprinkle over the mixture.

ABOUT CURRY

When a recipe says, "Add curry powder to taste," how much is likely to be right? Well, tastes vary, and brands of curry vary in strength, but in general it is "safe" to use at least 1/2 teaspoon of curry powder for each cup of liquid or sauce. You may need as much as 1 to 1 1/2 teaspoons per cup of sauce, particularly if a large amount of chicken or sea food or the like is to be mixed with it. If in doubt, try the small amount first, and add more later if needed. . . . When to add curry powder? Sometimes it is mixed with the dry ingredients in making the sauce. Sometimes it is sprinkled over the onion, et cetera, during the preliminary simmering in butter. Sometimes it is blended smooth with a little water or milk or cream and stirred into the cooking mixture. It doesn't matter a great deal which method is followed, so long as you make sure the curry doesn't go in in lumps, and that it does have a chance to cook long enough to blend the flavors of the 16 ingredients that make up this pungent seasoning.

OVEN FRICASSEE

Cut up a fricassee hen, sprinkle with salt and pepper, but do not flour. Brown in a small amount of oil or shortening with a peeled clove of garlic in skillet. Transfer to casserole (preferably a Mexican-type pottery one), and add:

1 1/2 cups diced celery	1/2 to 1 cup diced onion
1 cup diced carrot	1/2 cup chopped parsley

Rinse skillet with 1/2 cup hot water (first discard garlic), pour over chicken and vegetables, add a little salt, cover, and bake slowly (300° F.) 3 hours or longer, until very tender. Drain off liquid, add 1/2 cup top milk or cream, thicken slightly with 1 tablespoon each butter and flour rubbed together, pour over chicken and serve. Serves 5 or 6.

TO STUFF AND ROAST A TURKEY OR CHICKEN

If possible get one of the new style turkeys, broad of breast and short of leg; or a chicken that is heavy and meaty for its size. Follow "By-law 3" in getting turkey or chicken ready for stuffing. Take it out of the refrigerator 2 or 3 hours before time to put it in to cook so it will come to room temperature. Slit skin at back of neck and cut off neck down close to the bird's "shoulders." Put neck, heart, and gizzard to simmer for a couple of hours in hot water to cover, with a sliced onion, a handful of celery tops, and a few sprigs of parsley, in a covered pan; add liver for last 15 minutes of simmering. Make stuffing (plenty of it), using part of giblet stock for moistening.

Fill the breast cavity lightly with stuffing, and sew or "pin" the neck skin to back of bird with skewer or nail. Fill the body cavity lightly. Close by sewing with white cord, or, better, by lacing it. (To lace, insert small skewers, nails or toothpicks horizontally across opening; then, using white cord, lace back and forth around the ends of the toothpicks as you would lace a pair of work shoes.) Tie legs to tail, and fasten wings snugly against the body; but don't bring cord across breast—it makes marks. Rub the skin all over with melted turkey or chicken fat or oil, place in a large shallow pan, cover with a cloth dipped in oil or fat, and roast according to the timetable on page 141. As the cloth dries, dip it in the drippings in pan. With this method no basting is necessary. Remove the cloth for the last half hour to permit deeper browning.

Should you roast the bird on its back, breast, or side? If you have one of those new roasting racks, you can roast it breast down. If the bird isn't too big, you can lay it on one side, and turn it over when it is half done. Personally, I am well satisfied to roast it flat on its back throughout. There are no marks or breaks in the skin to mar its beauty, and I doubt if a blindfold test would show up any great difference in juiciness of the breast meat. I am inclined to feel that the temperature and the length of time of roasting have more bearing on juiciness than has position during roasting.

Unorthodox Note. One of the best roast turkeys I've ever tasted was roasted by the old Italian short-time high-temperature method! It was a 10-pound turkey, and was roasted breast down in a wire rack just 2 hours in hot (400° F.) oven, with frequent basting. It was beautifully golden and crisp outside, beautifully tender and juicy inside.

Another Unorthodox Idea. An outstanding French cook I know gives her turkeys and chickens a scalding shower before stuffing them. She puts the thoroughly cleaned and washed bird in the sink, and pours a big kettle of boiling water over and through it. After draining, she stuffs and roasts bird as usual. She says it plumps the fowl, cuts down roasting time a bit, and improves the flavor. Try it and decide for yourself.

REALLY GOOD TURKEY GRAVY

When neck and giblets are tender take them out and chop the meat fairly fine. Set meat and broth aside. When the bird is tender and golden brown, lift onto a hot platter, using cloth holders. Pour off most of fat from roasting pan, leaving about 1 tablespoon fat for each cup of gravy wanted. Add an equal number of tablespoons of flour, place pan over direct heat, and stir until lightly browned. Stir in giblet broth plus water to make required amount and consistency and cook, stirring, to dissolve all those browned bits on the pan. Add chopped giblets, season just right, and let cook very slowly for at least 15 minutes. Thin with boiling water if necessary. Serve boiling hot.

BREAD-AND-BUTTER STUFFING

These quantities will stuff a 4 to 5-pound chicken. For a turkey weighing around 12 pounds multiply by 3. (Rule of thumb is, allow 1 to 1 1/2 cups stuffing for each pound the bird weighs.)

4 cups fluffy white bread crumbs or cubes
1/2 teaspoon sage or poultry seasoning
1 teaspoon salt
1/4 teaspoon pepper
1 tablespoon minced onion

1/2 cup diced celery
1/2 cup melted butter
(Yes, that's right! Use part margarine or turkey fat if you wish)
1/4 to 1/2 cup giblet stock

Combine dry ingredients, mixing well; add butter and just enough stock to moisten slightly. It should be fluffy, not soggy! Fill lightly into bird. For *Oyster Stuffing,* add raw oysters (whole if small, chopped if large) in whatever amount you feel inclined to use. For *Nut Stuffing,* add chopped walnuts, almonds, filberts, or pecans ad lib.

Old-Timers Say: "Hang wild game for three days in cold place before using. Before cooking, bring the birds into the kitchen long enough in advance for them to reach room temperature. Game having white meat should be well cooked; dark-meated game should be served rare."

CORN BREAD STUFFING FOR TURKEY

6 cups white bread crumbs
4 cups corn bread crumbs
1 1/2 teaspoons salt
1/2 teaspoon celery salt
1/2 teaspoon pepper
1/2 teaspoon thyme

1 1/2 teaspoons sage
1 cup finely chopped celery
1/4 cup chopped parsley
1/4 to 1/2 cup finely
    chopped onion
1/2 cup butter (or more)

Combine ingredients, simmering onion in butter a few minutes before adding. Taste, to check on seasonings. Use dry, or moisten lightly with a little of the stock in which neck and giblets have been cooked. Makes enough for a 10 to 12-pound turkey. For a 15 to 16-pound bird, increase quantities 1/3 or 1/2.

WILD RICE STUFFING FOR TURKEY

1 cup butter
2 medium-sized onions,
    minced
2 medium-sized carrots,
    minced
2 cups diced celery
1/2 cup minced parsley
2 to 2 1/2 quarts fluffy
    bread crumbs

1 tablespoon salt
1/2 teaspoon pepper
1/2 teaspoon or more
    rubbed sage
1/2 teaspoon thyme
1/2 teaspoon marjoram
1/2 pound wild rice, cooked
Broth from giblets (about 1
    cup)

Cook onion, carrot, celery, and parsley in butter about 5 minutes over low heat. Mix seasonings with bread crumbs. Add the onion mixture, and toss until well mixed. Add cooked wild rice (see Index for methods) and mix well. Taste, add more seasonings if necessary. Add just enough hot broth to moisten the mixture lightly—it should still be fluffy. Pack lightly into breast and body cavities of turkey. Makes enough for a 14 to 16-pound bird.

HOT TURKEY SALAD

A good luncheon specialty is this. It has a slight resemblance to Deviled Crab.

2 cups diced cooked turkey or chicken
1/4 cup consommé or water
1 1/2 cups thinly sliced celery
1 cup coarsely chopped salted almonds
1 pimiento, cut in strips
1 cup mayonnaise

2 tablespoons lemon juice
2 tablespoons grated onion
Salt and pepper
6 baking shells or grape-fruit shells
3/4 cup crushed potato chips
1/2 cup grated American cheese

Heat the turkey or chicken with consommé or water in a covered pan over low heat, stirring occasionally, until thoroughly hot. Remove from stove and add celery, nuts, and pimiento, and mayonnaise blended with lemon juice and onion. Toss with a fork, adding seasoning to taste. Fill into the shells. Mix crushed potato chips and cheese and sprinkle over the salads. Bake in hot oven (450° F.) about 10 minutes, until well heated and lightly browned. Makes 6 generous servings.

TIMETABLE FOR POULTRY ROASTING

Do western-grown turkeys require shorter roasting times than eastern ones? Or do Westerners prefer their turkeys not quite so well done as Easterners like them?

Whatever the reason, hundreds of good western cooks report that they prefer either a shorter time or lower temperature than many eastern roasting charts give.

The timing suggested here represents my own ideas of turkey roasting, western style. If you are an Easterner, you may want to add an extra hour to the total allowance for each weight.

Starting with either a turkey cold from the refrigerator or

a just-thawed one, freshly-stuffed, estimate cooking time for
the stuffed bird on the basis of its ready-to-cook weight as
purchased, *before* stuffing. Here's how to figure:

10 to 16 pound turkey—3 1/2 to 5 hours at 325° F.*
18 to 25 pound turkey—6 to 7 hours at 325° F.*
4 to 8 pound junior turkey—2 1/4 to 3 1/2 hours at 325° F.*
3 to 5 pound chicken or duck—2 to 3 hours at 325° F.*

(*Start roasting at 325° F. But if bird is browning too fast at
end of first 30 minutes, turn heat down to 300° F. or even
lower. . . . To roast a turkey *without* stuffing, see page 145.)

The above recommendations are intended as guides, not as
hard-and-fast rules. For turkeys—and tastes—vary, and oven-
controls sometimes need adjusting. It's wise to allow the
longer time suggested, but start testing for tenderness 45 minutes or so before that time is up. Test by gently pressing thick
part of drumstick and by twisting the leg slightly. If meat
feels tender, and if joint gives easily, the turkey is done.

It's best, too, to put the turkey in to roast 30 to 45 minutes
earlier than you figure would be necessary. This allows some
leeway in case longer cooking should be needed. Also, carving
will be easier and slices more attractive if the turkey stands
on its platter 20 to 30 minutes before serving, while you make
gravy and finish other details.

About Small Turkeys. All over the country young turkeys
weighing only 4 to 9 pounds are being marketed. They can be
roasted, but make mighty good eating when fried just as you
fry chicken. Be sure to allow plenty of time for the big pieces
to cook.

TO ROAST WILD DUCK

Clean and dress as for chicken, removing those stubborn pinfeathers with tweezers. (Ducks are notorious for "5-o'clock
shadow.") Dig out every bit of buckshot, too.

If you like your ducks rare (as most California hunters seem to prefer them), stuff each duck with chopped celery, onion, apple, and orange (skin and all), to add flavor. Rub the breast with butter or margarine and place on a rack in a shallow pan. Roast in very hot oven (500° F.) for 15 or 20 minutes, basting every 5 minutes with melted butter or margarine mixed half-and-half with Burgundy or claret wine, and with plenty of salt and Worcestershire sauce added. Remove the temporary stuffing and rush duck to table.

If you like duck well done, roast it about 45 minutes at 450° F., basting as described. Ducks done this way may be stuffed with bread or rice stuffing before roasting.

For stuffing wild or tame duck, a simple wild rice stuffing is excellent. Wash a cup of wild rice, cover with plenty of boiling water, and set aside to soak for several hours or overnight. Drain off any excess water. Simmer a minced onion in a little butter or margarine until soft; mix with the soaked rice, add salt and pepper to taste, stuff lightly into the bird, truss and roast as usual.

Wild Goose should be roasted until well done in an uncovered pan in moderate (350° F.) oven. It will take 1 to 2 1/2 hours, according to size and tenderness of bird.

ROAST PHEASANT

A young hen weighing about 3 pounds makes the best roaster. Prepare and stuff as for chicken, rub with oil or butter, and roast uncovered in moderately slow oven (325° F.), about 1 hour, or until tender. Cover with a cloth dipped in oil, or baste frequently with oil and hot water while roasting. One pheasant will serve 3 or 4.

QUAIL ON TOAST

Split birds, allowing 1 per person. Roll in seasoned flour and brown in butter, then add 1 cup hot water, cover skillet, and let simmer until tender. Add 1/2 to 1 cup top milk or cream, simmer 10 minutes longer, and serve on toast.

ROAST SQUAB

Allow a whole squab for each person. Dress, wash, and truss as for roast chicken. Rub with soft butter. Sprinkle inside and out with salt and pepper, and stuff with celery tops. Place in a shallow pan on a bed of chopped onion and celery, also a small clove of garlic, chopped, and a sprig of rosemary if wished. Roast in fairly hot oven (425° F.) about 45 minutes or until tender, basting occasionally with a few spoonfuls of white table wine.

GOOD WAYS WITH RABBIT

The meat of the domestic rabbit or Belgian hare is fine-grained and white, like white meat of chicken. Prejudice against it, I suspect, is due principally to the shape of the pieces. If it is boned or cut to disguise those shapes and fixed in any of the ways chicken is cooked, and if it is not announced as rabbit, it will be accepted usually without question. Fried rabbit is especially good seasoned with onion, garlic, and celery salt before cooking. Most of the books say that rabbit is a dry meat. Most persons, however, find it rather rich. For that reason, many prefer it without gravy. Whatever way you cook rabbit, use plenty of chopped parsley with it. After frying young rabbit, strew chopped parsley and onion over it when you put it into the oven to finish cooking in a covered pan. When you make a rabbit casserole or fricassee, add plenty of parsley, too.

One of the best ways of fixing rabbit, to my way of thinking, is in a simple curry, such as the one that follows.

RABBIT CURRY

Cut up a plump rabbit and simmer in a closely covered kettle in 1 cup water and 1 cup white table wine, with parsley, celery tops, and a sliced onion and carrot. Season to taste with salt and pepper while cooking. When tender, let cool in the broth, then remove meat from the bones, and cut in medium-sized pieces. Strain the broth, and skim off as much fat as you can. For the curry sauce, you will need:

3 tablespoons butter or margarine	**2 to 4 teaspoons curry powder**
1 medium-sized onion, chopped	**4 1/2 tablespoons flour**
	1 cup broth from rabbit
1 raw apple, pared and chopped	**1 1/2 cups rich milk**
	Salt and pepper to taste

Melt butter in large heavy saucepan, add chopped onion and apple, sprinkle with curry powder, and simmer until soft. Stir in flour, then gradually add broth and milk, stirring constantly, and cook slowly until smoothly thickened. Add diced rabbit meat. Taste. If more curry powder is needed, blend it with a little liquid and stir in. (You may find that adding a tablespoon of lemon juice improves the flavor.) Serve with rice and the usual accompaniments.

One attractive way to serve a curry dinner is to heap a mound of rice on a platter, and surround it with small bowls, sauce dishes, or thin glass custard cups, each containing one of an assortment of accompaniments—chutney, chopped crisp bacon, chopped hard-cooked egg, preserved ginger, nuts, toasted coconut, seedless raisins. Serve the curry separately in a bowl. Another way is to spoon hot steamed rice to form a rough ring on a platter and pour the curry in the center of the ring. In this case the accompaniments may be arranged on a relish plate.

———

When Serving Turkey. You haven't a platter big enough to hold a turkey? Then use an aluminum cooky sheet, or a big shiny tin jelly-roll pan from the dime store. (Better set the pan on the big bread board or molding board, or it will bend and buckle when you carry it in.) You can use a low hedge of parsley and celery tops around the edge, to glamorize it.

To Roast a Turkey without Stuffing. Just sprinkle inside with salt, pepper, and a bit of poultry seasoning, then roast as usual. Allow 30 to 45 minutes less time than if it were stuffed. (See page 141.) Mix and shape Walnut Stuffing Balls (recipe follows), or make plain ones, using recipe for Bread and Butter Stuffing on page 138. When turkey is done, take it out, turn up oven heat to 400° F., and bake.

WALNUT STUFFING BALLS

5 cups soft, fluffy bread crumbs or cubes (about 1 pound)	1/4 cup finely chopped onion
1 cup chopped walnuts	1/2 cup melted butter
1/2 cup chopped parsley	1/4 cup water or giblet stock
1/2 cup finely chopped celery	

Mix all ingredients. Press and shape into 2-inch balls. Arrange on greased baking sheet. Bake at 400° F. about 20 minutes, until crisply browned. Makes 8 to 10 balls. Serve piping hot, with turkey gravy.

When Making Stuffing. To crumble bread quickly for stuffings: If it's unsliced bread, cut the loaf in half, and pull out the crumbs with a fork. If it's sliced bread, stack several slices on the bread board and cut off the crusts; cut through all the slices at once, making narrow strips, then cut through all the strips, making small cubes.

By-laws of Casserole Cookery

These suggestions apply not only in making casserole dishes, but in putting together any combination of foods for top-of-stove cooking or for oven baking.

1. Don't combine too many ingredients in one dish. Men in particular have a distinct aversion to conglomerate mixtures.

2. Have some one food dominant and recognizable in the mixture. In preparing a dish, as in composing a painting or a piece of music, you need one major interest and one or more minor themes.

3. Make it a point to include something colorful in each combination. Strips of pimiento or green pepper, slices of tomato or carrot, pitted ripe olives, chopped parsley—these give contrast and character to a mixture. It's a good idea to arrange the various foods in layers, when feasible.

4. Try to have something definitely chewable in every mixture. Cubes of meat or balls of ground meat, whole-kernel corn, coarsely chopped nuts—these make a pleasant break in the monotony of an otherwise soft, smooth mixture.

5. Give real thought to the flavor and seasoning of every mixed dish. Sometimes a tiny bit of fried ham or bacon will supply what is needed; sometimes a pinch of herbs will do the trick. And don't forget to use garlic as well as onion in practically all meat dishes. It does wonders for them.

6. Allow plenty of time for slow baking or simmering to develop a rich, well-rounded flavor.

Chapter 6

Hearty Dishes
with Little or No Meat

N o CALIFORNIA buffet or barbecue menu is complete without a huge casserole or kettle of something bubbling hot and savory. Often it is beans, pink, red, lima, or navy, seasoned in some special manner and served as a supplement to the meat. Equally often it is white or brown rice, or spaghetti, macaroni, noodles, or any one of the amazing other shapes and designs of Italian pastes, combined with the meat.

Whatever its place and purpose in the meal, a made dish needs to be thoughtfully assembled, not thoughtlessly thrown together. It takes a little time and care to have a casserole really good. True, it isn't always necessary to follow an exact recipe for such dishes, but you do need to use your sense of proportion and sense of taste.

In deciding on the hearty dish for a barbecue or buffet supper, it's smart to select one that can be put together the day before it is needed, or at least several hours in advance, ready to bake or simmer unwatched during the last hour or so before serving. And do pick one that will be improved, rather than ruined, by an extra half-hour of cooking. Save such touchy show-offs as soufflés for times when you can be sure the people will be ready to eat when the soufflé is ready to eat!

There are, of course, hundreds of excellent possible combinations for casseroles and other hearties. Since there isn't space for all of them, I'm including only those that I believe you'll find quite (but not too) unusual, and unusually good.

Don't let those occasional foreign names stop you from trying them! You'll miss a lot of cooking and eating fun if you do.

TURKEY TETRAZZINI

1/2 pound uncooked spaghetti (2 cups broken)
3 tablespoons butter
1/2 cup sliced fresh mushrooms
3 tablespoons flour
1 cup broth made from turkey bones, or canned consommé
3/4 cup white table wine or milk

1/2 cup cream or evaporated milk
Celery salt, salt and pepper
1 to 1 1/2 cups coarsely diced cooked turkey
1/2 cup fine dry bread crumbs
1/4 cup grated Parmesan cheese

Cook spaghetti in plenty of well-salted boiling water until barely tender, drain, and rinse with hot water. While this is cooking, fry mushrooms in butter about 5 minutes, blend in flour, then stir in broth and wine, and cook, stirring, until smooth. Add cream, and season to taste. In a buttered baking dish put first a layer of spaghetti, then of diced turkey, then of mushroom sauce. Repeat; finish with a thin layer of spaghetti. Sprinkle with crumbs mixed with grated cheese, dot with butter, and bake in top of hot oven (450° F.) 20 to 30 minutes, until brown and bubbling. Serves 5 or 6. Naturally, Chicken Tetrazzini can be made in the same way.

SPAGHETTI WITH CHICKEN AND MUSHROOMS

4 tablespoons butter
1/2 cup diced smoked ham
1 medium-sized onion, minced
1 cup chopped celery
1/2 green pepper, chopped
1 cup sliced mushrooms, canned or fresh
3 cups diced chicken

1 No. 2 1/2 can (3 1/2 cups) tomatoes
2 teaspoons chili powder
3/4 pound uncooked spaghetti (3 cups broken)
Salt and pepper
1 cup grated Parmesan cheese

Fry onion and ham a rich brown in butter. Add celery, green pepper, mushrooms and chicken, fry a few minutes, then add tomatoes and chili powder, season to taste, cover, and let simmer about half an hour. If it gets too dry, add a little chicken broth or water. Cook spaghetti tender (10 to 15 minutes) in plenty of boiling salted water, drain. In a greased large casserole put alternate layers of spaghetti and chicken mixture, cover, and bake 1 to 1 1/2 hours in slow oven (300° F. to 325° F.) so that flavors may blend. Pass grated Parmesan cheese to sprinkle over servings. Serves about 8.

HOW TO FIGURE HOW MUCH TO COOK

Rice and beans swell to about 3 times their original size in cooking. One cup weighs about 1/2 pound, makes about 3 cups cooked; serves 2 to 4 depending upon what you are serving with it. . . . *Spaghetti and macaroni* double in size during cooking. A 1/2-pound package of either of these pastes broken into short lengths measures about 2 cups before cooking; about 4 cups after; serves 3 or 4. . . . *Noodles* measure almost the same before and after cooking. A half-pound package of noodles measures about 4 cups before cooking, and between 4 and 5 cups after cooking.

TAGLIARINI STUDIO SUPPER

1/2 pound tagliarini
4 tablespoons butter
1 cup fresh mushrooms, sliced
3 or 4 chicken livers, coarsely chopped
1 pimiento, cut in strips

1 tablespoon flour
1 can (8 ounces) tomato sauce
1/2 cup water
1 or 2 bouillon cubes
Grated Parmesan cheese

Tagliarini is a narrow type of noodle, sometimes colored red or green. Cook it in plenty of boiling salted water about 25 minutes, until tender, then drain. While it is cooking, fry mushrooms in butter 5 to 10 minutes, until lightly browned, take out and keep hot. In remaining butter, in same skillet, fry chopped chicken livers, seasoning them while they cook. Take them up and put with the mushrooms. Stir flour into butter that remains in skillet (add a little more butter if necessary) and brown lightly. Add tomato sauce, water, and bouillon cubes, and stir until smoothly and slightly thickened. To the hot drained tagliarini add chicken livers, pimiento, mushrooms, and a big spoonful of grated cheese. Mix well and heap on a hot platter. Pour the tomato sauce over all, sprinkle with more cheese, and serve at once. Serves 3 or 4.

JANIE'S SUPER MACARONI

6 ounces (1 1/2 cups) uncooked short-length macaroni
1 large egg or 2 small eggs
2 tablespoons milk or water

1/2 lb. well-aged, sharp Cheddar cheese
Salt and pepper
1/2 pint dairy-made sour cream

Cook macaroni in plenty of boiling salted water until just tender; drain thoroughly. Using fork, beat egg with milk or water; pour over the hot macaroni and mix well. Cut about 1/4 of the cheese into thin slices; dice the rest. In a buttered small (1 quart) casserole or pie pan spread about 1/3 of the macaroni. Sprinkle lightly with salt and pepper, then cover with half the diced cheese. Repeat. Top with final layer of macaroni. Drizzle over all of whatever egg mixture is left in the pan, then arrange slices of cheese over top. Bake at 350° F. (moderate) 25 to 30 minutes, or until brown. Cut in wedges and serve with sour cream spooned over it. 6 servings.

TEXAS DISH FOR TWO

1 small bag corn chips, crushed
1 can chili con carne

3 or 4 green onions
2 ripe tomatoes, sliced
1 cup grated cheese

Spread chips over the bottom of a buttered pie pan. Over this spoon the chili con carne mixed with the chopped onions. Lay slices of tomato over this. Top with grated cheese, and bake in a moderate oven (350° F.) about 20 minutes.

SUPERIOR SPAGHETTI CASSEROLE

One of the secrets of superiority of this dish is that you use bacon or ham (or better yet, both) in its making. Like most good casserole concoctions, it takes a while to fix, but when that is out of the way, your buffet supper is practically ready. These amounts serve 6; multiply as necessary to fit your crowd.

4 slices bacon or 4 table-spoons oil
1/2 pound smoked ham
1 medium-sized onion, chopped
1 green pepper, chopped
1 clove garlic, mashed with
1 teaspoon salt

1/2 pound ground beef
1 quart (or No. 2 1/2 can) tomatoes
1/2 pound (2 cups broken) uncooked spaghetti
1 cup grated or chopped American cheese

Fry bacon crisp in a large skillet, take up. (Or heat the oil.) In the same skillet fry the slice of ham until lightly browned, take up. To fat in skillet add chopped onion, pepper, and garlic with salt. (See "About Garlic" on page 6 for just how to chop and mash garlic with salt.) Cook slowly until onion is soft and yellow. Add ground beef and cook, stirring frequently, until it loses its redness. Crumble or chop bacon, and cut fried ham into small strips or cubes, and add to the mixture. Add tomatoes, cover, and let simmer for an hour, seasoning to taste while cooking. (This long simmering blends the flavors as brief cooking cannot do.) Now cook spaghetti in plenty of boiling salted water until it is almost but not quite tender. Drain, rinse with hot water, and mix with the sauce and half the cheese. Taste—it may need a little more salt. Pour into a 2-quart casserole, sprinkle with rest of cheese, cover, and bake slowly (at 300° F.) at least an hour. Uncover for the last 15 or 20 minutes to let it brown slightly. Serves 6 to 8.

BUFFET SUPPER CASSEROLE

This dish is wonderful to serve for small or large gatherings. It contains practically the entire meal in one dish, and can be made the day before, ready to be baked slowly, with no watching, while you fix the salad and other things. Here is the recipe as we make it, for small and for large groups. The amounts do not need to be exact:

	To Serve	
	8 to 10	30 to 35
Fricasseeing hens	1 (about 4 to 5 pounds)	4 or 5 (20 to 25 pounds)
Chopped onion	1/3 to 1/2 cup	1 1/2 cups
Chopped green pepper	1/3 to 1/2 cup	1 1/2 cups
Chopped pimiento	3 or 4 table- spoons	3/4 to 1 cup
Ripe olives	1 cup	3 cups
Medium-wide noodles or broken spaghetti	3/4 pound	2 1/2 pounds
Green peas, cooked	1 cup	3 to 4 cups
Sharp cheese, grated	1 1/2 cups	1 pound

	To Serve	
	8 to 10	30 to 35
Smoked ham, diced and fried	1/4 to 1/2 cup	1/2 pound
Mushrooms	1 small can	2 large cans
Celery salt, savory salt, pepper and salt to taste		

Don't disjoint the hen or hens. Cover with boiling water, add celery tops, sliced onion, and bay leaf, cover, and simmer until tender. Remove chicken and let cool. Cool and chill the broth, skim off the fat, and use part of it for frying the chopped onion and green pepper about 5 minutes. Drain olives and mushrooms, adding their liquid to the chicken broth, add the mushrooms to the onion and pepper. Measure the broth, add water to make 7 cups for the smaller amount or 7 quarts for the larger amount. Heat to boiling, cook noodles or spaghetti barely tender. Don't drain. Cut up chicken coarsely and add to noodles. Add peas, cheese, and part of the ham and olives. Pour into big pans, top with remaining ham and olives to make it look pretty, and bake 1 hour in fairly slow oven (325° F.)

VEAL AND NOODLE CASSEROLE

Here's a dish that is fine for a buffet supper or for a church supper or a picnic.

1 1/2 pounds lean veal, cut in inch cubes
1 large onion, chopped
Water to cover
1 pound wide noodles

1 large can (about 1 1/2 cups) mushrooms
1 cup sour cream
Salt and pepper
Buttered bread crumbs

Simmer veal and onion in water to cover until very tender, about 1 hour, adding salt to taste. Cook the noodles just 3 minutes in boiling salted water, drain, and add to veal. Add also the mushrooms and their liquid, and sour cream. Season well, pour into a large casserole or baking pan, cover with crumbs and bake half an hour or longer in moderate oven (350° F.). Serves 8 to 12, depending upon the occasion and the rest of the menu.

BAKED TUNA-NOODLES

Cook a half-pound package of wide noodles tender in boiling salted water, drain, and put into a greased baking dish. Over the noodles spread the coarsely flaked contents of a 7-ounce can of tuna. Over all pour either a can of condensed cream of mushroom soup or 1 cup freshly soured cream. Sprinkle with salt and pepper and grated cheese and bake 20 minutes in fairly hot oven (400° F.). Serves 4 or 5.

EASY CHEESY MACARONI

Boil 1 cup short-length macaroni or spaghetti 10 to 15 minutes in salted water. Drain, and stir in a 3-ounce cake or jar of cheese sandwich-spread—pimiento, chive, or olive, or plain; or add 1/2 cup milk, 1/4 teaspoon dry mustard, and 1 cup grated American cheese. Season with salt and pepper to taste, stir until cheese is melted and blended with the macaroni, and serve to 2 or 3.

GENUINE SPANISH RICE

This is far removed from the too usual nondescript mixture that passes for Spanish rice. Try it and you'll see what I mean!

1 frying chicken
1/2 cup oil
1 cup uncooked rice
1 small onion, chopped
1 clove garlic, minced
1/4 cup tomato purée

2 1/2 cups boiling chicken broth
Salt and pepper
2 cups peas
2 pimientos, cut in strips

Cut chicken in pieces. Do not flour it, but fry in oil until delicately browned. Take up chicken, and to oil in frying pan add the unwashed, uncooked rice, and fry until golden, stirring frequently. Add onion, garlic, tomato purée (that is, solid-pack canned tomatoes which have been forced through a wire strainer), and boiling chicken broth. Season to taste, add the browned chicken, cover, and let simmer slowly 30 minutes without uncovering. About 10 minutes before serving time, cook the peas in very little boiling salted water; when done, add to the rice. Add also 1 of the chopped pimientos, mix lightly, and serve on a platter garnished with strips of remaining pimiento. Serves 4 to 6.

If it's more convenient, you can transfer the browned chicken to a casserole, pour the rice mixture around it, cover and bake slowly (at 300° F. or 325° F.) about 45 minutes, or until both rice and chicken are tender. Then either mix the peas and pimientos with the rice, or garnish the rice with strips of pimiento and serve peas separately as a vegetable.

ITALIAN RISOTTO

Don't try any short-cuts on this recipe. It's well worth making in this traditional Italian way. The recipe, incidentally, was given me by a Mexican friend, Elena Zelayeta—who, in spite of the fact that she lost her sight some years ago, is one of the best cooks I know.

2 cups uncooked rice	2 cups canned tomatoes
12 dried mushrooms	4 to 5 cups hot chicken or
2 cloves garlic	meat broth
A little minced parsley	Salt and pepper
(about 2 tablespoons)	Grated Parmesan cheese
Olive oil (about 1/2 cup)	

Cover rice with cold water and let soak about 1/2 hour. Wash dried mushrooms, cover with warm water, and let soak about 20 minutes, until soft, then drain and chop fine. Mash garlic and mix with minced parsley. Cover bottom of a saucepan with olive oil, heat, put in garlic, parsley, and mushrooms, and fry gently a few minutes. Add tomatoes, cover, and let simmer half an hour. Drain the rice and put into another saucepan with 1/2 cup broth. Cook, covered, until the broth has been absorbed, then add another 1/2 cup, and so on, until rice is tender. Stir in the tomato mixture, season to taste, and let cook about half an hour longer. Serve sprinkled with cheese. Serves 8. This takes altogether about an hour to prepare, depending on the type of rice used.

CHINESE FRIED NOODLES

Drop noodles into boiling salted water and cook just until they are soft enough to bend—no longer. Drain and spread on paper towels or cloth to dry. Pick up a forkful of the noodles, and whirl into swirls in deep hot fat (375° F.); when brown, drain. Serve hot.

RICOTTO RAVIOLI

Don't be alarmed at that word "ravioli." These are not the usual little pillow-shaped kind. They are much simpler to make, and simply delicious to eat. The ricotto cheese, found in Italian markets, is similar to cottage cheese, but smooth.

2 cups well-drained cooked spinach, chopped very fine	1/2 cup grated Parmesan cheese
1 cup ricotto cheese	Salt and pepper to taste
	2 eggs, beaten

Mix ingredients thoroughly, shape into small balls like large marbles, and roll in flour. Drop balls into boiling salted water and cook 20 minutes. Lift out with a skimmer onto hot platter, pour over them the following sauce, and sprinkle with additional Parmesan cheese. Serves 6.

RAVIOLI OR SPAGHETTI SAUCE

2 cloves garlic, minced	1 No. 2 1/2 can (3 1/2 cups)
1 onion, minced	tomatoes
1/3 cup oil	1/4 teaspoon sugar
1/2 cup chopped celery	Salt and pepper
1 pound ground beef	Minced fresh basilica
1 cup red table wine	(about 1 teaspoon)

Fry garlic and onion in oil until golden, add celery to meat and cook, stirring often, until meat is brown. Add remaining ingredients, cover, and simmer slowly for 2 hours. Pour hot over cooked ravioli or spaghetti. Serves 6.

ARROWHEAD CASSEROLE

Cook 1/2 pound spaghetti 15 to 20 minutes in boiling salted water, until tender. While it cooks, fix the sauce:

2 pounds ground beef	1/2 cup chopped celery
1/4 cup melted suet or	1 green pepper, chopped
shortening	1 can whole-kernel corn
2 teaspoons salt	1 cup grated American
1/2 cup water	cheese
1 large onion, chopped	1 can (10 1/2 ounces) con-
2 tablespoons chopped	densed tomato soup
parsley	

Cook ground beef in suet 5 to 10 minutes, stirring, adding salt and pepper while cooking. Add water, onion, parsley, celery, and green pepper, and cook 5 minutes. Add corn, cheese, and soup, mix with drained spaghetti, add more seasonings if needed, and bake in a casserole in slow oven (300° F.) for 1 to 1 1/2 hours. Serves 8 to 10. This is an exceptionally rich, meaty spaghetti dish.

MEAL-IN-ONE

Arrange in layers in a casserole, in the following order, sprin
kling each layer lightly with salt and pepper:

1 cup uncooked rice,
 washed and drained
1 cup whole-kernel corn
2 cups tomato purée or
 juice

1 cup finely chopped sweet
 onion
3/4 pound uncooked ground
 beef
4 or 5 strips bacon

Cover and bake in slow oven (300° F.) for 40 minutes, then
uncover and continue baking, uncovered, 40 minutes longer.
Serves 4. With this, serve a mixed green salad and hot French
bread or corn bread.

SYRIAN STUFFED EGGPLANT

I got this recipe in a decidedly unusual way—from a friendly
Western Union operator who liked the sound of a recipe I was
describing in a wire to *Good Housekeeping,* and who offered
this one in exchange for a copy of mine! Try it, and I think
you'll mark it as one of your special favorites, as it is mine.
To serve 6 to 8, you will need:

1 pound lamb shoulder, cut
 in small cubes (or 1 to
 2 cups diced cold
 cooked lamb)
4 tablespoons olive oil
1/2 cup uncooked rice
1 large eggplant (or 2 small
 ones)
1 clove garlic, minced
1 small onion, minced
2 tablespoons diced green
 pepper

1/4 cup piñons (pine nuts)
1 tomato, peeled and diced
Salt, celery salt, and pepper
A tiny sprinkle of cinnamon
1/4 to 1/2 cup red table
 wine
1 cup crumbled goat cheese
 or 1/2 cup grated
 Parmesan

Brown lamb slowly in olive oil in a heavy skillet. (If uncooked meat is used, cover after browning and let it braise until tender.) Meanwhile boil the rice tender, drain, and set aside; also parboil the whole eggplant for 15 minutes in boiling salted water. After parboiling, cut eggplant in half lengthwise, and hollow out, leaving a shell about 1/4 inch thick. (Save the part you have removed; it is to be added to the meat a little later.)

When the meat is well browned and tender, add garlic, onion, and green pepper, and let braise until almost brown. Then add piñons, rice, tomato, chopped eggplant, season to taste with salt, celery salt, pepper, and that tiny touch of cinnamon, and stir in just enough red wine to make a rather loose mixture. Fill eggplant shells with this, spread cheese over the top, and bake in an uncovered pan in moderate oven (350° F.) 30 to 40 minutes. Finally, slide the whole thing under the broiler to brown the top lightly.

BUFFET OR OTHERWISE

Syrian Stuffed Eggplant   Boiled Potatoes with Sour Cream
French Bread, Heated   Butter
Mixed Green Salad
Mild Cheese   Fresh Fruit
Demitasse of Very Sweet, Very Strong Coffee

ARMENIAN RICE PILAF

Related to Risotto, but different as cousins are likely to be, is this flavorsome rice dish, which I first ate and enjoyed in Fresno.

1 1/2 cups uncooked rice   3 cups boiling broth
4 tablespoons butter   (chicken, lamb, or
Salt and pepper   beef)

Wash rice thoroughly and dry between towels. Melt butter in a heavy skillet or Dutch oven which can be put into the oven. Add the rice, and heat until it is golden, and butter begins to

bubble. Add broth, season to taste, heat to boiling, then cover
and bake in fairly hot oven (400° F.) for 30 minutes. Stir well,
cover, and bake 10 minutes longer. Serves 6.

VEGETABLE RICE TORTE

Serve this semi-hearty main dish with any meat for dinner, or
with a vegetable salad for lunch. It is simple, yet really de-
lectable.

1/3 cup uncooked rice	1/2 cup grated cheese (any
2 eggs	kind)
1 1/2 cups cooked spinach,	5 tablespoons oil
chard, or asparagus, or	Salt and pepper
other vegetable,	A pinch of dried marjoram
drained and chopped	and basilica

Cook rice tender in plenty of boiling salted water, drain and
rinse it with hot water. Beat eggs, add the vegetables, rice,
cheese, oil, and seasonings to taste, and mix well. Bake in an
oiled and floured shallow baking dish or loaf pan in moderate
oven (350° F.), from 35 to 45 minutes, until firm. Turn out,
cut in slices or squares, and serve plain or with tomato sauce.
Serves 6.

KIPPERED SALMON WITH RICE

1 1/2 cups uncooked rice	1/2 pound kippered salmon,
1 No. 2 can peas	boned and flaked
2 cups medium-thin cream	2 hard-cooked eggs,
sauce	coarsely chopped
Salt, pepper, and paprika	Minced parsley

Add rice and 1 teaspoon salt to 2 1/2 cups boiling water, cover
tightly, and cook over very low heat about 25 minutes. While
it cooks, drain peas, to their liquid add milk to measure 2
cups, and use with 3 tablespoons butter and 3 tablespoons flour

to make cream sauce; season to taste. When rice is tender, turn
it into a greased casserole. Over it spread the flaked salmon,
peas, and eggs. Pour the cream sauce over all, sprinkle with
chopped parsley, cover, and bake in fairly hot oven (400° F.)
about 15 minutes, or until bubbling hot. Serves 6.

TAMALE LOAF

1/2 cup oil
1 large onion, chopped
1 clove garlic, chopped
1 pound ground beef
2 1/2 teaspoons salt
3 teaspoons chili powder
Dash of cayenne or Tabasco
  sauce

1 No. 2 1/2 can (3 1/2 cups)
  tomatoes
1 cup corn meal
1 cup milk
1 No. 2 can cream-style
  corn
1 cup pitted ripe olives

Cook onion and garlic in oil 5 minutes, add ground meat and
cook until slightly browned, stirring frequently. Add salt, chili
powder, cayenne, and tomatoes. Cook 15 minutes. Mix corn
meal with milk and stir in, then cook 15 minutes longer, stirring constantly. Add corn and olives, mix well, pour into a
greased 8 x 12-inch pan, brush top with oil, and bake in moderately slow oven (325° F.) 1 hour. Serves 8 to 10.

TAMALE PIE

1 1/2 cups yellow corn meal
1 1/2 teaspoons salt
6 cups boiling water
1/2 pound bulk sausage
1 clove garlic, minced
2 large onions, chopped
1 small green pepper,
  chopped
1 cup chopped celery
1 1/2 pounds ground beef

2 teaspoons salt
3 teaspoons chili powder
Dash of cayenne
1 No. 2 1/2 can (3 1/2 cups)
  tomatoes
1 No. 2 can (2 1/2 cups)
  whole kernel corn
1 cup pitted ripe olives
1 1/2 cups grated American
  cheese

Stir corn meal and salt slowly into boiling water in top of a large double boiler over direct heat. Cook, stirring, until smoothly thickened, then place over hot water, cover, and let cook half an hour or longer. In a large skillet or Dutch oven fry sausage, stirring, until some of the fat is cooked out; add garlic, onion, green pepper, and celery and cook about 5 minutes, then add ground beef and cook, stirring, until lightly browned, adding salt, chili powder, and cayenne while cooking. Add tomatoes and corn and let simmer 15 minutes. Grease a large shallow baking pan (about 10 x 14-inch size) and line the bottom and sides of it with about 2/3 of the hot mush. Fill with meat mixture and press ripe olives into it here and there, then drop remaining mush by spoonfuls over meat, and sprinkle with cheese. Bake in moderate oven (350° F.) about an hour. Serves 10 to 12.

CHINESE CHICKEN WITH ALMONDS

6 tablespoons peanut oil
1/2 cup sliced fresh or canned mushrooms
1/2 cup minced onion
1/2 cup thinly sliced celery
1/2 cup diced canned water chestnuts
1 cup bean sprouts
1 cup diced cooked or canned chicken
1 can (10 1/2 ounces) condensed consommé, or 1 1/4 cups strong chicken broth
1/2 cup blanched almonds
1 teaspoon cornstarch
1/4 teaspoon salt
1/4 teaspoon sugar
2 tablespoons cold water
1/2 teaspoon soy sauce

Brown mushrooms, onion, celery, water chestnuts, and bean sprouts, lightly in 2 tablespoons of the oil, stirring. Add 1/2 cup water, cover, and simmer 10 minutes. Brown diced chicken lightly in 2 tablespoons of the oil. Add consommé, cover, and let simmer 10 minutes. Brown almonds slightly in remaining 2 tablespoons oil and set aside. Mix cornstarch, salt, sugar, water, and soy sauce, add to chicken and cook, stirring, until slightly thickened and smooth. Add vegetables (there should be no liquid left on them), heat thoroughly, add almonds, and serve with steamed rice or fried noodles. Pass soy sauce at table. Serves 3 or 4.

KITCHENETTE CHOP SUEY

1/2 pound lean pork or veal, cut in small strips	1 1/2 cups meat stock, or water with 2 bouillon cubes
2 tablespoons oil or butter	1 teaspoon soy sauce
1/2 cup sliced mushrooms	1 tablespoon flour
2 medium-sized onions, sliced	3 tablespoons warm water
1 cup thinly sliced celery	

Brown meat thoroughly in oil or butter. Add mushrooms, and cook 5 minutes. Add onion and celery, and cook a few minutes, then add stock, cover, and simmer until meat is tender, or about 30 minutes. Add soy sauce. Mix flour to thin paste with the warm water, stir into meat mixture, and cook, stirring, until slightly thickened. Add more seasonings if needed. Serve with hot steamed rice or boiled noodles. Serves 4.

MEXICAN CHILES RELLENOS

These cheese-stuffed green chile peppers, so popular at the best Mexican restaurants, look difficult to make, but are really easy as can be. What is more, they can be stuffed, dipped, and fried several hours or even a day ahead of time, then heated in the tomato sauce just before serving.

To make them, cut Monterey cream cheese, or mild American cheese, into domino-shaped pieces, about 1/2 x 1 x 2 inches. Wrap each piece in a strip of peeled green chile pepper, fresh or canned. Make a fluffy batter, allowing 1 egg and 1 tablespoon flour for each 2 whole green chiles: beat the egg whites stiff, beat the yolks, fold in the flour, then fold yolks into whites. Drop a cheese-stuffed pepper into the batter, lift out with a spoon, and place in moderately hot oil (375° F.) about 1 1/2 inches deep in a frying pan. Turn immediately. (If you don't, you'll find it hard to make them stay turned over!) Fry until golden brown all over. Drain on paper towels and let stand. The puffy coating will deflate, but don't let that worry you.

Shortly before serving time make a thin sauce this way: Mince 1 small onion and 1 clove garlic fine, and fry in a little oil until transparent. Add 2 cups tomato purée (solid-pack canned tomatoes forced through a wire strainer), and 2 cups chicken broth or meat stock. When boiling, season with 1 1/2 teaspoons salt, 1/2 teaspoon pepper and 1 teaspoon oregano (rub this between the palms of your hands into the sauce). Drop the stuffed chiles into the boiling sauce and heat about 5 minutes, until they are heated through and puffed up again. Serve with some of the sauce. Allow 2 (or more!) chiles rellenos per person.

ITALIAN STUFFED PEPPERS

3 large green peppers, cut
  in halves lengthwise
1 large onion, chopped
2 cloves garlic, chopped
3 tablespoons oil or butter
1 No. 2 1/2 can tomatoes (or
  1 quart) forced through
  wire strainer
1 teaspoon salt
1/2 teaspoon pepper
1/2 teaspoon sugar
4 slices French bread
1/2 pound American cheese,
  chopped
3 eggs, not beaten

Remove seed cores and parboil green peppers 5 minutes. Fry onion and garlic in the oil or butter until transparent. Add tomatoes, salt, pepper, and sugar, heat, then pour into a broad, shallow casserole. Dip bread into water, squeeze dry, and add. Fill the drained green pepper shells with chopped cheese and arrange in tomato sauce in the casserole. Bake in moderate oven (350° F.) about 25 minutes. Then break the eggs and drop them into tomato sauce between the peppers, and continue baking until eggs are as firm as you want them—perhaps 8 to 12 minutes. Serves 3. Serve from the baking dish.

POLENTA WITH CHEESE

Make a thick mush by stirring 1 1/2 cups coarsely ground yellow corn meal (polenta) and 2 teaspoons salt into 4 1/2 cups boiling water in a large kettle. Cook for about an hour, stirring almost constantly with a long wooden spoon. Cut a pound of fresh Monterey cheese or mild American cheese in half-inch cubes and add just before taking from the heat; stir in also 3 tablespoons butter, and salt and pepper to taste. Turn out onto a big plate. Serve with any good meat-and-tomato sauce, such as you would use for spaghetti. Serves 6, usually. A big green salad and red wine with this make it "polenta good!"

CHEESE BALLS WITH TOMATO SAUCE

1 3-ounce package cream cheese

1/2 pound grated American cheese

1/2 teaspoon salt

1/2 teaspoon paprika

1 teaspoon Worcestershire sauce

2 egg yolks, beaten

1 cup soft bread crumbs

2 egg whites, beaten stiff

1 cup (or more) fine dry bread crumbs

Blend both kinds of cheese with the seasoning, egg yolks, and soft bread crumbs, fold in half the beaten egg whites. Shape into balls, roll first in the beaten egg white that remains, then in the fine dry bread crumbs. Set aside until shortly before serving time, then brown the balls in semi-deep hot shortening. Serve hot with this tomato sauce, which you can make in advance:

Creamy Tomato Sauce

Make 2 cups of fairly thick cream sauce (using 5 tablespoons each butter and flour to 2 cups milk). To an 8-ounce can (1 cup) tomato sauce add a bay leaf, 1 teaspoon sugar, and about 2 tablespoons chopped parsley, let simmer slowly 15 to 20 minutes. Just before serving, stir a tiny bit of soda (about 1/8 teaspoon) into the tomato sauce, then stir that slowly into the hot cream sauce. Strain if you wish, and serve with cheese balls. The cheese balls and sauce will serve 6. With a salad of fruit or vegetables or lettuce, and a simple dessert, you have a most interesting luncheon.

RICE AND CHEESE

2 cups cold cooked rice
2 eggs, beaten
2 cups grated American
    cheese
2 cups milk
1/4 cup oil

1 medium-sized onion,
    chopped fine
1 cup minced parsley
1 teaspoon Worcestershire
    sauce
Salt, pepper, paprika, and
    chili powder to taste

Mix the ingredients in the order given, pour into a greased baking dish, and bake in moderate oven (350° F.) about 40 minutes, until firm. Serves 6.

FRITTATA

This soul-satisfying dish is simply a baked puffy omelet with chopped vegetables in it. I doubt if any Italian cook ever follows an exact recipe for making frittata, but these general proportions will help you make it the first time. After that, you'll be ready to follow your own ideas.

Allow 2 eggs and about 1 cup of chopped cooked vegetables per person. Any mixture may be used—spinach, artichoke hearts, zucchini, string beans, peas, green limas, or whatever you have; a slice or 2 of bread soaked in milk may be added, too. Mix with the beaten egg yolks, and add salt and pepper and minced garlic, parsley, fresh marjoram, or other herbs to suit your taste. (Add some grated dry Monterey or Parmesan cheese, too, if you have it—say 2 or 3 tablespoons for 6 eggs.) Fold in the stiffly beaten egg whites. Heat plenty of olive oil (3 or 4 tablespoons) in a heavy skillet, pour in the frittata mixture, and bake in moderate oven (350° F.) 15 to 25 minutes, or until firm. Cut in wedges and serve straight from the skillet.

CHEESE BAKE

Easier and more certain than a soufflé for the amateur is this baked bread-and-cheese custard. It's attractive done in an oblong oven-glass baking dish, so there'll be plenty of crusty brown for everyone.

Cut 7 or 8 slices of bread (or the equivalent of broken pieces) into medium-sized strips or squares. Slice half a pound of American cheese thin. Arrange bread and cheese in alternate layers in a greased shallow baking dish. Mix together:

3 eggs, beaten	1/4 teaspoon dry mustard
1/2 teaspoon salt	2 1/2 cups milk
1/2 teaspoon paprika	2 tablespoons melted butter

Pour over the bread and cheese, let stand an hour, then bake in a rather slow oven (325° F.) 1 hour. Serves 3 or 4.

If you're a little short on cheese, chop up about 1/2 cup of canned chicken or tuna and spread over the bottom layer of bread and cheese, sprinkle with pepper and a little finely chopped onion, and finish as described.

EGG BOWL FOR TWO

Hard-cook 4 eggs, and shell and slice them hot into a warm bowl. Add salt and pepper, a generous tablespoon of butter, and 3 or 4 chopped green onions, tops and all. Toss together, and serve at once. For a springtime supper, serve this Egg Bowl with crusty hash-browned potatoes, garden lettuce and radishes, and toast or heated rolls. And how about strawberries and cream with walnut meringues or cookies for dessert?

SWISS CHEESE FONDUE

A deep heavy French or Mexican type pottery casserole suitable for top-of-stove cooking is most attractive to use for this genuine French fondue, but any heavy saucepan will do.

Shred well-aged Swiss cheese coarsely; either Wisconsin Swiss or imported may be used. Put it into the casserole or saucepan, and barely cover the cheese with white table wine—sauterne, Chablis, or the like. Add no salt; the cheese is salty enough. Set the saucepan on an asbestos pad over very low heat, and stir constantly and patiently until the cheese is smoothly melted, which will take probably 30 to 45 minutes. Stir in Kirschwasser (cherry-flavored brandy) to taste—about a tablespoon to a pint of the mixture. Take the fondue to the table in its cooking dish and keep it hot on a coffee warmer; or pour it into hot individual pottery casseroles and set one on each plate. Dip chunks of hot French bread into the fondue and eat with a tossed green or mixed vegetable salad and coffee.

TACOS DE CREMA

Because I like this Mexican dish so well, I am giving it in preference to a recipe for enchiladas, which require somewhat more elaborate preparation. To serve 6, fry 6 tortillas (bought at a Mexican store) lightly in a generous amount of oil in a skillet. Spread each with thin strips of Monterey cream cheese or American cheese, using 1/2 pound cheese for 6 tortillas, and strips of canned green chile peppers. Roll up and place side by side in a pan. Chop fine 1 onion and 1 clove garlic, and brown in a little oil. Add 1 1/2 cups tomato purée and 1 teaspoon each salt and oregano, cover, and simmer 30 minutes. Add 1 pint sour cream (or a pint of thin cream and two 3-ounce packages of cream cheese). Pour over the rolled tortillas and bake, covered, in moderate oven (350° F.) 30 minutes.

BETTER THAN SCRAMBLED EGGS

It's really a French omelet you make this easy way. To serve 2, beat 3 or 4 eggs slightly with a fork, adding salt and pepper, and 1 tablespoon milk or cream for each egg. In a skillet melt a tablespoon of butter, margarine, or bacon drippings. Pour in the egg. As soon as it begins to look firm around the edges, begin pulling those edges toward the center, letting the uncooked portion run down onto the skillet. Continue cooking until lightly browned underneath and as firm as you like it. Then roll or fold, and serve immediately.

TOASTED HAM AND TOMATO BUNS

Make a rich cream sauce, add plenty of grated American cheese, season well, and keep hot in double boiler. Split and butter English muffins, and toast buttered sides lightly under broiler. Lay a thin slice of baked or boiled ham on each muffin and a slice of tomato on that; sprinkle with salt and pepper, and bake 10 minutes in hot oven (450° F.). Serve with the cheese sauce poured over all.

EGGS MONTE CARLO

On each toasted English muffin half put a slice of baked or fried ham, top with a poached egg, then pour well-seasoned hot cream sauce over all.

MIXED BEAN CASSEROLE

This original combination of different sizes and colors of beans, originated in our country kitchen at Inverness, makes a mighty

good-looking as well as good-eating dish for a buffet or barbecue dinner.

2 thin slices ham (about 1/2
  pound)
1 clove garlic, minced
1 medium-sized onion,
  chopped
1 large can baked beans
  (without tomato sauce)
1 large can kidney beans,
  drained
1 large can green lima
  beans, drained

1 tablespoon brown sugar
1 teaspoon dry or prepared
  mustard
1/2 cup catsup
1/2 cup claret or Burgundy
  wine, or 1/2 cup water
  and 3 tablespoons
  vinegar
Salt and pepper to taste

Trim fat from ham and fry out in heavy skillet, cut ham in
small strips and fry in the hot fat. Add garlic and onion and cook
until limp. Add other ingredients, heat thoroughly, and serve;
or turn into a big casserole, top with onion slices, and bake
in moderate oven (350° F.) 45 to 60 minutes. Serves 8.

LIMAS WITH LAMB SHANKS

1 1/2 cups dried lima beans
4 small lamb shanks or 2
  large ones, sawed in
  halves

4 tablespoons oil or
  drippings
1 onion, sliced
Salt and pepper

Add 3 cups cold water to limas and let soak 4 or 5 hours or
longer. About 2 1/2 hours before dinner, brown the shanks
in oil, sprinkling with salt and pepper while browning. Then
put into a large casserole, add a cup of hot water, cover, and
bake in moderate oven (350° F.) about an hour. Take out
meat temporarily, and into the casserole pour the limas and
their soaking water, add onion and a teaspoon of salt, put the

lamb shanks on top of the beans, cover, and bake 1 1/2 hours longer or until both lamb and limas are very tender, and most of the liquid has been absorbed. Serves 4.

Breast of lamb may be used instead of the shanks. Pour off excess fat before adding the beans.

OTHER GOOD LIMA WAYS

Mix thick creamed dried beef with undrained cooked dried limas, heat thoroughly and serve; or pour the mixture into a casserole, top with buttered crumbs, and bake until brown. (See Vegetable chapter for directions for cooking limas.)

Mix leftover stew with cooked limas, heat and serve.

Scallop cooked dried limas with sliced cooked or canned corned beef, or fried ham, and a medium-thick cream sauce. Bake until crumbed top is brown and mixture bubbling.

Mix canned or home-cooked limas with chopped onion, celery, parsley, and condensed tomato soup. Pour into a casserole, top with crumbs and squares of bacon, and bake in moderate oven (350° F.) until bacon is crisp and crumbs browned.

Cook soaked dried limas until almost tender (about 30 minutes). Season to taste with salt and pepper, a little dry mustard, a little sugar, plenty of chopped onion, and catsup. Put into a shallow baking dish, top with browned (but not thoroughly cooked) pork chops, cover, and bake 45 minutes to an hour at 325° F., until chops are tender.

Mix cooked limas with well-seasoned tomato sauce, made with ground beef as for spaghetti. Top with grated cheese and bake slowly (at 325° F.) for 30 to 45 minutes.

OLD-FASHIONED SPANISH BEANS

From a friend's private cook book that is filled with many a good recipe handed down from the Virginia City days of her mother and grandmother, I expropriated this extra-good way with beans.

Wash and pick over a pound of dried cranberry beans. Cover with cold water, heat to boiling, drain; again cover with cold water, add a sliced onion, a ham bone, and a tablespoon of whole cloves tied in a bag, and simmer 2 hours. Remove the cloves, and add an 8-ounce can of tomato sauce, a tablespoon of Worcestershire sauce, and 2 tablespoons molasses or syrup. Salt to taste. Simmer an hour longer, adding a little boiling water if the beans cook down too dry. Serves 4 to 6.

BARBECUE BEANS

There are uncounted shades of opinion as to just how Spanish beans should be cooked and seasoned. Here is one really good fundamental way of fixing them, followed by a few of the possible departures from it.

2 cups (1 pound) pink or
    red beans
2 or 3 cloves garlic, minced
1 large onion, chopped
1 can (8 ounces) tomato
    sauce
1/3 cup oil or bacon
    drippings

2 teaspoons salt
2 to 4 teaspoons chili
    powder
1/4 teaspoon powdered
    cumin seed or comino
    (may be omitted)

Wash and pick over beans. Soak overnight in cold water, if you wish, or cover beans with boiling water and let stand until cool. In either case, drain, cover with fresh boiling water, add rest of ingredients, cover, and simmer gently 2 or 3 hours, until beans are tender and sauce is thick and rich. Stir occasionally. It may be necessary to add a little boiling water from time to time. When done, the beans should be neither dry nor soupy. Served with grilled meat, this amount of beans will be enough for 6 to 8.

OTHER WAYS WITH PINK OR RED BEANS

To soaked beans add garlic, onion, and water to cover; also a 10 1/2-ounce can of condensed tomato soup and 6 or 8 Italian garlic sausages, sliced. Cook until beans are tender.

Cook soaked beans in water to cover until about half done, adding salt but no other seasonings. Skin 2 Mexican sausages (Chorizos), crumble and fry a few minutes with chopped garlic and onion in oil, then add to the beans and finish cooking. Season to taste and serve.

Cook the beans with water and salt until tender. Drain, saving the liquid. Heat 1/3 to 1/2 cup bacon drippings in a heavy skillet. Add some of the beans and mash thoroughly. Add more beans, mash, add some of the bean liquid, and repeat, until all the beans and liquid are used. Continue cooking, stirring frequently, until mixture is thick. These are the standard Mexican *Frijoles* (free-HOLE-es), or fried beans. To make *Frijoles Refritos* (refried beans) for another meal, heat additional oil or drippings in a skillet, add the mashed and fried beans, and cook, stirring, until the beans are dry. Cubes of Monterey or American cheese added during the refrying make the beans even better. To serve, shape the beans roughly into a roll or loaf on a hot platter.

Start beans cooking with water and salt. Brown garlic, onion, and ground beef lightly in bacon drippings, add chili powder and tomato sauce, then add all to the beans and finish cooking.

Ever bake navy beans overnight? It works fine, if your oven has a temperature control. Set it at 250° F., see that there is plenty of liquid around the beans, put them in about 9, and at 7 the next morning they'll be beautifully baked, with no watching. (But the rich fragrance of them may waken you from time to time during the night!)

By-laws for Vegetable Cooking

1. Start with really fresh vegetables. Second-rate raw ones make second-rate cooked ones.

2. *Wash vegetables quickly.* Don't soak them. Don't pare or peel unless there's a really good reason. Do whatever fixing is necessary—scraping, paring, husking, shelling, cutting up—*just before cooking.* Flavor and food value are lost when prepared vegetables are exposed to air or left standing in water.

3. Put the vegetable on to cook in the *smallest possible amount* of boiling salted water, preferably in a wide, rather shallow, fairly heavy saucepan. (Don't over-salt. Remember, you are using very little water and it will, or should, be all absorbed.) Cover pan, bring quickly to boiling, then turn heat low and *let cook in its own steam until just tender.* By that time the water should be all gone, or practically so. Don't cook a minute longer than necessary—in fact, don't cook quite as long as you think you should!

How much water? About 1/2 inch deep in pan, or 1/2 to 1 cup water for family-size amounts of most quick-cooking succulent vegetables. Use more water for those which are strong flavored or those which require long cooking. If water boils away too soon, add a little more boiling water. If too much is left, remove lid and let excess evaporate.

How much salt? About 1/2 teaspoon per pound of vegetables, or per cup of water used.

4. With a few exceptions (covered under individual vegetables in Alphabet of Vegetable Cookery), no draining should be necessary. Just season lightly and rush to the table. Letting a delicate cooked vegetable stand even a few minutes can undo much of your good work.

Chapter 7

Newest and Best Ways
of Cooking Vegetables

A NEWSPAPERMAN who has been a foreign correspondent for many years observes: "Good cooking is the art of not spoiling good food." Certainly a true statement, and certainly one that applies to the cooking of vegetables. It explains why considerable space is given here to just-right directions for cooking each vegetable, as well as to unusual combinations. (See pages 214 to 217 for new vegetable recipes not featured in previous editions of this book.)

ALPHABET OF VEGETABLE COOKERY

Artichokes, Globe—Italian or French. Most plentiful from October through May. *To buy.* Look for smooth fresh-looking tightly closed heads. The Italian variety (choice of most cooks) is long and cone-shaped; the French is more nearly round with slightly flattened top. Allow 1 per person unless artichokes are extremely large, then 1 can be split lengthwise to serve 2 persons. *To prepare.* Wash thoroughly, remove outside bottom leaves, trim stem, leaving 1/2-inch stub. If artichokes are thorny, cut off 1 inch of tops, straight across, using a heavy knife on a cutting board, or trim off tips of leaves, using scissors. *To Cook.* Favorite California way is to drop whole artichokes into plenty of boiling salted water containing 2 or 3 peeled cloves of garlic, 2 or 3 tablespoons salad oil, and several slices of lemon or 2 or 3 tablespoons lemon juice or vinegar. (These extras may be omitted if preferred.) Weight them down with a plate to keep them from floating. Cover pan, and boil 30 to 45 minutes. Test by pulling out a leaf, or by piercing bottom of artichoke with fork. Turn upside down to drain, cut off stubs of stems, and stand upright on plates. Serve hot with little cups of melted butter, plain or mixed with lemon juice, into which to dip the tender end of each leaf before eating; or pass Hollandaise sauce. Or serve cold with mayonnaise mixed with lemon juice and prepared mustard. When the leaves are all eaten, the fuzzy choke is removed with knife and fork and the bottom eaten with fork.

For simple home dinners, most Californians prefer their artichokes cooked plain, as directed above, and served hot or cold as described. For luncheons and special occasions, however, the vegetable is likely to make its appearance in various other ways, for example in combination with sea food, as in the recipe that follows:

CREAMED ARTICHOKES WITH CRAB

To serve 4, cook 6 large artichokes tender as directed above, in plain boiling salted water. Remove from water, turn upside down to drain. Cool. Remove leaves and scrape pulp from fleshy part of each leaf, using a spoon. (This doesn't take as long as you might think.) Cut out feathery choke from bottoms that are left, and arrange these bottoms in a buttered baking dish. On each lay a thick piece of crab meat (fresh-cooked or canned). Add the pulp that has been scraped from the leaves to 1 1/2 cups of rich, well-seasoned cream sauce. (Add sherry to taste, if you like—and you will like.) Pour this sauce over the artichoke bottoms and crab in baking dish. Sprinkle all with 2 tablespoons grated American cheese and bake in moderate oven (350° F.) for 15 to 20 minutes, or until mixture is heated through and delicately browned. Makes a just-right luncheon dish when accompanied by a green salad and hot rolls.

BAKED STUFFED ARTICHOKES

Cut off and discard about 1 inch of tops of large artichokes, and cook almost tender. Drain, cool, then with fingers gently spread the leaves apart to make a cup. Pull out small center leaves and with a teaspoon remove the choke. Fill artichoke cups with thick, very well-seasoned, creamed sea food, chicken, or turkey, and sprinkle tops with buttered crumbs or grated cheese. Place in a deep baking dish with 2 tablespoons oil and about 1/4 cup water in it. Cover, and bake in fairly hot oven (400° F.) about 20 minutes, then uncover and bake about 10 minutes longer to brown tops lightly. The filling is eaten with a fork, the artichoke leaves with the fingers, and finally the bottom, of course, with the fork.

ARTICHOKE HEARTS WITH MUSHROOMS

Allow 2 baby artichokes per person. Wash, remove coarse outer leaves, leaving only the hearts. Trim tops rather ruthlessly, cutting through the thick portion of leaves. Cut each artichoke heart in half lengthwise, and remove choke. Into a shallow baking dish, with cover, pour salad oil to cover bottom of dish, add a finely minced clove of garlic and 2 tablespoons minced parsley, and sprinkle with salt and pepper. In the dish, place artichoke hearts, cut sides down; cut washed fresh mushrooms in halves lengthwise and arrange among the hearts. Brush tops with more oil, sprinkle again with salt and pepper, cover, and bake in moderate oven (350° F.) for 35 to 40 minutes. Precooked or canned artichoke hearts may be baked in similar fashion, allowing less time for baking.

For artichoke salad ways see chapter on Salads.

Artichokes, Jerusalem. The Jerusalem artichoke—a very different sort of vegetable from the Globe artichoke—is really a root or tuber, something like a knobby potato. Common in the East for years, it is now making its appearance more and more in California markets from late summer to the next spring. One pound serves 4. *To prepare.* Wash, pare thinly, cook 15 to 30 minutes in a small amount of boiling salted water, until tender. Drain, dress with parsley butter, season to taste, and serve.

Asparagus. Most plentiful and most popular from end of March through May. While some cooks still prefer the blanched white stalks, the trend is very definitely toward the green "grass" as it is sometimes marked in California markets. *To buy.* Many Eastern cookery charts call for 1 pound of asparagus to serve 3 or 4. But the way it is eaten here in California, 1 pound is scarcely enough for 2. *To prepare.* Break off tough bottom ends, wash stalks quickly in cold water. Trim off the scales—they hold sand. *To cook.* For creamed asparagus, break tender portions of prepared stalks in inch lengths, drop into boiling salted water about 1 inch deep in pan, cover, and boil 12 to 15 minutes. Use the cooking liquid (or part of it) with evaporated milk or top milk to make cream sauce.

If asparagus is to be served "long," either tie stalks in serving-sized bundles before cooking, or, if you have kitchen tongs, lay the stalks into a pan of boiling water about 1 inch deep and cook, covered, 15 to 20 minutes, until barely tender. Lift out onto plates and serve with butter or with Hollandaise sauce. (See recipes for sauces at end of this chapter.) Fresh asparagus rightly cooked is good with no seasoning except the necessary salt and pepper. For a company touch, serve that creamed asparagus in a ring of steamed rice that has been mixed with buttered mushrooms and chopped parsley.

Beans, Green and Wax. Green or snap beans (ordinarily called "string beans," although very few have strings these days) and yellow wax beans are in the market from March through December, but most plentiful in summer and fall months. *To buy.* Look for slender, not too well-filled pods that snap crisply. Allow 1 pound to serve 4. *To prepare.* Wash, trim off ends, and remove strings, if any. Lay a handful of beans on cutting board and cut crosswise or diagonally into inch lengths, or less; or, if you have a bean slicer, sliver them lengthwise. Add cut beans to boiling salted water 1/2 inch deep in pan, cover, and cook 15 to 20 minutes. Season, and serve.

BETTER GREEN BEANS

A real improvement over plain cooked beans are these: heat 2 tablespoons butter, margarine or bacon drippings in a big skillet with a tight-fitting cover. Put in 1 pound green beans cut in inch pieces. Sprinkle with salt and pepper and add 4 tablespoons water. Cover and cook on high heat until they steam, then turn heat low as possible and let cook 20 to 25 minutes. Don't let them burn! When barely tender, add 1/4 cup cream and serve at once. Serves 4.

Beans, Fresh Shell. Included in this group are green limas, green horse beans or fava, green soy beans, and fresh cranberry or bayou beans. *Green Limas.* In the market from July through September. Better allow 1 1/2 pounds (as purchased in the pod) to serve 2. *To prepare*. Wash pods; shell. (To shell easily, trim off thin outer edge of pod with sharp knife, then pop out the beans.) *To cook*. Drop beans into boiling salted water about 1 inch deep in pan, cover, and cook 20 to 25 minutes. Watch carefully and add more water if necessary. Season and serve. *Horse Beans or Fava*. Fresh horse beans are found in Italian markets during the same period as green limas. Shell and cook the same as green limas, allowing about 20 to 25 minutes for cooking. Season with butter, salt and pepper, and serve sprinkled with chopped chives and parsley. Garlic and onion are often cooked with them, also bacon or ham for flavoring. *Green Soy Beans*. Not often found in markets, but sometimes grown in home gardens. Pick when pods are well filled but have not begun to turn yellow. They are rather difficult to shell. Covering the hairy pods with boiling water and boiling for 5 minutes makes the job easier. One pound of soy beans in the pod yields about 1 cup shelled. After shelling, proceed as for green limas, boiling the beans 15 to 25 minutes or until just tender. Season with salt, a little sugar, and top milk, and serve. *Cranberry or Bayou Beans*. In market in August and September. Pods and beans are creamy white speckled with red. Pods should be well filled. One pound in the pod yields 1 1/3 to 1 1/2 cups shelled. Since these beans are more mature than green limas, they need different treatment, longer cooking; for example:

CRANBERRY BEANS, WOODSIDE

Shell and wash beans, cover with plenty of cold water, and heat to boiling. (They lose their bright red color and turn a purplish-gray at this stage.) Then, for 2 pounds beans, stir in 1 teaspoon soda and let boil up well. (Nutrition researchers say that this does no appreciable harm, and it does get rid of that raw-beany flavor.) Drain, then wash the beans thoroughly through 3 or 4 waters. Drain, cover with boiling water, having it about an inch deep above the beans in the kettle.

Cover and simmer gently for an hour, adding 1 1/2 teaspoons salt during the last half of the cooking time. While they are finishing, put about 3 tablespoons bacon drippings or chicken fat (that left in skillet after frying chicken is extra-good) into a 1 1/2 quart casserole, and slice in a good-sized onion, a sweet red one if possible. Cover casserole and put into oven to heat for 10 to 15 minutes. When beans have finished cooking, pour them, liquid and all, into the casserole. Break up and add 2 small dry red chile peppers (chili tepines). If necessary, add boiling water, so that beans are well covered with liquid. Cover casserole and bake in slow oven (300° F.) for 2 1/2 to 3 hours, or until very tender. If they cook down too dry, add a little boiling water during baking. Serves 4.

Bean Sprouts. French bean sprouts are often found in Chinese markets. And dried soy beans and Mung beans (tiny round green beans) are frequently sprouted at home these days. They are exceptionally rich in protein and in vitamin C. *To cook.* Cook quickly in a small amount of boiling salted water—10 to 20 minutes is usually long enough to remove the "raw bean" flavor, which is all that is necessary. Dress with butter or with chopped onion fried in butter, or with tomato sauce; or add to chop suey or other meat-and-vegetable mixture; or use the sprouts instead of cabbage in the recipe for Skillet Cabbage given later in this chapter. For use in salad, drain and chill the cooked sprouts and add a little soy sauce to the salad dressing used.

Beans, Dried. Dry beans in all colors, shapes, and sizes bewilder one in the large California markets. Most plentiful are the familiar small white navy or pea beans; marrow beans, slightly larger, in red as well as white; dried limas, both the baby and giant size; cranberry beans, white speckled with red; red kidney beans; the small pink and red Mexican beans and their relatives, pinto beans, which are buff-colored sprinkled with brown. Then there are the huge white horse beans, the dried soy beans in green and yellow, and occasionally there are some black or turtle beans, and black-eyed peas or cowpeas, which are really beans. All, of course, are cooked in much the same way, chief difference being in the length of time they require to cook tender.

TO COOK DRIED BEANS

Wash and pick over 2 cups beans, cover with 4 cups cold or warm water, and let soak overnight or for several hours. (Navy, pink, and red, and cranberry beans may be cooked without soaking, but soaking cuts down the cooking time.) Heat to boiling in the soaking water, or in fresh water if the soaking water tastes strong; skim, then turn heat very low and let simmer slowly until tender but not mushy. Add 2 teaspoons salt when the beans are about half done. Ordinarily dried limas will need only 35 to 45 minutes' cooking. Navy, cranberry, and the various pink and red beans and black-eyed peas will take 1 to 2 hours. Soy beans require 2 to 3 hours' cooking, and even then they will be firm and crunchy, not soft like navy beans. Black beans will have to be simmered all day to make them tender enough to force through a sieve. Navy beans and soy beans swell the most in soaking and cooking, 1 cup of dry beans making 3 cups cooked. Limas increase about 2 1/2 times in bulk. Red, pink, and kidney beans increase to a little more than twice their original measure.

For various recipes for baked dried beans and baked bean combinations, see chapter entitled "Hearty Dishes with Little or No Meat."

Beets. Allow 1 pound to serve 2. *To prepare.* Wash, cut off tops leaving 2 inches of stem so beets won't bleed. Leave tap root on for same reason. *To cook.* Boil in water to cover until tender when tested with fork—1/2 to 1 hour for young beets, 1 to 2 hours for old. Drain, run cold water over them, slip off skins, stems, and tails; slice or dice, or leave whole if small.

Reheat with seasonings, including 1 or 2 tablespoons lemon juice or vinegar to help both color and flavor.

What about cooking beet tops? If they are tender and crisp, yes. Cook them as you would greens. See paragraph later in this chapter on greens in general.

STANFORD BEETS

1 teaspoon grated orange
   peel
1/2 cup orange juice
2 tablespoons lemon juice
1/4 cup sugar
1 tablespoon cornstarch

1/2 teaspoon salt
2 tablespoons butter or
   margarine
3 cups diced cooked or
   canned beets, drained

Heat grated peel, orange and lemon juice, in double boiler. Mix sugar, cornstarch, and salt; add all at once, and stir until thickened and clear. Add butter and beets, and heat in double boiler 15 to 20 minutes. Serves 4 to 6.

SAVORY BEETS

3 tablespoons butter or
   margarine
2 tablespoons chopped
   onion
1 tablespoon sugar

3 tablespoons vinegar
1 teaspoon salt
1/4 teaspoon cloves
1 No. 2 can diced beets,
   drained

Cook onion in butter until clear. Add seasonings, and cook 5 minutes. Add beets, heat thoroughly, and serve. Serves 4.

Broccoli. Most plentiful from September through April. In buying, look for crisp, heavy heads of tightly closed green flower buds; yellow flowers indicate that broccoli is too mature and will taste rather strong. Allow 1 pound to serve 2 to 3. *To prepare.* Wash, trim off the woody end of stem and any rough lower leaves; split end of stem with knife so it will cook as quickly as the tender upper part. If heads are large, cut lengthwise into halves or quarters. Lay broccoli in pan containing boiling salted water 1 inch deep, cover, and boil about 15 minutes, until barely tender. Lift out onto plates or serving dish. Serve immediately, dressed with butter or melted butter blended with lemon juice, or mustard mayonnaise or other sharp sauce. (See recipes for sauces at end of this chapter.) Garnish with generous wedges of lemon.

Brussels Sprouts. Most plentiful from October through February. One pound ordinarily serves 3; if in perfect condition, may serve 4. *To prepare.* Trim off wilted leaves, inspecting carefully for worm holes. Wash in cold water. Cook in boiling salted water about 1 inch deep in covered pan, not more than 12 to 15 minutes. Drain, season with a little butter and lemon juice or top milk, salt and pepper, and a dash of paprika or nutmeg, if desired. Serve immediately. Sprouts lose their bright green color and fresh flavor very fast after cooking. Twosome families who have difficulty using up a head of cabbage find these tiny "cabbages" a good bet.

Cabbage. There's always cabbage of one or more kinds and colors in the markets: young green or older white, pale green Chinese, frilly dark-green savoy, and deep maroon red cabbage. The greener the green cabbage, the richer it is in vitamins and minerals. A pound of cabbage, cooked or raw, will usually serve 3. *To prepare.* Wash and trim the head, and keep it covered in refrigerator until cooking time. Then shred, not too fine, and cook quickly with a little water in covered pan. Season while cooking, and serve at once. *Cooking time.* Chinese cabbage will need only 3 to 5 minutes' cooking; young green cabbage, 5 to 7 minutes; older white cabbage and crinkly green savoy, 10 to 12 minutes; red cabbage a little longer, usually 15 to 25 minutes, though some recipes call for twice that time. Always add 1 or 2 tablespoons lemon juice or vinegar to red cabbage before **or during** cooking, to keep or restore its brilliant color. Never overcook cabbage! Long cooking destroys its flavor and vitamins.

SKILLET CABBAGE

1 tablespoon butter or bacon drippings	1 or 2 large ripe **tomatoes,** peeled and chopped
1 onion, chopped	4 cups shredded cabbage
1 green pepper, chopped	1 teaspoon salt
1 cup thinly sliced celery	Pepper

Melt butter or drippings in large skillet or saucepan. Add vegetables, sprinkle with salt and pepper. (Tomatoes may be omitted.) Mix well. Cover snugly and let steam 5 or 6 minutes, stirring once or twice during cooking. Serve at once, Serves 4 or 5.

RED CABBAGE WITH WINE

2 tablespoons butter or margarine	Salt and pepper
2 tablespoons minced onion	4 tablespoons red table wine
4 cups shredded red cabbage	2 tablespoons lemon juice or vinegar
4 tablespoons brown sugar	

Fry onion in butter 3 or 4 minutes. Add cabbage, and sprinkle with brown sugar, salt and pepper, then add wine and lemon juice. Cover and cook slowly for 20 to 25 minutes, stirring occasionally. Serves 3 or 4.

Cardoon. (Sometimes known as Cardoni.) This rough-looking customer is shaped like a head of celery, but is larger and much coarser and has a prickly surface. It belongs to the artichoke family—in other words, the thistle family. To prepare, wash and scrape the thick ribs, cut in short lengths, boil until tender, and serve with butter; or parboil, then dip in batter and fry in deep fat.

Carrots. Allow 1 pound to serve 3. *To prepare.* Simply scrub young carrots with a stiff brush; older ones may need scraping. If small, leave whole; if thick, cut in halves or quarters lengthwise. (Did you ever notice how many persons who despise sliced or diced carrots will eat "long" ones happily?) Cook in boiling salted water about 1/2 inch deep in covered pan. Young carrots, whole, will cook tender in 15 to 20 minutes; older ones, quartered, in 20 to 30 minutes; shredded carrots in 8 to 10 minutes on top of stove, about 25 minutes in a covered casserole in moderate oven (350° F.), or in less time in a hotter oven. A good way with young carrots is to put them in a casserole with about 1/2 cup water and a little butter or bacon drippings, cover, and bake until tender, about 30 to 40 minutes in a moderate oven. Sprinkle with chopped parsley before serving.

Carrots, grated and baked, or butter-steamed, or creamed, are improved by combining with sliced or minced onion—up to 1/4 as much onion as carrot. Both vegetables cook in the same length of time.

CARROT-BEAN COMBINATION

Drain into a wide saucepan the liquid from a No. 2 can of green beans. Heat to boiling, add 2 tablespoons butter or margarine and 4 or 5 carrots which have been scrubbed and cut lengthwise into thin strips. Cover pan and cook about 7 minutes. Bring carrots to center of pan, and arrange string beans around them. Sprinkle lightly with salt and pepper, cover pan, and cook gently about 5 minutes, just long enough to heat beans thoroughly. Serve directly on dinner plates, or group vegetables around meat on platter. Serves 4 or 5. This is a vitamin-and-mineral-saving way of combining a canned and a fresh vegetable.

CARROT RING

2 1/2 cups riced or mashed
    cooked carrots
1 teaspoon salt
Pepper to taste
1 tablespoon finely minced
    onion

2 tablespoons melted butter
    or margarine
3 eggs, well beaten
1 cup milk

Mix ingredients in order given, and pack into well-buttered 8-inch ring mold. Set mold in shallow pan containing hot water 1/2 inch deep and bake in moderate oven (350° F.) about 40 minutes, until firm when tested with a knife. Remove from oven, let stand a few minutes, then loosen edges and invert on a hot plate. Fill center with buttered or creamed peas, or creamed tuna or chicken. Garnish with parsley and tomato wedges, and serve. Serves 6.

Cauliflower. Most plentiful from October through June. A small head weighing about 1 1/2 pounds will serve 2 or 3; a large head, 4 to 6. Look for a firm, compact, snowy-white head, with fresh green leaves. Loose, seedy-looking heads, yellowish in color, are likely to be strong-flavored and rather tough. *To prepare.* Trim the head (but don't discard those thick outer stalks; save them to cut up and cook another day). Wash and cut cauliflower into florets so they will cook quickly and evenly. Cook in boiling salted water about 1 inch deep in covered pan, until barely tender when tested with fork—not more than 12 to 15 minutes. Drain, dress with butter and/ or top milk, reheat quickly, season well, and serve immediately. Especially good if fixed with top milk and butter and served in "side dishes" to be finished with a spoon. If cauliflower is to be left whole, tie it in a square of cheesecloth before cooking, and allow 20 to 25 minutes' cooking time.

Remember that the raw tender florets of cauliflower make a good-tasting addition to the relish plate (see salad section). Remember, too, that cooked cauliflower, broken into florets or cooked whole, is delicious served with a cheese sauce. (See recipes for sauces at end of this chapter.)

Venetian Cauliflower. Venetian cauliflower, which is gorgeous bronze-purple, almost iridescent, is cooked the same as white cauliflower. Personally, I rather prefer to use it raw for decorative purposes, together with eggplant and other colorful vegetables, for a table centerpiece!

Celery. Most celery these days is the Utah type, green rather than white, crisp and tender, delicate in flavor. A stiff brush speeds up the washing of the grooved stalks. Make it a point to use every bit of every head of celery. Add tops, fresh or dried, to soups, stews and pot roasts; cut the outer stalks in short lengths and cook 15 to 20 minutes in bouillon or stewed tomatoes or salted water; or slice thin for salads. Eat the crisp inner stalks as is, of course.

BAKED CELERY VICTOR

Cut outside stalks of celery into pieces 3 to 4 inches in length. Cook gently in meat stock or consommé until tender and stock is almost evaporated. Arrange in neat piles in a shallow baking dish, brush with butter, sprinkle with grated Parmesan cheese and heat in oven until cheese is lightly browned. (For recipe for traditional Celery Victor, see salad section.)

Celery Root, or Celeriac. Most plentiful through winter months. One pound will serve 3. *To prepare.* Scrub and trim the rough, tough-looking root, and cook in plenty of boiling salted water 30 to 40 minutes, or until tender. Drain, plunge into cold water, then peel and slice or dice or mash, and reheat with seasonings. If celery root is being cooked for salad, dress the hot diced or sliced cooked root immediately with lemon juice or lemon French dressing, to keep it white. Its usual color is a bit dingy. (See "Salad Dressings" for an extra-good way to use celery root in salad.)

Chard. (See "Greens.")

Chayote. (Pronounced chi-O-ti.) This pale green squash that looks like a pear is frequently found in the markets in summer and fall. Unlike other summer squash, it has just one tender, edible, almond-shaped seed. *To prepare.* Wash, cut crosswise through seed and all, into 3/4-inch thick slices, cut into cubes if you wish, cook 15 to 20 minutes in boiling salted water 1/2 inch deep in covered pan. Drain, serve with butter or tomato sauce or cream sauce. Almost any of the recipes given for summer squash (later in this chapter) may be used for cooking chayotes.

Corn. Available from May or June through September. Buy corn that is obviously tender and fresh-picked. How many ears to allow per person is usually dictated by the price per ear and the appetite per person. *To prepare.* Don't husk corn until just before cooking; do keep in refrigerator until cooking time. A brush helps in removing silks. *To cook.* For corn on the cob, drop enough ears for the first round (about 8 minutes before serving time) into plenty of rapidly boiling salted water, bring to boiling again, and boil just 3 to 5 minutes. Serve immediately. Cook the second round while the first ears are being eaten. *Corn off the cob.* It takes 3 or 4 medium-sized ears to make a cup, or 6 to 8 ears to serve 3. Slice off kernels, using care not to cut too closely to the cob; then scrape cob with back of knife. Add a little top milk and let simmer in covered saucepan until barely tender—about 5 minutes. Don't let it stick and scorch. Season to taste and serve.

FRESH CORN SAUTE

Cut whole kernels from cob, but do not scrape cob. In a heavy skillet heat 2 to 3 tablespoons butter and in it cook 2 to 3 cups of cut corn for 5 or 6 minutes, stirring constantly. When kernels are tender and delicately browned, add 1/4 cup sweet cream and salt and pepper to taste. Serve at once. For a Spanish touch, add chopped green or red pepper and cook gently with the corn. Serves 4 to 6.

GARLIC-BUTTERED ROASTING EARS

Remove coarse outer husks and loosen inner husks, removing silk carefully; trim ear if necessary. Brush kernels generously with garlic butter or margarine. Tie inner husks into their original position, and lay on grill above glowing coals. Turn frequently. It will take anywhere from 10 to 25 minutes to roast the corn.

To fix "garlic butter" slice 3 or 4 cloves of garlic and add to 1/4 pound soft butter or margarine. Mix well and let stand at room temperature an hour or longer, stirring occasionally.

SUCCOTASH

When combining corn cut from the cob and shelled green lima beans for succotash, cook each vegetable separately, then combine just before serving. Both appearance and flavor are really better than when the two are cooked together.

CORN ROSETTES

Cut uncooked corn-on-the-cob crosswise into inch pieces. You'll need a sharp, heavy knife, but it can be done. Cook as usual, then add to serving dish of hot green beans (fresh-cooked or canned). The little rosettes of corn add a festive touch to the beans, and make for good eating, too.

Eggplant. Most plentiful from July through September. Look for shiny, smooth, rich purple ones (a dull-looking eggplant is a sign that it has lost much of its goodness). A medium-sized eggplant weighing about 1 1/2 pounds will serve 4 or 5. Bantam-sized eggplants weighing about 1/2 pound or less are sometimes seen in the markets. These are especially attractive to stuff and serve individually. *To prepare.* Wash, slice crosswise or cut in pieces, according to the way it is to be used. Unless the skin is tough, it is not necessary to peel the eggplant; neither is it necessary to soak in salt water before cooking, nor to salt it and place under a weight, as old recipes used to direct. *To broil.* Wash unpeeled eggplant and slice crosswise in 1/2 inch slices. Brush slices with bacon drippings or oil (use garlic-flavored oil, if you like), sprinkle with salt and pepper, and broil until lightly browned on both sides. Excellent broiled along with chops or thin slices of ham.

TO PAN-FRY EGGPLANT

Dip slices in seasoned flour and brown in hot butter or bacon drippings in skillet. Or dip slices first in flour, then in slightly beaten egg, then in fine bread crumbs, and brown in a fairly generous amount of bacon drippings, oil, or shortening, seasoning with salt and pepper.

EGGPLANT SPANISH

3 tablespoons shortening	Pepper
1 small onion, minced	1 No. 2 can tomatoes or an
1 medium-sized eggplant, diced	8-ounce can tomato sauce and 1/2 cup
1/2 teaspoon salt	water

Melt shortening in heavy skillet and in the hot fat brown onion and eggplant. Sprinkle with salt and pepper. Add tomatoes, and continue cooking until eggplant cubes are tender and liquid mostly boiled away—20 to 30 minutes, usually. Add a little boiling water if mixture boils dry. Serves 4.

Finocchio, or Italian Fennel, or Anise. The licorice-flavored vegetable. Its crisp stalks may be eaten like celery; the bulb sliced thin and used raw in salad, or cut in inch pieces, cooked in a small amount of boiling salted water 15 to 25 minutes, and served with butter and lemon juice. Good with fish. Allow 1 small to medium-sized bulb per person.

Grape leaves. For preparing certain Armenian and Greek meat-and-rice dishes, pick large, tender, perfect leaves of Thompson seedless grapes. Wash, wrap a spoonful of meat and-rice mixture in the leaf, making a neat bundle, place on a rack in a kettle, add boiling water or meat stock to cover, and simmer 30 minutes.

Greens. Young beet and turnip tops, Swiss chard, mustard, spinach, and the dark outer leaves of chicory and escarole—yes, even radish tops and tender carrot tops—go under the heading of greens. Generally speaking, 1 pound of any kind of greens will serve 2. *To prepare.* After removing any bad outer leaves, wash the bunches through a couple of baths of lukewarm water. Then remove roots and tough stems and wash the leaves, a few at a time, through 2 or 3 more lukewarm baths. Always lift greens out of the water, rather than run water through them, so that grit and soil and sand will stay in the pan. *To cook.* Directions used to call for cooking greens in only the water that clings to the leaves after washing. Now, many nutritionists consider it better to cook spinach in a moderate amount of boiling salted water, and drain before seasoning and serving. The reason is that spinach contains a good deal of oxalic acid, which combines with the calcium in the spinach to form an insoluble calcium salt; this sometimes causes headache or other disturbance. Using extra water and draining spinach gets rid of the trouble. Actually, you can do just as you like, and find plenty of authority for either method! Whether or not you add water, do cook the greens until just tender, in a covered pan, salting lightly before cooking. Chicory, escarole, Swiss chard, and spinach need only 10 to 15 minutes' cooking; beet tops, turnip tops, dandelion greens, mustard, and kale need from 15 to 30 minutes. Radish and carrot tops are not particularly important, but may be added to any other greens that are going into the pot.

SPEED-UP TRICK

When you want hard-cooked eggs to slice over a dish of chard or spinach or other greens, just wash the eggs carefully and lay them on top of the greens when you put them on to cook. By the time the greens are tender, the eggs will be ready to shell and slice. Saves getting out another saucepan!

One Way to Season Spinach. When tender, slash through the greens with scissors, add the juice of half a lemon, a dash of nutmeg, and enough cream (sweet or sour) to hold the mixture together. Serve immediately.

Kohlrabi. Allow 1 medium-sized kohlrabi per person. Cut off leaves, wash, pare, and slice or dice. Cook uncovered in generous amount of boiling salted water for 25 to 35 minutes, until tender. Drain, season with salt, pepper, butter and lemon juice; or serve creamed or scalloped.

Lettuce. Since lettuce is primarily a salad standby, it is discussed in the salad chapter. The coarse, dark green outer leaves of any type of lettuce or salad greens—particularly escarole and chicory—may be cooked like spinach, or with spinach or other greens. (See discussion of Greens.) Wilted lettuce is really served as a vegetable rather than a salad, hence this recipe.

WILTED LETTUCE, LA JOLLA STYLE

Oakleaf, or green leaf lettuce ("local lettuce" they call it in California markets), makes superior wilted lettuce. Wash, drain, and heap lettuce into a bowl. To serve 2 or 3 you will need, besides the required amount of lettuce, plus a generous sprinkling of chopped green onions, if you wish:

3 or 4 strips bacon	1 teaspoon sugar
2 or 3 tablespoons vinegar	Salt and pepper
1/2 teaspoon dry mustard	1 or 2 hard-cooked eggs, hot

Fry bacon crisp; remove, crumble, and set aside. Pour off part of bacon fat if necessary, leaving about 3 or 4 tablespoons in the skillet. To this hot fat add vinegar, mustard mixed with sugar, salt and pepper. Let boil up once, stirring, then taste and adjust seasoning to suit yourself. Add crumbled bacon and pour boiling hot over lettuce. Toss well, then slice hot hard-cooked eggs over top, and serve at once. Amounts given are approximate, for ideas about how wilted lettuce should be seasoned are varied indeed. Incidentally, shredded green cabbage is very good treated in this way.

Mushrooms, Fresh. Allow 1 pound to serve 4 to 6, if to be broiled or fried; if mushrooms are to be creamed or used in a sauce, you can make them go further. Firm white mushrooms, free from spots, are nicest. Keep them dry until just before cooking. *To prepare.* Wash quickly and drain—don't let them soak. Don't peel unless skin of cap is tough and brown. Leave whole, or slice lengthwise, or cut stems in pieces and leave caps whole. *To broil.* Marinate in a little olive oil that has been salted and peppered, then broil slowly. *To fry.* Cook in a fairly generous amount of butter in a covered saucepan 8 to 10 minutes, stirring occasionally. Season and mix with peas or other vegetables, or serve on toast; or sprinkle lightly with flour, stir, then add thin cream and cook.

SERVE THESE MUSHROOMS WITH FRIED CHICKEN

1 pound fresh mushrooms
5 tablespoons (2/3 cube) butter
1 teaspoon finely chopped green onion (or onion juice)

Salt and pepper
2 tablespoons sherry
2 tablespoons brandy
1/3 cup heavy cream

Wash and drain mushrooms, but don't cut them up. Heat butter in saucepan. When it begins to bubble, add onion, cover and cook until soft and lightly browned. Add mushrooms, sprinkle lightly with salt and pepper, and cook uncovered 7 minutes, stirring occasionally. Sprinkle sherry over all, then add brandy and cook about 5 minutes. Stir in cream and cook a few minutes longer. Serve on toast, to accompany fried chicken. Serves 4.

Mushrooms, Dried. Cover with hot water and let soak about 20 minutes, then pour off water and let stand, covered, in a warm place to steam, for about 10 minutes. Use in sauce for spaghetti and the like. Or add butter and salt to taste and a little cream if you wish and simmer, covered, for 20 minutes; serve on toast. For dehydrated mushrooms, follow directions on the package.

Okra. Now found frequently in California markets in the autumn months. Allow 1 pound to serve 3 or 4. *To prepare.* Wash pods, cut off stem ends. If pods are young and tender, leave whole; if not, cut in thick slices crosswise. Cook in boiling salted water 1 inch deep in covered pan until barely tender, 15 to 25 minutes. Drain and season with salt, pepper, butter, and vinegar. *To fry.* Fry 1 medium-sized onion in a small amount of butter in a skillet, add sliced okra and cook until almost tender, then add fresh peeled and sliced tomatoes ad lib. Continue cooking until the tomatoes are heated through, season, and serve.

Onions. Tiny delicate chives or larger shallots; young green onions or scallions; thick leeks; small white boiling onions; white, yellow, and red-skinned cooking onions; huge, sweet flat-round red Spanish; or big creamy Bermuda; or long red Torpedo onions; take your pick in California markets at almost any time of year. *To boil onions.* Allow 1 pound to serve 3. To avoid weeping, pour boiling water over onions before skinning, then drain and run cold water over them. Skins slip off easily. Cook in plenty of boiling salted water, uncovered (they perfume the house less that way), 30 to 45 minutes, or until tender. Drain. Serve buttered or creamed. For holiday serving, the onions may well be boiled the day before, then reheated thoroughly in cream sauce in a big double boiler.

To bake onions. Whole onions may be baked in their skins like potatoes, in hot oven (450° F.), then skinned, cut in quarters lengthwise, and dressed with butter. Medium-sized onions will require almost an hour to bake. I don't guarantee that you'll be enthusiastic about this method, but some people are!

To fry onions. For that old favorite, *liver and onions,* fry onions separately rather than in the hot fat left after cooking the meat—less danger of onions sticking and burning. Or, simmer onions gently in a small amount of bouillon or consommé and heap around the meat at serving time. Or fry onion slices in butter or oil, then douse fairly generously with soy sauce, and serve at once. These are wonderful!

FRENCH FRIED ONIONS

The large, mild-flavored, creamy white or yellow onion, found in the markets in early fall, is best for French frying. Allow 1 onion per person. Peel, cut in slices about 1/4 inch thick, and separate into rings. Have ready a cup of salted milk in a shallow bowl (2 teaspoons salt to 1 cup milk). Let onion slices stand in the milk a few minutes, then lift out and into a paper bag containing about 1/2 cup flour. Shake bag until the rings are well coated. In a heavy saucepan heat shortening 1 to 2 inches deep. How hot? Well, 370° F. to 380° F. if you have a frying thermometer; otherwise, use your judgment, but don't have the fat smoking hot. Drop in onion rings, not too many at a time, and fry 4 to 6 minutes, or until lightly browned. Drain on paper towels; keep hot in the oven until all are fried; sprinkle with salt, and serve. If everything else needed for the dinner is ready or under way, or if you have a helper, you can manage to broil a steak and French-fry onions at the same time.

SHERRIED CREAMED ONIONS

12 small white winter
    onions
3 tablespoons butter
1/4 teaspoon salt
2 tablespoons flour

1 cup milk
1/4 cup sherry
1/4 cup chopped walnuts or
    filberts

Peel onions and cut in thick slices. Melt butter in saucepan, add onion slices, sprinkle with salt, cover tightly and cook slowly until tender, about 20 minutes; add a little water if necessary. Sprinkle with flour and stir carefully. Add milk and cook gently until thickened, about 3 minutes. Add sherry and nuts cut in fairly large pieces. Serves 3 or 4.

TO COOK LEEKS

Allow 2 bunches to serve 3 or 4. Wash, trim, cut off all but about 2 inches of their green tops. Cook in plenty of boiling salted water, uncovered, about 15 minutes. Drain and serve with butter.

Parsnips. Allow 2 young parsnips per person, or about 1 pound for 3 servings. Wash, scrape, leave whole or cut lengthwise in halves or quarters. Cook in boiling salted water about 1 inch deep in covered pan, 30 to 40 minutes, or until tender. If parsnips have woody cores, boil them whole, then cut in halves lengthwise and strip out the tough fibers. Drain, season, and serve; or brown quickly in butter or bacon drippings; or cut in cubes and dress with cream sauce; or mash, season, shape into patties, and fry.

CARAMEL PARSNIPS

Parboil scraped parsnips for 10 minutes. Cut in halves length-wise, and arrange in greased shallow baking pan. Spread with soft butter, and sprinkle generously with brown sugar. Bake in fairly hot oven (400° F.) about 20 minutes.

Peas, Green. "In" every day of the year in California city markets. Allow 1 pound to serve 2. Shell and wash just before cooking. Cook in boiling salted water about 1 inch deep in covered pan, not more than 8 to 12 minutes. Don't drain! Just season and serve at once. They'll stay bright green in color, fresh and sweet in flavor. Yes, many eastern cookery charts do recommend much longer cooking time for green peas, but when quickly grown under California conditions, long cooking is neither necessary nor desirable.

PEAS WITH CORN

Combine approximately equal amounts of cooked green peas and sautéed corn (see recipe for Fresh Corn Sauté under Corn earlier in this chapter). Season and serve. An appropriate vegetable dish for Thanksgiving dinner.

PEAS WITH MUSHROOMS

Cook green peas as directed. While they are cooking, slice fresh mushrooms, allowing 1/2 pound for 4 to 6 servings, and cook gently in butter about 8 to 10 minutes, until golden. Mix with hot cooked peas, season, and serve.

Peas with Edible Pods. They are best when about 2 inches in length. Allow 1 pound to serve 3 or 4. Prepare as you do string beans, breaking off tips of pods and removing any strings. Don't cut the pods. If they are large, break them in halves. Cook in a small amount of boiling salted water in a covered pan for 5 to 10 minutes, until barely tender. Season lightly, and serve. Chinese restaurants usually mix them with bits of cooked pork, but they are delicious simply buttered.

Peas, Garbanzos, or Chick Peas. Allow 1 pound (2 cups) to serve 6. Soak overnight in lukewarm salted water. Drain, add 6 cups water, salt to taste, and simmer covered until tender, or about 2 hours. Minced garlic and onion are often cooked with garbanzos to flavor them.

Peas, Dried Split. To serve as a vegetable, add 2 cups quick-cooking green or yellow split peas to 4 cups boiling water; add 1 teaspoon salt, and boil, covered, about 45 minutes, until tender and mushy. Uncover, and let excess water boil away. Season, mash if you wish or leave as they are, and serve as you would mashed potatoes. Makes 4 cups, serving 4 to 6. Being rich in protein and iron, the peas make a good supplement to small servings of meat. (Recipe for Split Pea Soup is given in the chapter on Soups and Chowders.)

Peppers. Like onions, California peppers come in a great range of sizes, shapes, colors, and temperatures. Most common here as elsewhere are the big, sweet, bell peppers, which are used chiefly while green, but also when ripened to a gorgeous red. Then there are the rather small, pointed, yellow-green wax peppers, and the long, slender chile peppers, which are only medium-hot when green, considerably more than medium-hot when ripened and dried. (This is the kind you see hung in long strings to dry outside the Mexican adobes in the desert.) There are also the tiny, dry, red-hot chili tepines (te-pins) used in pickling, and a variety of others seen most often in Mexican grocery stores. Used ordinarily only as salad makings or as seasonings in cooking, bell and pimiento and green chile peppers are ever so good served as a vegetable. *To prepare.* Early in the summer the skin on these peppers is too delicate to remove successfully. All that needs to be done then is to wash the peppers, cut out stem and seed cores, and drop them into boiling water for a few minutes until wilted. Drain, drop into cold water, drain, then fry or stuff, as desired. Later in the season, when the skin has toughened, they should be peeled before using. To do this, put the peppers under the broiling unit and turn frequently until the skin is well blistered. At once put into a paper bag, close it, and let the peppers stand 15 minutes to steam; then peel.

QUICK PEPPER RELISH

To make a delightful relish to serve with meats, skin or scald sweet red pimiento or green bell peppers as directed above, remove seeds, and cut peppers into strips. Rub a bowl with garlic, put in the pepper strips, and add oil, vinegar, salt and pepper to taste. Let stand 2 hours before serving.

You'll find Baked Stuffed Peppers and Mexican Chiles Rellenos in Chapter Six, "Hearty Dishes with Little or No Meat."

Potatoes. In buying white potatoes, specify whether they are to be used for boiling or baking. Allow 1 pound to serve 2 or possibly 3. (Even if you are reducing, don't cut out potatoes entirely; their vitamins and minerals are important in the diet —and, remember, it's the gravy or butter you eat on them, rather than the potatoes themselves, that add most of those pounds!) *To prepare.* Don't peel potatoes, unless there is really a good reason; you waste a high proportion of their vitamins and minerals when you do this. Just scrub with a brush and cook tender in covered pan in enough boiling salted water almost to cover them. Whole potatoes will take 20 to 30 minutes. Drain, and slip off skins.

TO BAKE POTATOES

Scrub extra thoroughly, so skins can be eaten. (I like to use a metal sponge for scrubbing them.) Bake in hot oven (450° F.) until tender when pinched between cloth-protected fingers.

This will take 40 to 55 minutes usually, depending upon their size. Take out of oven, slash a big X in top of each, then roll and squeeze gently in cloth or paper towels, until potato pops fluffily through the X. Serve at once. If baked potatoes must stand after baking—which is a pity—go ahead and fluff them as directed, then turn oven down to 275° F. and put them back to keep hot. That way, they won't get soggy.

Serve a small dish of chopped green onions, tops and all, to spoon into those baked potatoes along with the butter. Paprika or coarsely ground black pepper too, of course.

STUFFED BAKED POTATOES

To serve 4, bake 4 medium-sized potatoes. When done, cut in halves lengthwise; scoop out contents; mash with butter and cream. Season. Whip until light. Refill shells. Shortly before serving, dot with butter and brown in 350° F. oven.

HOLLYWOOD POTATOES

For a buffet supper, indoors or out, serve these butter-broiled potatoes right in the baking dish in which they were browned. *To prepare.* Boil medium-sized potatoes in their jackets. While still hot, peel, and roll each in melted butter, then in grated cheese. Place in well-buttered shallow baking dish or pan and heat under the broiler until lightly browned. They make a good surprise dish for a barbecue supper. No spuds are in evidence at the grill. Then, presto, as the chops are distributed, the big dish of potatoes arrives from the kitchen, piping hot!

MUSHROOM SCALLOPED POTATOES

To serve 3 or 4, peel and slice 6 good-sized potatoes, 3 or 4 carrots, and 1 medium onion. Mix 1 can cream of mushroom soup and 1 cup milk. In a greased baking dish put a layer of potato and onion, sprinkle lightly with salt, pepper, and flour or crumbled crackers, and add part of the soup-and-milk. Repeat until everything is used. Add more milk if necessary, so that it comes up over top of potatoes. Cover and bake in moderate oven (325° F. to 350° F.) about 45 minutes; uncover and bake 30 to 45 minutes longer, until potatoes are tender and well browned.

PINECREST POTATOES

Dice 4 or 5 potatoes and 1 medium-sized onion, add 1 teaspoon salt, and enough boiling water to about half cover vegetables. Cover pan and cook 10 to 15 minutes, until potatoes are tender. Uncover pan and cook until most of the remaining water has boiled away. Add about 1/2 cup top milk, heat, and serve sprinkled generously with chopped parsley. Makes enough for 3 or 4.

This is a good camp special; it is equally good whenever and wherever you're cooking in a hurry. And remember, the fact that the potatoes aren't drained means that you get all their goodness in this dish.

CHEESED POTATOES

Leftover baked potatoes are the foundation of this superb dish. Potatoes boiled in their jackets may, of course, be used. but they do not have quite the flavor of the baked ones. Peel and dice the potatoes into a buttered shallow baking pan, making a layer about 1 1/2 inches thick. Sprinkle generously with salt and pepper, dot with butter, then dribble cream or evaporated milk over them, until potatoes are well moistened but not drowned. Cover with a thick layer of coarsely grated or thinly sliced American cheese. Bake in moderate oven (350° F.) for 30 to 40 minutes, or until nicely browned. These go beautifully with ham loaf for a company dinner that is as easy to prepare and serve as it is good to eat.

WALNUT CREEK CREAMY POTATOES

Boil potatoes in their jackets, cool, then dice or chop fine. For about 4 cups potatoes, melt 3 tablespoons butter or margarine in a skillet, add potatoes, sprinkle with salt and pepper, stir, then gradually dribble over them just as much cream (thick or thin) as they will absorb, usually about 1/2 cup. Don't brown the potatoes. When they have taken up as much cream as you feel is right and are thoroughly hot, they are ready to serve to 3 or 4 persons.

"FRENCH FRIES" THE OVEN WAY

Wash and pare small potatoes, cut into eighths lengthwise and soak in cold water 1/2 to 1 hour. Drain, pat dry between towels, spread in a greased shallow baking pan and brush thoroughly with oil or melted butter or shortening, turning to coat both sides. Bake in hot oven (450° F.) for 20 to 30 minutes, or until browned, turning occasionally and adding more oil if needed. Sprinkle with salt and pepper, and serve.

For potato soups see chapter on Soups and Chowders. For potato salad see Salad section.

Radishes, Chinese. Like other radishes, these long slender ones are good cooked as well as raw. *To prepare.* Wash, slice or shred coarsely, and cook in covered pan with a very little boiling salted water 5 to 10 minutes or until just tender. Season and serve.

Radishes, Red. Cut tails off little red radishes and remove any bad leaves. Wash thoroughly and cook whole, tops and all, in a small amount of boiling salted water. They'll be done in 5 minutes. Dress with butter and serve.

Rice, Brown, White, and Wild. Rice is one of the big crops of the Sacramento and San Joaquin Valleys in California.

Brown Rice is natural rice, with only the coarse outer husk removed, and so it is classed as a whole-grain cereal. *White Rice* has had all the brown coating removed in milling. It may be polished (usually coated with glucose and talc) or left unpolished. *Wild Rice* is really not rice at all, but the seed of a grass that grows with its feet in the water, as rice does. It comes chiefly from Minnesota, but is especially popular in California for serving with wild fowl. In figuring how much to cook, remember that 1 cup of raw rice of any variety makes about 3 cups cooked, serving 3 or 4. *To prepare.* Wash thoroughly in cold water, unless directions on package say *not* to do so. (Some brands of white rice have been treated with vitamin B_1 to replace the loss in milling.) Polished rice should be washed through several waters, rubbing the grains between the hands to remove the coating. After washing and draining, it may be either boiled or steamed. Steaming is really simpler and gives a better product, in my opinion.

STEAMED WHITE RICE

To 2 cups boiling water add 1 cup rice and 1 teaspoon salt. When water again reaches boiling, cover pan tightly, turn heat as low as possible and let steam 20 to 25 minutes without lifting cover. By that time water should be all absorbed and rice light and fluffy. For something really special, use consommé or chicken broth instead of water for steaming rice.

To keep Steamed Rice fluffy, if it must wait after cooking, put a doubled cloth over the saucepan underneath its lid. Place the pan in boiling water to keep hot without scorching.

STEAMED BROWN RICE

Follow directions for steaming white rice, but allow 40 minutes for steaming. If softer rice is preferred, use 2 1/2 cups boiling water for 1 cup brown rice, and let steam 45 to 50 minutes. If too moist when done, remove cover and leave over low heat for a few minutes. To cut down cooking time, brown rice may be soaked 3 or 4 hours, using 2 cups cold water for each cup rice. Cook in same water, to conserve vitamins and minerals. Simply add salt, heat to boiling, cover, reduce heat and steam about 30 minutes.

FEATHERED RICE

This wonderful recipe came to me from a Santa Barbara friend. Spread 1 cup dry white rice in a shallow pan, place in fairly hot oven (375° F. to 425° F.), and bake, stirring occasionally, until golden brown. Then wash rice (if necessary), put into a casserole with tight-fitting cover, add 1 1/2 teaspoons salt and 2 1/2 cups boiling water and bake, covered, 20 minutes at 400° F., or 30 minutes at 350° F. The rice puffs up into something light and fluffy, quite unlike ordinary rice, and has a wonderful toasted flavor. Brown rice may be done the same way, but allow 30 to 40 minutes at 400° F. for baking. A pound or so of rice may be browned at one time and stored in a jar ready to bake.

GREEN RICE

Steam 1 cup white or brown rice as directed. When done add 1 or 2 tablespoons butter and 4 tablespoons chopped parsley, and toss with fork until well mixed but not mashed. Serves 3. Coarsely chopped walnuts or blanched almonds may be added ad lib. Mighty good with chops or chicken.

TO COOK WILD RICE

Take your choice of these 3 ways, according to the amount of time you have. The slower processes result in a more delicate texture and flavor. First, wash the wild rice thoroughly in cold water. If possible, soak it several hours in cold water to cover.

To Steep Wild Rice. Start about 2 hours before dinnertime.

Wash 1 cup wild rice in cold water, then pour 4 cups boiling water over it and let stand 20 minutes. Drain, add another 4 cups boiling water and let stand 20 minutes. Repeat 3 or 4 times more, adding 2 tablespoons salt to the last water. Drain and keep hot in double boiler until serving time. Season with butter, salt and pepper. Serves 4 to 6.

To Cook in Double Boiler. Start about 1 hour before serving time. Put 1 cup washed wild rice in double boiler, add 1 teaspoon salt and 4 cups boiling water, cover, and cook over hot water 45 minutes or longer, until water is all absorbed. Season and serve. If a can of condensed consommé or bouillon is substituted for 1 1/4 cups of the water, the flavor will be improved.

To Steam Wild Rice. Stir 1 cup washed wild rice slowly into 4 cups boiling water, add 1 teaspoon salt, cover, turn heat low, and let steam 35 to 45 minutes, until rice is tender and water all absorbed. Season and serve.

Salsify, or Vegetable Oyster. Looks something like parsnips, but the skin is darker. Allow 1 pound to serve 3. It must be handled quickly to keep from discoloring. Wash, scrape, and plunge at once into cold water with 1 tablespoon vinegar or lemon juice added for each quart of water. Slice or dice, and cook 15 to 20 minutes, in a small amount of boiling unsalted water, until tender. Drain and at once add cream or cream sauce, season to taste, and serve.

Squash, Summer Varieties. Visitors to California remark about the small size of the summer squash in our markets and on our tables. Some of these are practically embryonic—literally so in the case of the squash blossoms for sale throughout the summer in Italian stores. Tiny pale-green scalloped "patty pans"; little yellow crooknecks, looking like baby ducks; slender dark-green zucchini or Italian squash; striped vegetable marrow—all are simply washed and trimmed but not pared or scraped before cooking. They are usually sliced or diced, and cooked briefly, 10 to 15 minutes, in 1/4 to 1/2 inch of boiling salted water in a covered pan, then seasoned and served; or they may be mashed, if preferred.

WAYS WITH SUMMER SQUASH

Season cooked diced or sliced squash with butter, salt and pepper and catsup to taste. . . .

To cooked summer squash, add a few spoonfuls each of French dressing and condensed tomato soup, and mix well. . . .

To cooked summer squash, add condensed tomato soup, a little brown sugar, and salt, pepper, and vinegar to taste. . . .

Cut small patty-pan squashes in halves crosswise, cook tender, drain. Place halves in greased pan, top each with a slice of tomato and a slice of cheese, and bake or broil until cheese melts. . . .

Cook patty-pans whole, hollow out, mix centers with fresh corn, a little cream, and seasonings to taste. Place patty-pan shells in greased shallow pan, and heap with corn mixture, sprinkling remainder in between the squashes. Sprinkle with grated cheese or buttered crumbs, and bake about 20 minutes in fairly hot oven (400° F.), until browned. . . .

Fry sliced zucchini or other summer squash slowly in a little oil or butter or bacon fat in skillet, turning occasionally, until lightly browned. (Put a peeled clove of garlic in with the oil if you like.) Sprinkle with salt and pepper, add a few spoonfuls of water, catsup, or tomato sauce, cover, and let steam 5 to 10 minutes. Remove garlic and serve. . . .

Tiny yellow crooknecks, cooked whole, then lightly browned in a little hot oil in a skillet, make a charming and edible garnish for a platter of chops. . . .

Thick (1 to 1 1/2 inch) slices of larger crooknecks cooked tender, hollowed out to make rings, placed on dinner plates, and then filled with green peas are easy to fix, highly decorative. Use cooky cutter or knife to cut out centers.

FRENCH FRIED ZUCCHINI

Cut zucchini lengthwise in medium-thin slices, dip in salted evaporated or fresh milk (1 teaspoon salt to 1/2 cup milk), then roll in flour. Fry a few pieces at a time until brown in hot fat (370° F.) 1 to 2 inches deep in heavy pan. Drain on paper towels and keep hot. Sprinkle with salt and pepper, and serve.

ZUCCHINI ITALIAN STYLE

4 tablespoons butter or margarine	2 large, ripe tomatoes, peeled and sliced
1 medium-sized onion, minced	6 small zucchini
	Salt and pepper

Melt butter in saucepan, add minced onion and brown lightly. Add tomatoes and continue cooking for 2 or 3 minutes, then add washed and sliced zucchini. Season with salt and pepper, cover, and cook 15 to 20 minutes, until zucchini is tender. Add a little boiling water if mixture cooks dry. Serves 6.

Squash, Winter Varieties. Included here are the small dark-green acorn or Danish squash, cream squash, Hubbard and banana squash. The *acorn squash* seems to have been designed especially for the family of 2. Easiest way with it is to wash it and pop it whole into hot oven (400° F.) for 30 minutes or so, until tender. Then cut it in half lengthwise, spoon out seeds and stringy center, and sprinkle with salt and pepper. Put back into oven to dry slightly for a few minutes. Serve with butter.

A little more work (but some like it better this way) is to cut the raw squash in half, remove seeds, sprinkle halves with salt and pepper, then turn cut sides down in a pan containing a little bacon drippings. Bake 30 to 40 minutes until tender and lightly browned on cut edges.

Acorn squash halves can, of course, be stuffed with meat concoctions, but I'd rather have my hamburger or sausage and my squash separately. The squash gets too soaked with fat to suit me.

Cream squash resembles the acorn variety, but has a medium-hard creamy white shell. Handle it as you do the acorn type.

Hubbard and banana squash are usually sold by the piece, by weight. Allow 1 to 1 1/2 pounds to serve 2. Cut into 2- or 3-inch squares, brush with butter or bacon drippings, sprinkle with salt and pepper, cover, and bake until tender in moderately hot oven (375° F. to 425° F.). Hubbard squash will take 45 to 60 minutes; banana squash, being thinner and more tender, will need only about 30 minutes' baking. Some cooks spread a little brown sugar or molasses over the squash before baking; some lay a thin slice of cheese over each square after baking and put back into oven until cheese is semi-melted.

Note: If ever you are confronted with a whole huge Hubbard squash and haven't a saw or cleaver with which to attack it, drop the squash on a concrete floor or driveway as the grocery boys do!

TO COOK A WHOLE SQUASH

When you wish to serve mashed squash to a large crowd, do this: Cut the big squash in half, remove its seeds, place the halves cut side down in a large pan, and bake slowly until the shells cave in. This will take 2 or 3 hours, usually, in moderate oven (350° F.). Scoop out pulp, then mash and season. Prepare pumpkin the same way.

If it is more convenient to pare potatoes a few hours ahead of time, just cover them with cold salt water, using 4 teaspoons salt to the quart of water. That way they will lose much less of their vitamin C than if they were let stand in unsalted water, according to recent research.

ORANGE SQUASH

2 cups cooked Hubbard or banana squash (baked or steamed)	2 tablespoons butter
	1/2 teaspoon salt
	Pepper
1/2 cup orange juice (more if squash is dry)	1/4 cup chopped almonds

Mash or rice the squash. Add orange juice, butter, salt and pepper and whip until light. Fill 4 orange shells with the squash mixture, heaping it roughly. Top with chopped almonds. Bake in hot oven (450° F.) until slightly browned.

Sweet Potatoes and Yams. It is easy to tell sweet potatoes from yams, both before and after cooking. The sweets are long and slender and usually rather small, and have rough, dry-looking skin, while yams are large and fat, with smooth reddish-orange skin. When cooked, the sweets are creamy-yellow in color, and mealy in texture, while the yams are bright orange, soft, and moist. They may be used interchangeably in recipes. Neither kind keeps as well as white potatoes, so they should be bought in fairly small amounts while they are in market, which is from August through March. Allow 1 medium-large or 2 small sweets or yams per person, or 1 pound to serve 2. They are at their best baked. *To bake.* Simply scrub and bake in hot oven (400° F.) for 30 to 45 minutes, until tender. Slash top, squeeze and press gently, and serve at once. *To boil.* Scrub thoroughly but do not pare. Almost cover with boiling salted water and cook 20 to 30 minutes until tender. Drain and peel, then mash, or candy, or serve plain, as you like.

WALNUT CANDIED SWEET POTATOES

Boil sweet potatoes or yams in their jackets until almost tender. Drain and spread out to cool until they can be handled. Peel and cut in halves, or in thick slices if very large. For 6 to

8 servings, have ready a syrup made by boiling together for 5 minutes in a large skillet:

1 cup brown sugar	2 tablespoons butter
3/4 cup water	Dash of cinnamon
1/2 teaspoon salt	1/2 cup walnuts

Put in the sweet potatoes and cook gently, turning occasionally, about 20 minutes, until syrup is fairly thick and potatoes well glazed. If you prefer, pour the syrup over the potatoes in a shallow pan and bake uncovered in moderately hot oven (375° F.) about 30 minutes, basting occasionally with the syrup.

HOME SHIFT SWEET POTATOES

Allow 1 medium-large sweet potato and 1 not too thin pork chop for each person. Trim off some of the fat from the chops, melt the fat in skillet, and use it to brown the meat well. While chops are browning, pare the raw sweets and cut in halves or quarters lengthwise. Tuck them in around the browned chops, sprinkle with salt and pepper, and add about 1/2 cup water. Put a thick slice of onion on each chop if you like. Cover tightly and let steam over low heat 20 to 30 minutes, or until sweets are tender and chops well done.

Tomatoes. Along with the large reds, the small round reds and yellows, and the small pear-shaped reds, the large deep golden Jubilee tomatoes are now appearing in markets and home gardens. Those small round and pear-shaped red ones are especially good peeled and used whole in salads, or as appetizers. The small yellows are best for making tomato preserves. The large yellow Jubilees can be used in the same ways that large red ones are used; i.e., fresh, cooked, baked, or broiled. In general, allow 1 pound to serve 3. *To prepare.* Wash and dip ripe tomatoes into boiling water for about 30 seconds to loosen skins, then plunge into cold water to cool. If to be used later for salad, put tomatoes into refrigerator without peeling. When wanted, skins can be slipped off in a moment. Always be careful to cut away every bit of hard core before serving raw, or cooking, or canning.

TOMATOES—BAKED, BROILED, OR PAN-BROILED

For an interesting addition to the dinner plate, add half a tomato, baked, broiled, or pan-broiled, depending upon how, or whether, you are using the oven. That is, if you're baking a casserole at 375° F., bake the tomatoes at the same time and temperature, first cutting each unpeeled tomato in 2 crosswise, and sprinkling the cut surfaces with a little sugar, salt and pepper, and some minced onion, too. Be sure to grease the baking dish. Bake about 20 minutes, or until heated through and lightly browned. . . .

If you are broiling chops or steaks, put tomato halves, cut side up, on broiler when you turn the meat; sprinkle with salt and pepper, dot with butter, and broil while the meat finishes cooking. Don't turn the tomatoes. . . .

If you aren't heating the oven, cut unpeeled tomatoes into thick slices, dip them into seasoned flour, and skillet-brown them in oil or butter, taking care not to break the slices when you turn them.

Oriental Touch. Blend 3 tablespoons butter with 1 teaspoon curry powder. Put a generous dab on each tomato half that is to be baked or broiled; add more after first few minutes of cooking.

SEPTEMBER TOMATOES

Chop 4 or 5 green onions, tops and all, and a tiny sprig each of fresh basilica, thyme, and marjoram, and cook gently for 5 minutes in 3 tablespoons butter or margarine. Add 6 peeled whole ripe tomatoes, sprinkle with salt and pepper, cover tightly, and cook over low heat for 15 minutes. Lift tomatoes carefully to dinner plates or into a serving dish, and pour the liquid in the pan over them. Serves 3 to 6, depending upon the size of appetites and size of tomatoes.

Turnips and Rutabagas. White turnips are usually sold by the bunch. If they are to be served mashed, allow 3 or 4 medium-sized turnips (about 1 pound) per person. (Turnips shrink, you know.) If to be served diced and buttered or creamed, 1 pound will probably serve 2. Pick firm, heavy roots. *To prepare.* Pare; dice, or if they are to be mashed, slice crosswise into thin slices. Cook in a small amount of boiling salted water in covered pan. Young turnips will be done in about 10 minutes. Drain if necessary, season and serve. For best mashed turnips, drain cooked sliced roots, mash with potato masher and let cook down a bit to boil off excess liquid. For 2 servings, stir in 1 teaspoon butter and 1/2 teaspoon sugar, sprinkle 1 teaspoon flour over all, and stir smooth. Then add about 1/4 cup top milk and stir until thickened. Season and serve. They're creamy and white.

Prepare and cook *rutabagas* as you do white turnips, but allow 20 to 30 minutes' cooking time. (They are especially good cooked in consommé instead of water.) For an excellent combination, add hot drained rutabagas to hot drained potatoes (about half as much rutabaga as potato), and mash together until light and fluffy, seasoning with butter, salt and pepper, and a little hot milk, if needed.

Zucchini. See summer squash.

VEGETABLE CASSEROLE FOR EIGHT

1 1/2 pounds green beans	2 1/2 cups canned tomatoes,
2 cups small white onions	seasoned highly with
4 large green peppers	salt, pepper, and
6 ears corn	Worcestershire sauce

An hour before serving time, cut green beans lengthwise into strips and cook 10 minutes in boiling salted water. Peel onions and cook until almost tender. Cut peppers in halves lengthwise and remove seeds. Cut corn from cob, season with salt and pepper, and fill into pepper shells. In a large, shallow baking dish (preferably a round one), arrange pepper shells like spokes of a wheel. Between peppers put the white onions. Drain the parboiled beans and place in a circle around the edge of baking dish. Pour tomato sauce over beans, dot all vegetables with butter (being especially generous when it comes to the corn), sprinkle with salt and pepper, cover dish, and bake in moderately hot oven (400° F.) 30 minutes. Bring baking dish to table so that all may admire the pretty arrangement.

MORE VARIATIONS AND COMBINATIONS

Ways with fresh, frozen and canned vegetables—all easy to fix; all good to eat!

BEANS WITH MUSHROOMS

Cook 1 pound green beans as directed in "Beans, Green and Wax" on page 179. While they cook, melt 2 tablespoons butter in a skillet; add 2 tablespoons finely chopped onions and one 3-ounce can sliced mushrooms. Heat gently about 10 minutes. Add to drained cooked beans, along with 1/2 cup cream and salt and pepper. Serve piping hot. Serves 4.

Use this mushroom sauce, too, to step up cooked, frozen green beans and heated canned ones.

GOLDEN CAULIFLOWER

Fry sliced ham as usual. Meanwhile cook broken-up cauliflower in boiling salted water. (See page 187.) When cauliflower is tender, take up ham, then carefully lift the florets into the hot ham skillet. Heat and turn until all are a delicate brown. Serve immediately. (A good way to flavor green beans, too.)

DON'S WAY WITH CORN

This way of doing sweet corn takes a little longer, but it's wonderful! For 2, break 2 or 3 ears of corn into chunks, put into a double boiler, add enough milk to completely cover, and cook over hot water about 30 minutes. Serve corn as usual. Next day, heat that corn-flavored milk and serve as soup.

ONIONS BAKED IN CREAM

Any large, dry onions can be used in this recipe—Bermudas are good. To serve 4, peel 4 large onions, cut crosswise into slices about 1/4 inch thick. Arrange in layers in well-buttered baking dish, sprinkling each layer with salt, pepper, and sugar. Pour in enough cream or top milk to come up over tops of onions. Cover and bake in a moderate oven (350° F.) about 1 hour until tender.

BETTER-THAN-EVER PEAS

Chop a large onion fine, put it into a saucepan, add 2 cups water and 1/2 teaspoon salt, and cook about 30 minutes, until onion is soft and mushy and most of water has cooked away. Add 3 tablespoons butter and a package of frozen peas (or 1 1/2 pounds fresh peas, shelled). Cover and cook 8 to 12 minutes. Add more hot water if needed. Makes 3 good servings.

TOMATOES PARMESAN

Put 2 or 3 tablespoons water into a skillet, along with 2 tablespoons butter. Then arrange, in a single layer, halves of unpeeled medium-sized tomatoes, cut-side up. Sprinkle them lightly with salt and pepper, then generously with grated Parmesan cheese. Cover skillet and cook over medium heat 5 to 10 minutes, until tomatoes are barely tender. Do not turn. Serve very hot. Allow 2 tomato halves (or more) for each person.

TOMATO EGGPLANT CASSEROLE

To serve 4, cut a medium-sized eggplant into cubes. (You don't need to pare it.) Spread in buttered casserole. Cover generously with sliced onion (1 large). Over the onion arrange tomato quarters; allow 2 or 3 medium-sized tomatoes. Dot generously with butter. Season with salt, pepper, and a suspicion of minced herbs—thyme, marjoram, and sweet basil make a good combination. Add 2 or 3 tablespoons water. Cover casserole and bake at 350° F. (moderate) about 45 minutes. The vegetables shrink during cooking.

EMILY'S CREAMED SPINACH

1 (12-ounce) package
    frozen chopped spinach
4 tablespoons butter
5 tablespoons flour

1 cup milk
1/2 teaspoon Accent
Salt, pepper, and nutmeg to
    taste

Remove frozen block of spinach from carton and let stand at room temperature 10 to 15 minutes. Meanwhile, melt butter in top of double boiler over direct heat; blend in flour, add milk, and cook, stirring constantly, until mixture boils and thickens. With a sharp knife, cut block of spinach into small chunks; add to hot sauce. Add Accent. Cover and cook over boiling water 15 minutes, stirring occasionally so that as spinach thaws it will blend with the sauce. Season to taste with salt, pepper, and nutmeg before serving. 4 servings.

ZUCCHINI MAIN DISH

To serve 4, cook 3/4 pound lean ground beef in a little butter or oil in a big skillet, stirring frequently. While it browns, cut 5 or 6 medium-sized zucchini into chunks and cook in boiling, salted water. To the beef add 2 or 3 peeled and chopped tomatoes and 1/2 to 1 cup grated sharp Cheddar cheese. Continue cooking, seasoning well with salt and pepper. When zucchini is barely tender, drain and combine

with the meat-and-tomatoes. Serve immediately, or pour into
buttered casserole and bake in a 350° F. oven 10 to 15 minutes.

SUMMER BROILER COMBINATION

8 to 12 small new potatoes
 or 4 larger ones
4 medium-sized zucchini
1 peeled clove garlic
3 tablespoons oil
2 large, firm tomatoes

Salt and pepper
1/4 cup grated Parmesan
 cheese
1/2 cup buttered fluffy
 crumbs

In advance, boil potatoes in their jackets; cool. Parboil zucchini in boiling salted water; cool, then cut in halves lengthwise. Mash garlic in a pie pan, add oil, coat zucchini with
the mixture, cover, and refrigerate. About 20 minutes before
serving, line broiler pan or large, shallow pan with foil. Slip
skins off potatoes; if large, cut in halves; brush with melted
butter. Cut tomatoes in halves crosswise; sprinkle with a little
sugar. Arrange potatoes, tomatoes, and zucchini on the foil;
sprinkle lightly with salt and pepper. Broil slowly, low under
broiling unit, turning potatoes but not the other vegetables.
When almost done, sprinkle the zucchini with grated Parmesan cheese, the tomatoes with buttered crumbs; brown
lightly. Serves 4.

For a Summer Supper. Feature this broiler combination,
along with slices of cold meat loaf and crisp, hard rolls.

SEASONINGS AND SAUCES FOR VEGETABLES

Good seasoning for any vegetable starts with good cooking. If
you have managed so that only a spoonful or 2 of liquid is left
when vegetables are done, you need only add pepper to taste
and a little butter or margarine and/or cream, if you like, and
serve immediately. Personally, I like them with just salt and
pepper. When I do serve a sauce, it's likely to be one of the
following:

HOLLANDAISE SAUCE

Real Hollandaise is not hard for even an amateur to make if you are careful never to let the water boil underneath the mixture, and if you work right along, not stopping at any point to do something else. Here is the recipe:

1/2 cup butter
2 egg yolks, unbeaten
1 tablespoon lemon juice or
    vinegar

1/4 teaspoon salt
Dash of cayenne

Divide the butter into 3 approximately equal parts. Put 1 piece of butter, egg yolks, and lemon juice or vinegar into top of double boiler, place over steaming hot but not boiling water about 1 inch deep in bottom part, and stir constantly until mixture is smoothly thickened. Add a second piece of butter and stir until it is melted; then add the third piece, continuing to stir constantly. When butter is all melted, remove from the heat, add seasonings, and beat with a spoon until glossy. Serve at once. Do not reheat. Makes about 1/2 cup sauce, serving 3 or 4. Especially good on asparagus, broccoli, and artichokes.

If the sauce should by any chance separate or curdle while making, add slowly a tablespoon of boiling water and stir vigorously until smooth; add a second tablespoon if necessary.

EASY-GOING HOLLANDAISE

1/4 cup butter
2 egg yolks
1/8 teaspoon salt
Dash of cayenne

1 tablespoon lemon juice or
    vinegar
1/3 cup boiling water

Melt butter over hot water; remove and add egg yolks one at a time, stirring until very well blended. Add salt, cayenne, and lemon juice or vinegar, then, very slowly, stir in the boiling water. Place over hot (not boiling) water, and stir constantly 7 to 10 minutes, until thickened as for custard. Serve at once; or make this sauce in advance if you like and then reheat about 5 minutes over hot but not boiling water. If it should curdle, slowly stir in 1 tablespoon boiling water. Makes about 3/4 cup, serving 4 or 5.

CREAMY SAUCE

This is a departure from and improvement on the orthodox white sauce. Adding the vegetable cooking liquid thins the sauce slightly and gives it richness of flavor and strength of character.

2 to 3 tablespoons butter or margarine
2 tablespoons flour
1 cup rich milk

3 to 5 tablespoons vegetable cooking liquid
Salt and pepper

Melt butter in a heavy saucepan, add flour, blend well, then stir in cold milk and cook, stirring constantly until smoothly thickened. Stir in vegetable liquid, then season to taste just right. (That means taste it and see!) Makes about 1 1/3 cups. Keep hot. Combine with hot vegetables and serve. You'll want to allow about half as much sauce as vegetable.

MUSTARD SAUCE

1 tablespoon butter or margarine
1/2 tablespoon prepared mustard

1/4 cup cream or evaporated milk
Salt and pepper
1 tablespoon lemon juice

Heat together butter, mustard, cream, and salt and pepper; stir in lemon juice and serve poured over hot broccoli. Makes just enough for 2. Good, too, on Brussels sprouts, spinach and other greens.

MUSTARD MAYONNAISE

Mustard mayonnaise is equally good with hot or cold artichokes or with hot broccoli. To 1/2 cup mayonnaise add 1 to 2 teaspoons prepared mustard, then stir in 1 to 2 tablespoons lemon juice or vinegar, to suit your taste. Serve in little nut cups or small fluted paper baking cups on the plate with the artichoke. Two paper cups, one inside the other, make a sturdier container! For broccoli, pass the sauce separately. Serves 3.

TWO QUICK LEMON SAUCES

Heat 3/4 cup mayonnaise with 1/4 cup lemon juice in double boiler, stirring. Serve hot with hot asparagus, broccoli, or other vegetable. Serves 4 or 5.

Heat 1 cup salad dressing in double boiler 10 minutes. Stir in 2 tablespoons lemon juice, and serve with any hot green vegetable. Serves 4 or 5.

TWO CHEESE SAUCES

Melt 1/2 pound processed cheese in double boiler. When melted, stir in 1/3 cup milk. Season to taste. Serves 6.

Make 1 1/2 cups thin white sauce, seasoning it well. Add 1 cup grated or thinly sliced American cheese; or add a 3-ounce cake of pimiento cream cheese. Stir occasionally until melted. Season to taste. Serves 6. Especially good on cauliflower or cabbage.

MUSHROOM SAUCE

Cook 1 cup coarsely chopped mushrooms (fresh or canned) 5 minutes in 3 tablespoons butter, stirring frequently. Add 2 tablespoons flour and stir until well blended. Add 1 cup top milk, or milk-and-cream mixed, and cook, stirring, until smoothly thickened. Season well with salt and pepper. Just before serving, add 3 tablespoons lemon juice and pour over hot cooked string beans. Makes enough sauce for 1 pound, or 4 servings, of beans. Good also with peas or carrots.

WHITE WINE SAUCE FOR VEGETABLES

1 tablespoon melted butter	1/2 cup top milk
1 tablespoon minced green onion	1/4 cup vegetable cooking water
1 egg yolk	1/4 cup white table wine
1 tablespoon flour	Salt and pepper to taste

Melt butter in top of double boiler; remove from heat and stir in onion, egg yolk, and flour; blend well. Stir in milk and vegetable water, place over boiling water and cook, stirring, about 5 minutes, until thickened. Add wine and salt and pepper, heat, and serve with any vegetable or with a vegetable plate—carrots, broccoli, green beans, summer squash, new potatoes, or whatever. Makes 1 cup, serving 4.

IDEAS FOR VEGETABLE PLATES

When serving a vegetable plate for lunch or dinner, these are things to keep in mind: (1) Look to the colors and forms of the vegetables when you buy them; consider how they will look when grouped together on a plate. (2) Don't serve more than 1 creamed vegetable; keep the others plain, or nearly so. (3) If feasible, feature a hot bread on the plate. (4) Include a protein food, such as cottage cheese, baked beans, deviled eggs, or sea food. (5) Don't overcook those vegetables. Serve them the minute they're done. Now for some combinations:

Buttered ear of corn; hot artichoke with cheese sauce; hot bun with thin meat patty, topped with tomato slice; stuffed celery; radishes. . . . Asparagus with mustard sauce; baked potato with crumbled bacon topping; hot biscuits; tomato stuffed with chive cottage cheese . . . New potatoes rolled in parsley; lettuce cup of cottage cheese sprinkled with grated raw carrot; buttered string beans; square of corn bread.

By-laws for Making Breads

1. Keep sponge or dough for yeast breads and rolls comfortably warm while rising. Let double in bulk at each rising. Keep dough for refrigerator rolls rubbed with oil and well covered to prevent drying; punch down with fist whenever dough rises to double its bulk.

2. Nut breads and other loaves made with baking powder or soda usually crack less on top if mixture is let stand in pan about 20 minutes before baking, but it is not essential that they stand. Such breads usually slice better when a day old than when fresh.

3. Don't beat muffin batter; beating causes holes and tunnels. Stir only until flour is dampened. Batter should look lumpy when put into the pans.

4. To make good baking powder biscuits, cut shortening into flour until very fine; use enough liquid to make a soft moist dough; knead the dough slightly (about 1/2 minute) before rolling and cutting. These techniques are the exact opposite of those used in making perfect piecrust.

5. To make really good flapjacks or hot cakes, be sure to have the griddle at the right temperature. That's as important as the recipe! Test by sprinkling a few drops of water on it: if they dance about, it is hot enough. Turn cakes just once, when the tops are full of bubbles and begin to look dull. Don't poke and pat them. For cakes that are to be rolled, use extra egg in the batter, so they won't crack.

6. Don't have waffle batter too thick. To prevent sticking, use enough oil or melted shortening in the batter and have the waffle baker at right heat.

Chapter 8

Breads and Little Breads—
Easy to Make, Good to Serve

SOMETIMES I wonder why we hostesses struggle so to plan "unusual" menus, when by merely serving a different kind of hot bread we can turn the most ordinary meal into something special. Think what garlic French bread or home-made rolls, hot from the oven, can do for any buffet supper; what a hit orange rolls or cheese-frosted biscuits are sure to make with a salad luncheon, or with coffee or tea for refreshments or snack.

The bread doesn't necessarily have to be home-baked, but it's smart to add some little home touch that gives it style and individuality. Merely heating in the oven will do a lot! French bread, bakery bread, hard or soft rolls, snails and cinnamon rolls, all are infinitely more appealing when they are served hot.

We'll begin with some favorite California ways with ready-baked breads, then go on to recipes for especially good breads and rolls, both yeast-raised and "quick" types, that you'll like to make at home.

GARLIC FRENCH BREAD

Peel and slice 2 or 3 cloves of garlic, mix with about 1/4 cup (1/2 cube) soft butter or margarine and let stand half an hour or longer. Slash a long loaf of sour French bread (or a round loaf of Italian bread) into thick or thin slices, but don't entirely separate the slices—leave them attached together along one side of the loaf. Between the slices and over the top spread the garlic butter. Heat in a fairly hot oven 10 to 15 minutes, until piping hot; serve at once, in a napkin-lined basket. Hard rolls may be done the same way. A "must" for barbecues and buffet suppers.

For Cheese Bread slip a thin slice of cheese between the buttered slices of bread; or spread nippy soft cheese between; or sprinkle grated Parmesan cheese between slices and over top of loaf. Dash top with paprika. Put loaf into a paper bag and heat in moderate oven about 15 minutes.

CHEESE-TOASTED ROLLS

Buy oval or long French rolls—the ones that have a fairly soft crust, if your baker or grocer has that kind. Cut them in halves lengthwise; spread cut surfaces with soft butter or margarine (garlic-flavored, if you wish), then sprinkle thickly with grated Parmesan cheese. Five minutes before they're wanted, slip them under the broiler to brown the cheese topping slightly while heating the rolls through. These are a great help when the meat or fish is a bit skimpy, and are equally good with a steak!

TOASTED ENGLISH MUFFINS

Split muffins crosswise, using 2 forks to pull them apart. Spread with butter, then toast buttered sides under broiler. At a garden club tea in Saratoga, each person was served a half-round of one of these toasty hot muffins spread with marmalade. Mighty good with tea or coffee.

TO FRESHEN BAKED ROLLS AND BREAD

Soft Rolls, Biscuits, or Muffins. Place in a baking pan, sprinkle lightly with water, and bake in hot oven (400° F.) 5 to 10 minutes. Heat snails, butterhorns and other sweet breakfast rolls, and doughnuts, without sprinkling.

Hard Rolls. Place in a pan, uncovered, and bake until heated through. If rolls are rather stale and dry, dip them quickly in water before heating.

Baker's Sliced Bread. Place a waxed-paper-wrapped loaf in moderate oven (325° F. to 350° F.) about 10 minutes, until hot. Don't let the paper burn.

Home-Baked Bread. Buy a chubby loaf of cracked wheat or white bread, unsliced, from a "home bakery." Brush the crust with butter, place it in a loaf pan if you have one, and heat in moderate oven (325° F. to 350° F.) 15 to 20 minutes. As an added attraction bring the loaf to the table on a small bread-board, and slice it as needed.

BUTTERY BREAD

This simple stunt always brings that gratifying query, "How do you do it?" Cut slices of bread in halves crosswise, and stand the half-slices with cut edges up in a loaf pan or casserole. Spread soft butter rather generously over the top edges, and bake in hot oven (450° F.) 10 to 15 minutes. The bread slices will come out with edges crisp and toasty and centers hot and buttery.

ORANGE TOAST

2 tablespoons soft butter or
  margarine
2 tablespoons grated orange
  peel

2 tablespoons orange juice
3/4 cup powdered sugar

Blend butter and grated peel. Work in juice and sugar alternately, a small amount at a time, beating smooth. Toast slices of bread on one side, spread untoasted side with this mixture, and toast under broiler until tinged with brown. Serve hot with afternoon tea, or in place of cookies with fruit for dessert, or with salad of cottage cheese and fruit for luncheon. Recipe makes enough to spread 4 to 6 slices of bread.

CINNAMON ORANGE TOAST

1 tablespoon grated orange
  peel
2 tablespoons orange juice

1/2 cup granulated sugar
Dash of cinnamon

Mix ingredients, spread on buttered toast, and brown lightly under broiler. Makes enough spread for 6 to 8 slices of toast. Serve with tea, coffee, or chocolate.

CINNAMON TOAST, POMONA STYLE

1/2 cup sifted powdered
  sugar
1 to 2 tablespoons cinnamon

4 tablespoons soft butter
3 tablespoons finely
  chopped walnuts

Mix sugar and cinnamon, stir into butter, add nuts, and mix well. Toast slices of bread on one side, spread the untoasted side with the walnut-cinnamon mixture, and toast slowly under the broiler until bubbly. Serve at once, with tea or coffee, or hot chocolate.

FROSTED ORANGE ROLLS

Want to build a reputation as a glamorous cook? Then serve these rolls warm with fruit salad and hot coffee for a luncheon or for afternoon or evening refreshments. They're easy to do, too. Allow about 3 hours for making and baking them.

1 package yeast, compressed or dry granular
1/4 cup lukewarm water
1 egg
2 tablespoons sugar
1 1/2 teaspoons salt
2 tablespoons melted butter
1 tablespoon grated orange peel
3/4 cup orange juice
3 cups sifted flour
1 orange, diced and sugared

Soften yeast in water. Beat egg in mixing bowl, add yeast, sugar, salt, butter, orange peel and juice, and flour. Beat until smooth, adding a little more flour if necessary to make a soft dough. Turn out on floured board and knead until smooth and elastic. Put back into greased bowl, grease top, cover, set bowl in pan of warm (not hot) water, and let rise for about 1 hour, or until double in bulk. Punch down, let stand a few minutes, then roll out about 1/2 inch thick, and cut with cooky cutter. Let stand on board 10 to 15 minutes, to "relax" (this is to keep them from unfolding later), then crease each circle with back of knife, brush with melted butter, place a piece of sugared orange on the circle, and fold over, Parker-house roll style, and press lightly. Place on greased baking sheets, cover with damp cloth, let rise again until double in size, then bake in fairly hot oven (425° F.) 15 to 20 minutes. Makes about 3 dozen. While still warm, cover liberally with:

Orange Butter Icing

1 tablespoon soft butter or margarine
1 teaspoon grated orange peel
1 cup sifted powdered sugar
1 tablespoon lemon juice
About 3 tablespoons orange juice

Add orange peel to butter. Gradually and alternately work in powdered sugar and juice, beating well after each addition, until of right consistency for spreading. Equally good for frosting cinnamon rolls or cakes or cookies.

TEAROOM REFRIGERATOR ROLLS

If you are starting from scratch, cook 1 1/2 cups diced raw potato in 2 cups boiling water without salt. If you are boiling potatoes for dinner, save the potato cooking water and force enough hot cooked potato through a wire strainer to make 1 cup. This recipe makes 4 dozen rolls:

1 cup hot sieved potatoes	2 eggs, beaten
1/4 to 1/2 cup sugar	1 1/2 cups lukewarm potato
1 1/2 teaspoons salt	water
1/2 cup shortening	About 7 cups sifted flour
1 package yeast, com- pressed or dry granular	

Add sugar, salt, and shortening to potatoes, and beat well. When lukewarm, crumble in the yeast, add eggs and potato water, then stir in flour to make a fairly stiff dough. Knead on floured board about 10 minutes, until smooth and elastic. Put into greased bowl, grease top, cover with damp cloth, and let rise about 2 hours, until double in bulk. Punch down.

(A) Shape part of dough into rolls at once if you wish, place on greased pans, cover with damp cloth, and let rise in warm place about 45 minutes until double in size, then bake in fairly hot oven (425° F.) 15 to 20 minutes.

(B) Grease top of dough remaining in bowl, cover with doubled waxed paper or with elastic-edged bowl cover, then with damp cloth, and place in refrigerator. Whenever dough rises, punch it down; redampen cloth as necessary. When you wish to bake rolls, take out the amount of dough needed about 2 to 2 1/2 hours before serving time, let it stand in warm place about an hour, until light, then shape into rolls and proceed as under "A" above. Don't keep refrigerator dough too long. The rolls will taste best when dough is used within 3 or 4 days.

RAISIN ROLLS

1 package yeast, com-
pressed or dry granular
1/2 cup lukewarm water
1 cup milk, scalded
1/4 cup shortening
1 teaspoon salt
1/2 cup sugar
1 egg, beaten

1 teaspoon grated lemon
peel
1 1/2 tablespoons lemon
juice
Dash of nutmeg
5 1/2 cups sifted flour
(about)
1 cup seedless raisins

Crumble yeast into lukewarm water. Pour hot milk over shortening, salt, and sugar in large mixing bowl; let cool to lukewarm, then add dissolved yeast, egg, lemon peel and juice, and nutmeg. Stir in flour and raisins, turn out on floured board and knead until smooth and elastic, about 7 minutes. Grease bowl, shape dough into ball and put back into bowl, turn dough over to grease top. Cover, let rise in warm place until double in bulk. Punch down, then shape into rolls (use part of dough for cinnamon rolls if you like), place on greased pans, and let rise in warm place until double in bulk. Bake in fairly hot oven (425° F.) 15 to 20 minutes. Makes about 3 dozen rolls.

For *Raisin Wreath Rolls,* place a single row of cinnamon rolls or plain raisin rolls to form a ring around the edge of a greased pie pan, leaving center empty. Let rise and bake. Frost while warm with powdered-sugar-and-cream frosting, lightly flavored with cinnamon.

OATMEAL PUFFINS

Start these simple yeast-raised muffins about 1 1/2 hours before serving time. They require no kneading.

1 cup milk, scalded
1/2 cup uncooked rolled oats
1/4 cup brown sugar, firmly packed
1 teaspoon salt
1 tablespoon shortening
2 packages yeast, compressed or dry granular
2 cups sifted flour

Pour hot milk over rolled oats, sugar, salt, and shortening in mixing bowl. Let cool to lukewarm, then crumble yeast into mixture, add flour, and beat well. Drop at once into greased muffin pans, filling them half full. Let rise in warm place until pans are full—about an hour—then bake in moderately hot oven (400° F.) 20 to 25 minutes. Makes 12 muffins.

ALMOND MUFFINS

Start these rich, fancy, yeast-raised muffins about 2 hours before serving time.

1/2 cup milk
1/2 cup mixed butter and shortening
4 eggs
6 tablespoons sugar
1 1/2 teaspoons salt
2 packages yeast, compressed or dry granular
4 cups sifted flour
1 cup almonds, blanched and chopped

Heat milk with butter and shortening, cool to lukewarm. Beat eggs, add sugar, salt, and warm milk. Crumble yeast cakes and add. Stir in flour and almonds, and mix well with spoon. Cover and let rise in warm place until double in bulk. Drop the soft dough by spoonfuls into greased muffin pans and let rise until doubled in bulk. Bake in fairly hot oven (425° F.) about 15 minutes. Serve warm. Makes 2 dozen muffins. Very good without the almonds, but better with them.

PANETONE

Whatever your nationality, you'll like this fruited Italian Christmas bread. It is wonderful fresh or toasted, at any time.

2 cups scalded milk
1 tablespoon sugar
1 package yeast, com-
    pressed or dry granular
6 cups sifted flour
5 tablespoons shortening
1 cup sugar
2 eggs, well beaten

1 1/2 teaspoons salt
1/2 cup raisins
1/2 cup thinly sliced citron
1 cup coarsely chopped
    walnuts
1/2 teaspoon anise extract
    or 1 teaspoon nutmeg

Cool milk to lukewarm, add sugar and crumbled yeast. Add 2 cups of the flour, and beat well. Cream shortening with sugar, add eggs, and beat well. Add to first mixture; add salt and remaining flour, mix well, cover, and let rise in a warm place about 1 1/2 hours, until very light. Work in remaining ingredients and knead on floured board until smooth and elastic. Put into greased bowl, grease top, cover, and let rise until double in bulk. Shape into round loaves, not too large, and place on greased cooky sheet or pie pans. Beat an egg slightly with 1 tablespoon water, brush over tops of loaves, and let rise until doubled. Bake in moderately hot oven (400° F.) for 15 minutes, then reduce heat to 350° F. and bake 25 to 35 minutes longer, depending upon size of loaves. Makes 2 medium-sized or 3 or 4 small loaves.

HOMEMADE BREAD

Good as all the fancy and foreign breads are, there are times when nothing else has quite the appeal of home-baked bread, fragrantly fresh from the oven. Time was, of course, when learning to make good bread was something that required years of application. Now, with this easy and exact recipe, I promise you that you'll turn out beautiful loaves at your very first try. Allow about 5 to 6 hours over all for the making and baking—but remember, you can be doing lots of other things while bread rises between mixings. For 2 loaves, you'll need:

2 cups lukewarm liquid
(milk; or milk-and-
water; or potato water)
1 package yeast, com-
pressed or dry granular
2 tablespoons sugar

1 tablespoon salt
6 to 6 1/4 cups sifted all-
purpose flour
2 tablespoons lukewarm
melted shortening

If you are using milk, scald it, then let it cool to lukewarm before using. Crumble yeast into a mixing bowl, add sugar, salt, and lukewarm liquid, and stir until dissolved. Add 3 cups of the flour and beat with mixing spoon until batter is smooth and elastic enough to fall from spoon in sheets. Beat in melted shortening, then stir in remaining 3 to 3 1/4 cups flour, using the hand to work it in when the dough gets too stiff to stir. Turn dough out onto a lightly floured board or table top, cover, and let stand 10 minutes, then knead it about 7 or 8 minutes, until it is smooth and elastic, using very little flour on the board—just enough to keep the dough from sticking. (Get an experienced bread maker to show you how to do the kneading, if you don't know how.) Grease the mixing bowl, put the neat ball of dough into it, cover with a damp cloth, and keep in a comfortably warm place for 1 1/2 to 2 hours, until it has doubled. Punch down the puffy mass with your fist, shape it into a ball again, cover, and let rise again until almost double. (It will take only about 30 to 45 minutes for this rising.) Punch down, then divide dough into halves, shape into balls on board, cover, and let stand 15 minutes. (This lets the dough relax, and makes it easier to handle.) Shape each piece into a loaf, place in a greased bread loaf pan (8 x 4 x 4 inches), cover with a damp cloth, and let rise 1 to 1 1/2 hours, until double in size. Bake in hot oven (450° F.) 10 minutes, then reduce heat to 375° F. and bake 30 minutes longer. Turn out on a rack to cool.

PIZZA

Part of the fun of eating Pizza (Peet-za) at a Neapolitan "Pizzeria" is listening to the slap, slap, of Eddie's hands as he flat-tens the ball of sour dough into a very thin flat cake; then watching him flip it onto a broad wooden paddle and spread the top first with lard—"pork to pork," he says—then with paper-thin bits of Italian ham, pieces of cheese, plenty of flavorsome tomato sauce with fresh basilica in it, and a grandiose sprinkle of salt and pepper; then watching while he slides the whole thing onto the floor of the big brick oven, beside the blazing wood fire. A few minutes more, and you are watching it cut in wedges, learning to fold one over, and eat it, hot as hot, as—of all things!—an appetizer for the veal scallopini or whatever is to come.

It's fun to try to reproduce Pizza in your own kitchen, using a ball of sour dough bought from an Italian bakery, or your own make of unsweetened roll or bread dough, and topping it with any combination similar to that described. It may not turn out to be orthodox, but it's bound to be good!

And for an entirely unorthodox, but mighty good, version of Pizza, split English muffins, spread them with butter, ham, cheese, and tomato sauce or catsup, and broil slowly until bubbling hot. Serve at once, with coffee.

FUGACCIO

This Italian bread comes in flat sheets, in two varieties, onion and raisin, at many Italian bake shops and grocery stores. To make a reasonable facsimile of the Onion Fugaccio, it's best to buy a ball of sour dough from an Italian or French bakery, if you can get it; otherwise use any good recipe for rolls, omitting or cutting down the sugar. Have the dough quite soft. When light, roll it out about 1/2 or 3/4 inch thick, and lay in a well-oiled pan. Spread olive oil generously over the top, then strew with coarsely chopped green onions, punching the pieces down into the dough. Sprinkle with salt and plenty of paprika. Let rise until doubled in bulk, then bake in fairly hot oven (425° F.) about 20 to 25 minutes, until well browned. Cut in squares and serve hot. Imagine it with steaks! For *Raisin Fugaccio*, use raisins liberally in the dough. Roll out, brush with oil, let rise, and bake. Fugaccio should look rather rough and bubbly, not smooth and flat.

MARTHA MEADE'S BAKED DOUGHNUTS

These unusual yeast-raised doughnuts, originated by the director of home economics of one of the West's large flour mills, resemble French doughnuts. Serve them warm, freshly baked or reheated. You can make them from start to finish in about 2 hours.

1 1/2 cups milk, scalded
1/3 cup shortening
4 tablespoons sugar
2 teaspoons salt
2 teaspoons nutmeg
1/4 teaspoon cinnamon
   (optional)

2 packages yeast, compressed or dry granular
1/4 cup lukewarm water
2 eggs, beaten
4 3/4 cups sifted flour

Pour hot milk over shortening, sugar, salt, and spices in mixing bowl. Cool to lukewarm. Stir yeast with water and add with eggs to lukewarm liquid. Stir in flour and beat until well mixed. Cover and let stand in warm place about an hour, until dough is doubled in bulk. Turn out onto well-floured board and turn dough over 2 or 3 times to shape it into a soft ball. (It will be very soft to handle.) Roll out lightly, about 1/2 inch thick, being careful not to stretch the dough. Cut with a 3-inch doughnut cutter, and place carefully 2 inches apart on greased baking sheets. Brush with melted butter or margarine, and let rise in warm place until double in bulk, about 20 minutes. Bake in fairly hot oven (425° F.) 8 to 10 minutes. Remove from oven, brush again with melted butter or margarine, and roll in granulated sugar. Makes about 3 dozen.

OLD-FASHIONED DOUGHNUTS

Secrets of superior doughnuts are: use whole eggs and yolks; use about 1/3 all-purpose flour, 2/3 cake flour; keep dough soft as possible (chilling before rolling helps here); roll out and cut all doughnuts before beginning to fry; keep frying fat right around 375° F. at all times; turn doughnuts almost constantly, to make them evenly round; drain on paper towels; warm them before serving.

1 cup sifted all-purpose flour	1/2 teaspoon nutmeg
	1/2 teaspoon vanilla
2 1/2 cups sifted cake flour	1 cup buttermilk
2 teaspoons baking powder	1 teaspoon soda
1 teaspoon salt	1 tablespoon melted short-
2 eggs plus 2 yolks	ening
1 cup sugar	

Sift flours with baking powder and salt. Beat eggs in mixing bowl, beat in sugar and nutmeg, add vanilla. Stir soda into buttermilk and add. Add melted shortening, then stir in flour. It will be necessary to add a little more flour, enough to make a soft dough that can barely be handled. Chill dough. Roll 1/2 inch thick on lightly floured canvas, cut, and place on floured waxed paper on cooky sheets until time to fry. Have a broad deep kettle about 2/3 full of hot fat (375° F.). Fry 3 or 4 doughnuts at a time until well browned, drain, sugar if you wish by shaking a few at a time with granulated or powdered sugar in a paper bag. Makes 2 1/2 to 3 dozen. It's fun to fry doughnuts and make coffee on the outdoor grill, at any time of day!

GOOD WAYS WITH BISCUITS

To "personalize" biscuits—whether you make your own, or use a prepared mix or packaged ready-to-bake type—try some of these tricks. They add a lot of interest to a simple meal.

Parsley Biscuits. Mix 1/4 cup chopped parsley with 2 cups biscuit mix, before adding milk. Roll 1/2 inch thick, cut, and bake as usual, to serve with salad. Or arrange on top of hot meat-and-gravy in casserole and bake as a meat pie.

Cheese Drop Biscuits. Mix 1/2 cup grated Cheddar cheese with 2 cups prepared biscuit mix. Stir in 2/3 cup milk. Drop by spoonfuls on greased baking sheet and bake in a hot oven (450° F.) 10 to 15 minutes.

Cheese-Frosted Biscuits. Cream together, or melt together over hot water, a small (3-ounce) package of nippy pimiento cheese and 1/4 cup butter. Cut biscuits small, place close together on baking sheet, and top each with a spoonful of cheese mixture, and bake as usual. *Or,* melt the cheese and butter together in a pie pan in the oven; blend well. Arrange biscuits close together over the mixture, and bake.

Oatmeal Drop Biscuits. Put 1/4 to 1/3 cup cooked rolled oats (left from breakfast) into measuring cup and add milk to measure 2/3 cup. Stir into 1 cup biscuit mix. (Add a little more milk if needed to make soft dough.) Drop by fat spoonfuls on greased baking sheet. Bake at 450° F. for 10 to 15 minutes.

Orange Biscuits. Arrange refrigerator or other biscuits in greased pie pan. Dip a cube of sugar into thawed but not diluted frozen orange concentrate and press into top of each biscuit. Bake as usual. Good with tea or coffee for refreshments.

SALAD BISCUITS

Serve these cheese-and-olive-filled biscuits straight from the oven, with a fish salad or other hearty salad. First, combine these ingredients for filling:

1 cup grated sharp cheese
1/4 cup chopped ripe or
    stuffed green olives
1/4 teaspoon celery seed
2 teaspoons grated onion

1 teaspoon prepared
    mustard
Dash of Worcestershire
    sauce
Salt and pepper

Mix well. Make baking powder biscuit dough, roll thin, cut out, put a dot of filling on one biscuit, top with a second, and place on baking sheet. Brush tops with melted butter and bake in hot oven (450° F.) 10 to 12 minutes. Makes 12 to 15 biscuits.

RAISIN SCONES

2 cups prepared biscuit mix
3 tablespoons sugar
3/4 cup seedless raisins

1 egg, beaten
1/2 cup top milk

Stir together biscuit mix, sugar, and raisins. Add egg mixed with top milk, and stir thoroughly. Divide dough into 2 equal parts; roll or pat out each part into a round cake about 1/2 inch thick, and cut (like pie) into 6 triangular pieces. Prick tops with fork, brush with milk, sprinkle with sugar, and bake on a greased baking sheet in hot oven (450° F.) 10 to 12 minutes. Serve hot with butter. Makes 12 scones.

For scones filled with jam, omit raisins, pat out dough into 2 round cakes about 3/4 inch thick, and bake; while hot, split, spread strawberry or blackberry jam between, put together, and serve at once. Mighty good with coffee.

POPOVERS FOR SALAD LUNCHEONS

Popovers, piping hot, make any luncheon, home dinner, or Sunday breakfast a real event. They're utterly simple to make, if you follow directions exactly. First, preheat the oven to 450° F.; also grease 8 or 9 custard cups or heavy iron or cast aluminum muffin pans and heat sizzling hot in oven.

2 eggs   1 cup sifted flour
1 cup milk   1/4 teaspoon salt

Beat eggs and milk together in mixing bowl, using rotary beater. Dump in flour and salt, and continue beating until the thin batter is smooth and light. Pour into the hot pans, and bake at 450° F. for 30 minutes, then reduce heat to 350° F. and bake 10 to 15 minutes longer, to finish baking thoroughly. Cut a slit in each popover to let steam escape, and serve promptly. Makes 8 large popovers.

PRUNE BRAN MUFFINS

1/2 cup pitted cooked   2 tablespoons sugar
    prunes   3 tablespoons shortening
1 1/4 cups sifted flour   1 cup bran
1/2 teaspoon salt   1 egg, beaten
1 tablespoon baking powder   1/2 cup milk

Snip prunes in coarse pieces, using scissors. Sift flour, salt, baking powder, and sugar into mixing bowl. Cut or rub in shortening, as for biscuits. Add bran. Add egg mixed with milk, mix slightly, then add prunes and stir just until blended but still lumpy. Fill greased muffin pans 2/3 full and decorate tops with quartered cooked prunes if you wish. Bake in fairly hot oven (400° F.) 20 to 25 minutes. If you want to glaze them, brush tops with honey for last 5 minutes of baking. Makes 8 or 9 medium-sized muffins, which are very good reheated.

For Fig Bran Muffins, cover 1/2 cup dried figs with boiling water and let stand 10 minutes to soften; then drain, snip off stems, and cut figs coarsely, using scissors. Proceed as for prune muffins. For *Date Bran Muffins,* simply pit and cut up fresh dates, and add to batter.

SPOON BREAD

This, my favorite spoon bread recipe, was given me by a good-cooking friend from Georgia. It goes mighty well with fried chicken and gravy, in California or any other state!

1 quart milk	1 teaspoon salt
1 cup white corn meal	4 to 6 eggs, separated
(water-ground, if you	4 tablespoons butter
have it)	

Scald milk in a double boiler. Gradually stir in corn meal and salt, stir until thick, then cook 20 minutes or longer, stirring occasionally. Remove from heat, let cool slightly, then stir in beaten egg yolks. Fold in stiffly beaten whites, pour into 2 medium-sized, well-buttered shallow baking dishes, dot with butter, and bake in moderate oven (350° F.) about 30 minutes. Serves 6 to 8. Serve in baking dish; eat as you would eat mashed potatoes.

SOUR CREAM CORN BREAD

This extra-good recipe came to me from Wyoming, but it has become a native Californian by now.

1 egg	1/2 teaspoon soda
1 cup sour cream or butter-	1 teaspoon baking powder
milk	1 tablespoon sugar
1/3 cup flour	1 1/3 cups corn meal
1/2 teaspoon salt	2 tablespoons melted butter

Beat egg in a mixing bowl and add sour cream. (If the cream is very rich, better use half cream and half milk, sweet or sour —otherwise the bread will be too crumbly.) Sift together flour, salt, soda, baking powder, and sugar, mix with corn meal, and stir into egg and cream. Melt butter in a shallow baking pan (8 x 8 or 7 x 10 inches), thereby greasing the pan; pour excess butter into corn meal mixture, mix well, then spread the stiff batter in the buttered pan. Sprinkle a tiny bit of sugar over the rough spots or little peaks in the dough so they will brown nicely. Bake in fairly hot oven (400° F.) 20 to 25 minutes.

GOLDEN CORN STICKS

2 cups yellow corn meal
1 teaspoon salt
1 teaspoon soda
1 egg, beaten

2 cups buttermilk or sour
milk
4 tablespoons melted bacon
or ham drippings

Stir together corn meal, salt, and soda. Combine egg and buttermilk, add to dry ingredients,. and mix well. Stir in melted shortening. Pour into well-greased corn stick pans that have been heated piping hot, and bake in fairly hot oven (400° F.) for 25 to 30 minutes. Makes 18 corn sticks.

CALIFORNIA STEAMED BROWN BREAD

1 cup corn meal
1 cup bran
1/2 cup cracked wheat or
    whole-wheat flour
1/2 cup white flour
1 1/2 teaspoons salt
1 1/2 teaspoons soda

1 cup raisins
1 cup chopped dried figs
1 cup chopped cooked
    prunes
1 1/2 cups buttermilk or
    sour milk
1/2 cup molasses

Combine dry ingredients in mixing bowl. Add fruits. (If figs are very dry, cover them with boiling water and let stand for 10 minutes, then drain, snip off stems, and cut coarsely, using scissors. Prunes may be simmered for 15 to 20 minutes, then pitted and chopped, if you haven't ready-cooked ones on hand.) Stir in milk and molasses, mix well, then pour into greased smooth-edged cans, filling them 2/3 full. Tie doubled waxed paper over tops, and place on a rack in a deep kettle. Pour in boiling water to come up 2 or 3 inches around cans, cover kettle tightly, and boil steadily for 2 hours if small cans are used; up to 3 hours for larger ones. Turn out, and dry off for 10 minutes in moderate oven (350° F.). Best served hot, fresh or resteamed.

ORANGE NUT BREAD

3 cups sifted flour
4 teaspoons baking powder
1 teaspoon salt
1 cup chopped walnuts
1 egg, beaten

1 cup milk
2 tablespoons melted
   shortening
1/2 cup orange marmalade

Sift dry ingredients into mixing bowl. Add nuts. Combine egg, milk, and shortening and add to dry ingredients, mixing well. Stir in marmalade. Pour into greased 8 x 4 x 4-inch pan, let stand 20 minutes, then bake in moderate oven (350° F.) 65 to 70 minutes, until done. Cool on rack.

APPLESAUCE NUT BREAD

2 cups sifted flour
3/4 cup sugar
3 teaspoons baking powder
1 teaspoon salt
1/2 teaspoon soda

1/2 teaspoon cinnamon
1 cup chopped walnuts
1 egg
1 cup smooth applesauce
2 tablespoons shortening

Sift first 6 ingredients together onto paper; add walnuts. Beat egg in mixing bowl; add applesauce (unsweetened or slightly sweetened—it doesn't matter) and melted shortening. Add dry ingredients and stir just until blended. Pour into greased 9 x 5 x 3-inch loaf pan, let stand 20 minutes, then bake in moderate oven (350° F.) 60 to 70 minutes, or until done.

RAISIN NUT LOAF

3 cups sifted flour
1/2 cup sugar
4 teaspoons baking powder
1 1/2 teaspoons salt
1 cup raisins

3/4 cup chopped walnuts
1 egg, beaten
1 1/2 cups milk
2 tablespoons melted
   shortening

Sift flour, sugar, baking powder, and salt into bowl. Add

raisins and nuts. Combine egg, milk, and shortening, add to dry ingredients and stir just until blended. Pour into greased 8 x 4 x 4-inch loaf pan, let stand 20 minutes, then bake in moderate oven (350° F.) about 1 1/4 hours. Cool on rack.

DATE AND APRICOT NUT BREAD

1/2 cup dried apricots	1/4 teaspoon soda
1/2 cup dates	1 cup brown sugar, firmly
3/4 cup chopped nuts	packed
3 cups sifted flour	1 egg, beaten
3 teaspoons baking powder	1 1/2 cups milk
1 1/2 teaspoons salt	

Cover dried apricots with boiling water and let stand 15 minutes, drain and snip them into strips, using scissors. Chop dates and nuts and mix with apricots. Sift flour, baking powder, salt, and soda into mixing bowl, add brown sugar, fruit and nuts, and mix well. Stir in egg mixed with milk. Batter will be rather thin. Pour into greased 8 x 4 x 4-inch loaf pan, let stand 20 minutes, then bake in moderate oven (350° F.) about 1 1/4 hours, until done. Cool on rack.

BUTTERSCOTCH NUT WAFFLES

2 cups sifted flour	1 1/2 cups milk
3 teaspoons baking powder	1/3 cup melted butter or
1/2 teaspoon salt	other shortening
3 tablespoons brown sugar	3/4 cup coarsely chopped
3 eggs, separated	pecans or walnuts

Sift flour, baking powder, and salt into a mixing bowl, and add brown sugar. Beat egg yolks, add milk and melted butter. Stir into the flour mixture and beat just until smooth. Add nuts, and fold in the stiffly beaten egg whites. Bake in a hot waffle baker. Makes about 8 waffles.

Have you ever tried mixing melted butter with honey—1 part butter to 3 parts honey—and heating the mixture to serve on waffles or hot cakes? And don't forget that practically any syrup tastes better hot than cold, on hot waffles or griddle cakes.

TO SERVE TORTILLAS

Buy tortillas at a Mexican store. (They require a special kind of moist corn meal called "masa" and a special technique for making, which we won't attempt to tell about.) When you get them, they are soft. Before serving, heat them on both sides on an ungreased griddle, serve in a napkin-lined basket. To eat, tear them in pieces, roll or fold, and eat with butter or with *frijoles*. To keep leftover tortillas, let cool, then stack, wrap in a dry cloth and store in the refrigerator. Dampen lightly with moistened hands before reheating.

CAMPFIRE CORN CAKES

1 cup corn meal	1/4 teaspoon soda
3 tablespoons flour	2 tablespoons shortening
3/4 teaspoon salt	Water

Mix or sift dry ingredients. Rub in shortening as for biscuits, then stir in just enough water to make a stiff dough. Shape into thin patties or pones and fry in a skillet in a little hot fat. Serve with fish.

QUICK CORN FLAPJACKS

Mix 1/2 cup corn meal with 1 1/2 cups prepared flapjack or pancake flour. Beat 1 egg, add 2 cups milk and 2 tablespoons melted shortening, stir in flour mixture. Bake on a hot greased griddle. If you like thicker cakes, use a little less milk or a little more flapjack flour.

BEST FRENCH TOAST

Beat 2 eggs slightly with a dash of salt, stir in 1/2 cup milk or sherry. Dip 5 or 6 slices of bread quickly into the mixture to coat both sides, but don't soak them; brown slowly in a small amount of butter or bacon drippings in a heavy skillet, adding more fat as necessary during cooking. (Plenty of egg and slow browning—those are the secrets of good French toast.) Serve hot, sprinkled with sugar and cinnamon, or plain with honey or jam. Serves 2 or 3.

SANDWICH FILLINGS

Chop fine or grind 4 large cooked frankfurters, add 4 tablespoons sweet pickle relish and 3 or 4 tablespoons cooked salad dressing. Add prepared mustard, if needed. Spread between rye bread slices.

Flake, but don't mash, I large can salmon; add 1 finely chopped cucumber, 1 tablespoon vinegar, a little chopped celery if you like, and salt and coarse black pepper to taste. Moisten with salad dressing. Spread between whole-wheat bread.

Chop contents of a 12-ounce can of corned beef; chop and add 6 hard-cooked eggs and 1/2 cup mustard pickles. Add mayonnaise to moisten, salt and pepper to taste.

Chop 1 cup cooked chicken, add 1/2 cup finely chopped almonds (blanched or not), or walnuts, 2 tablespoons chopped capers, and 1 to 2 tablespoons chicken broth or consommé. Add mayonnaise to moisten, season to taste and spread between buttered white or whole-wheat bread.

Under "Canapés and Hors d'Oeuvres" in Chapter Ten, page 303, you will find dozens of ideas that can be adapted to plain or fancy sandwich making. Best guide in making really good sandwiches is your own sense of taste.

Campfire Toast. After frying bacon, pour off fat, then brown slices of bread slowly in the hot greased skillet. Or, rake red coals into a flat pile, drop a slice of bread onto them, turn immediately to brown on other side.

To toast fancy shapes of bread without having them buckle out of shape, spread one side lightly with butter and brown that side only on a hot griddle or skillet; or, toast one side quickly under the broiler. Spread the untoasted side with the canapé mixture.

FAMILY-SIZED SANDWICHES

Baked Salmon Sandwich. Cut a loaf of unsliced French or Vienna bread in halves lengthwise. Spread cut surfaces with soft butter, sprinkle with garlic salt. Drain a 1-pound can red salmon and flake coarsely. Mix with 1/2 cup celery, a little chopped onion, and just enough mayonnaise to hold mixture together. Spread on buttered bread, sprinkle thickly with grated Cheddar cheese, and bake in a hot oven (425° F.) about 10 minutes. Cut in chunks and serve piping hot, garnished with olives. With fruit salad (made with French dressing), and hot coffee or tea, you have a mighty good lunch or supper for 4 to 6.

Meat Ball Special. Cut a loaf of unsliced bread in two the long way. Spread cut surface of each half with butter and sprinkle with garlic salt. Open a 1-pound can of meat balls with gravy. Mash, mix with 1 tablespoon Worcestershire sauce. Spread bread with this mixture and heat in hot oven (400° F.) about 10 minutes, until hot and bubbly. Sprinkle with grated cheese, if you have it at hand. Cut in chunks to serve.

By-laws of Dessert Serving

Whether for everyday or for special occasions, plan a dessert that fits in well with the rest of the meal in all respects. In particular, look out for these points:

1. Choose a dessert that will contrast with the preceding courses in texture, form, and flavor. For example, to follow a spaghetti-meat casserole, you might well serve something like chilled fresh pears and cheese, but not a starchy pudding. To follow a soufflé or baked egg-and-cheese dish, you could perhaps choose apple or mince pie, but not pumpkin or other soft pie. To follow a roast, you might serve ice cream or a light fluffy pudding or a fruit gelatin dessert, but preferably not mince pie or steamed pudding. (Oh, of course, go ahead and have these for holidays, if you want to!) Generally speaking, it's good to follow a hot main course with a cold dessert, or vice versa, but this is not so important.

2. Avoid overelaborateness. The simplest sort of dessert, if it is attractive to look at and really good to eat, has infinitely more charm than a fussy creation that doesn't live up to its looks.

3. From the management standpoint, it's smart to decide on a company dinner dessert that can be made the day before, or at least several hours before serving.

4. For everyday dinners, see that the dessert contributes something besides sweetness and calories. If the main course is low in protein, balance it with a dessert rich in eggs, milk or nuts, or serve cheese with crackers and fruit or with pie. If the day's meals have been light on salads and fruit, make the dessert a fruity one.

Chapter 9

Favorite Desserts for All Occasions

A s MIGHT be expected, California desserts are likely to center around fruits. Often dessert is a tray of polished fresh fruits and nuts, which serves as table decoration during the first course and is eaten with crackers and cheese at the proper time. Or the dessert may be a fruit compote—a glass bowl of fresh, canned, or frozen fruits combined and served in heavy syrup, perhaps flavored with a dessert wine or a liqueur, or with white or red table wine. Or it may be a pudding or ice cream made with fruit or served with a fruit garnish or sauce.

This chapter then quite naturally runs largely to fruity desserts, plus some extra-special cakes and cookies and puddings that I know you will like to use over and over, as I do. One thing I should like to recommend is this: do try out the new methods of making pie crust and of mixing cakes that the test kitchens of various food manufacturers have recently been working out. Among them you are sure to find some methods and recipes that you like especially well. I am not giving them here because they are designed for use with particular brands of flour and shortening, and you should follow the recipes exactly as they are given for those brands.

PINEAPPLE PLATES

Wash a ripe, perfect, medium-sized fresh pineapple. Cut into quarters lengthwise, right through its green top. Trim out core, then with a grapefruit knife cut the meat from the shell, but leave it in place. Now carefully cut down through the meat, making medium-thin slices. Sprinkle with sugar and chill until serving time, then serve on plates with forks. Serves 4. Maybe you'd like to pour a little rum or sherry over the pineapple before sprinkling with sugar. It's an idea!

PEACHES CARDINAL

Served in a big glass bowl this colorful dessert is really a peachy one. For 8, allow 8 ripe freestone peaches (I like to use the big J. H. Hale's) and a box of red raspberries. Peel peaches carefully, cut in halves, remove pits, and cook 5 or 6 halves at a time gently in syrup made by dissolving 2 cups sugar in 1 cup hot water, with 1/4 teaspoon vanilla and a dash of salt added. As soon as peaches are barely tender, remove from syrup to a wide bowl. When all are cooked, boil the remaining syrup down to about half the original amount. (It should be quite thick.) Let cool, then add washed and drained raspberries; they will dilute the syrup to the right consistency. Pour over peaches in the bowl. Chill. Serve with angel cake or sponge cake.

BUYING AND STORING FRUITS

When you are marketing, don't pinch and squeeze fruits on display; it bruises them, causes spoilage. . . . The best citrus fruits are heavy for their size, full of juice. . . . The best peaches, apricots, strawberries, and cantaloupe are richly fragrant. Learn to know favorite varieties by name, such as Banner strawberries, J. H. Hale peaches. . . . All pears are picked green; they spoil at the core if let ripen on the tree. To hold back ripening, keep them in the refrigerator. . . . Chill cherries, grapes, apples, pears, melons, and peaches before serving, but not for too long a time. . . . To keep a ripe cantaloupe, Persian, Casaba, or other such melon from perfuming the entire refrigerator and its contents, put it into a tightly covered can or pan to chill. . . . To keep berries or other soft fruits overnight, spread on waxed paper on trays in the refrigerator. When possible, however, serve these and other delicately flavored fruits unchilled. And remember, it's an old ranch custom to serve ripe figs and apricots sun-warmed. . . . Wash berries just before using. Drop them gently into a pan of cold water, swish around, lift out with the fingers into a colander to drain. Wash strawberries before stemming. Sugar them shortly before serving, so all their juice won't be drawn out. . . . Keep dried fruits in covered glass jars. . . . Keep frozen fruits frozen solid until just time for them to thaw before serving.

ARTISTIC FRUIT PLATTER

A dessert beautiful for a summer luncheon or buffet supper is this, created and served by an artistic friend who lives in Mill Valley.

The day before the party, make a big sunshine, sponge, or angel cake (see recipes later in this chapter), and this *Fruit Sauce:*

1 cup water
2 cups sugar
2 baskets strawberries, crushed

1 basket loganberries or youngberries, crushed
6 sprigs of mint (may be omitted)

Boil water and sugar 10 minutes. Then add crushed berries

and mint, and boil 15 minutes longer. Strain, and chill syrup in refrigerator overnight so it will thicken somewhat. If mint is not used (or if it is, for that matter), you may like to add 1/4 cup sherry to the sauce.

Shortly before serving time, arrange various fresh fruits individually in groups or mounds on a huge turquoise blue pottery platter. You might use 2 mounds each of sliced peaches, strawberries, blackberries, and red raspberries, with cantaloupe and watermelon balls piled high in the center. To serve, have someone bring in and pass the sunshine cake, already cut in wedges. You follow with the fruit platter. Then pass the bowl of fruit sauce. Each takes a slice of cake, a helping of mixed fruits, then spoons the sauce over all.

BROILED GRAPEFRUIT

Allow half a grapefruit for each person. With a curved knife or sharp paring knife loosen flesh from membranes, but don't cut through those membranes themselves! Snip out the center core, using scissors. Place the halves in a baking pan, cut sides up, and on each put a tablespoon of brown sugar and a small dot of butter. Add 1 or 2 tablespoons sherry or rum, if you like. Broil slowly 5 to 8 minutes, until tinged with brown. Serve hot, as dessert or as first course.

If you don't want to heat the broiler to do 1 grapefruit, try skillet-broiling it. Melt about a tablespoon of butter in the skillet, sprinkle with brown sugar, then put in grapefruit, cut sides down. Heat gently until warmed through and lightly browned, then take up and pour syrup from pan over the fruit.

FOR PERFECT BAKED PEARS

Wash 4 firm-ripe pears. Cut out the blossom ends but leave the stems on. Place, upright if possible, in a deep casserole. Heat together 1/3 cup sugar, 1/2 cup water, a dash of salt, and a few strips of lemon peel; pour over the pears, cover, and bake in fairly hot oven (400° F.) for 1 to 1 1/2 hours, until tender. Take up the pears into individual dishes, boil down the syrup fairly thick, let cool, then spoon over the pears to glaze them. Serve warm or cold, with or without cream or chilled custard sauce. Serves 4.

STUFFED PEARS, S.P.

Many a person who has eaten stuffed baked pears in one of the dining cars of the Southern Pacific will welcome this recipe, provided by the head chef.

4 firm-ripe pears	2 tablespoons sugar
1/4 cup raisins	1 tablespoon lemon juice
2 tablespoons chopped	2 tablespoons water
walnuts	1/2 cup light corn syrup

Peel and core pears, leaving stems intact. Mix raisins, walnuts, sugar, and lemon juice, and stuff into the cavities of the pears. Place in a deep baking dish or pan, add water, and pour syrup over pears. Cover the baking dish. (If it does not have a tight-fitting lid, cover snugly with aluminum foil.) Bake in moderate oven (350° F.) for 1 1/2 hours. When done, remove cover, sprinkle pears lightly with sugar, and place low under the broiler, until nicely browned. Serves 4.

FOR BAKED APPLES

Pare the upper third of each apple, remove core, then place in a casserole, add the syrup made as directed for Perfect Baked Pears, and bake, covered, for about 30 minutes in moderately hot oven (375° F.). Glaze if desired. If you want them wine-flavored, pour 2 tablespoons port or sherry into each apple in its dish.

ROSY RHUBARB

Hothouse rhubarb, deep pink in color, delicate in flavor, comes in early in the new year. Don't you dare to peel it! Just wash and trim, then lay several stalks together on a board and slice into about 3/4-inch lengths. Put into a saucepan with 3 or 4 tablespoons water for 1 pound rhubarb, cover and cook gently about 5 minutes, until tender but not cooked to pieces. Add 1/2 to 1 cup sugar, and cook, stirring gently, just until sugar is dissolved. Cool, pour into a pottery or glass bowl (a blue one, if you have it!) and serve cold for dessert. Chocolate cake goes well with this. Makes 4 to 6 servings.

GUAVAS FOR DESSERT

Cut off the blossom ends of chilled thoroughly ripe guavas, peel them, and cut in halves. Scoop out pulpy centers and force through a wire strainer to remove seeds. Sweeten the pulp to taste, heap in the guava shells (or mix with the cut-up shells), and serve in dessert glasses with cream and sugar, accompanied by crisp cookies.

Peeled ripe guavas, put through a food mill or wire strainer, are excellent to use in place of other fruits in ice creams or sherbets.

All of the "strange fruits" described in the Salad chapter (see Index) are equally good to use for dessert, alone or in combination with other fruits. Follow the general directions for preparing them as given under Salads; then try them in various ways. Most of them are improved by a squeeze of lemon or lime.

TWO SPANISH DESSERTS

Orange Cup. Peel and slice or dice chilled oranges, sprinkle lightly with powdered sugar and cinnamon, and serve.

Sherried Peaches. Slice peeled peaches (clings are good) into a bowl, sugar to taste, then pour in sweet sherry almost to cover, and chill. Serve as is, or over ice cream.

AMBROSIA à la HAWAII

Mix sliced or diced oranges and diced fresh pineapple with plenty of shredded fresh coconut, adding powdered sugar to taste and a dash of salt; then flavor to taste with rum, sherry, or Curacao. Chill for several hours. Serve in small dessert dishes; no cookies or cake are needed with this.

BANANA FRITTERS

Bananas aren't produced in California, but banana fritters certainly are, in tremendous quantities! Practically every good Italian and French restaurant from border to border and Sierra to coast features them, served straight from the frying kettle, topped with a drift of whipped cream and a sharp shake of powdered cinnamon. Whether you serve them that way, or with brandy sauce or lemon sauce or some other kind of sauce, you'll find them easy to make this way.

4 or 5 ripe bananas
Lemon juice
2 tablespoons powdered
   sugar

Fluffy Batter:
1/2 cup sifted flour

2 teaspoons sugar
1/2 teaspoon baking powder
1 egg, separated
1/4 teaspoon salt
1/2 cup milk
2 teaspoons melted butter
   or margarine

First put shortening on to heat (have it about 2 inches deep in a broad, heavy pan). Next, get the bananas ready: peel and cut each banana crosswise into 3 or 4 fat chunks, coat the pieces with lemon juice and sprinkle with powdered sugar, and set aside while you quickly mix the batter as follows: Sift flour, sugar, and baking powder together. Add salt to egg white and beat stiff. Set aside briefly, while you beat egg yolk with the same beater, add milk and melted butter, then dry ingredients, and beat just until smooth. Fold in beaten white. Drain bananas. Dip each piece into the fluffy batter, and fry in deep hot fat (375° F.) about 2 minutes, or until golden brown all over. Drain on paper towels. Serve hot with whipped cream or sauce. Serves 4 or 5.

LIQUEUR SAUCE FOR BANANA FRITTERS

1/4 cup sugar
1 tablespoon cornstarch
Dash of salt
3/4 cup cold water

Brandy, Benedictine, or
   Cointreau or other
   liqueur to taste
1 tablespoon butter

Mix sugar, cornstarch, and salt in a saucepan, stir in water, and cook, stirring, until transparent. Add butter and 2 to 4 tablespoons (or more) of any liqueur (or combination). Makes about 1 cup, serving 4 or 5. Serve hot.

BRANDIED APRICOT SAUCE

3/4 cup apricot jam
About 4 tablespoons brandy

1 tablespoon butter

Stir enough brandy (or other liqueur, or rum) into jam to taste just right. Add butter and heat almost to boiling. If too thick, thin with a little hot water. Serves 4 or 5.

EGGNOG SAUCE

2 egg yolks
Dash of salt
1 cup sifted powdered
   sugar

3 to 4 tablespoons brandy or
   sherry
1/2 cup heavy cream,
   whipped

Beat egg yolks with salt, stir in sugar and brandy alternately, mixing well. Fold in whipped cream and serve with banana fritters or any hot steamed pudding. Serves 5 or 6.

PARTY PIE

This dessert, which is a form of torte, looks difficult but is really ever so easy to do. It has to be chilled overnight in the refrigerator to soften the meringue "crust" and make it easy to serve. First, make the meringue as follows:

4 egg whites	1/4 teaspoon salt
1/2 teaspoon cream of tartar	1/2 teaspoon vanilla
	1 cup sugar

Add cream of tartar, salt, and vanilla to egg whites in large, deep bowl, and beat stiff, using a rotary beater. Add sugar gradually, beating all the time. When very stiff, heap in a well-buttered 8-inch or 9-inch oven-glass pie pan, and bake very, very slowly (at 275° F.) for an hour. The meringue should not brown at all, but should be a delicate cream color, and dry and firm to the touch. Let cool thoroughly before spreading with this lemon filling:

4 egg yolks	4 tablespoons lemon juice
2 teaspoons grated lemon peel	1/2 cup sugar
	Dash of salt

Combine ingredients and cook over hot water, stirring constantly, until thick and smooth. Cool. Spread over center of cold meringue, then cover the lemon filling with a topping made by combining 3/4 cup whipped cream, 2 tablespoons sugar, 1/2 teaspoon vanilla, and 1/4 cup shredded coconut. Sprinkle a little more coconut over all and put into the refrigerator for 12 to 24 hours. Serve at the table, placing the pie pan on a large plate. Serves 6 generously; 8 adequately.

MILL VALLEY ICE CREAM CAKE

For this imposing dessert you have 2 layers of Sunshine Cake put together with an equally thick layer of Lemon Cream

Sherbet, and you serve it at table, passing a bowl of fluffy Orange Sauce. You can have everything made in advance, ready for final putting together. This recipe makes a cake just the right size:

Sunshine Layer Cake

4 egg whites
1/4 teaspoon salt
1/8 teaspoon cream of
    tartar
1 cup sugar

3 egg yolks
2 tablespoons water
1 teaspoon vanilla
1/2 teaspoon lemon juice
1 cup sifted cake flour

Add salt and cream of tartar to egg whites and beat until stiff but not dry. Add gradually 1/2 cup of the sugar, beating at first, then folding in the last additions. Beat egg yolks with remaining 1/2 cup sugar and the water, vanilla, and lemon juice until thick and light-colored. Fold into egg whites, then gradually fold in the flour. Pour into 2 ungreased 8-inch layer pans, and bake in very moderate oven (325° F.) 25 minutes. Invert pans on a rack until cool, then remove the cakes from the pans.

Lemon Cream Sherbet

2 eggs, beaten
1 teaspoon grated lemon
    peel
1/2 cup sugar

1/2 cup light corn syrup
1 1/2 cups top milk
1/4 cup lemon juice
1 cup heavy cream, whipped

Beat eggs; gradually beat in lemon peel and sugar. Add syrup, milk, and lemon juice. Pour into freezing trays and freeze until mushy. Remove from trays to a chilled bowl, beat until fluffy, fold in stiffly whipped cream, then return to trays and freeze until firm.

Fluffy Orange Sauce

1/2 cup sugar
2 egg yolks, beaten

Grated peel and juice of 1
    medium-sized orange

Cook in a double boiler, stirring, for 10 minutes. Cool. Just before serving, fold in 1 cup whipped cream.

TO SERVE: Put 1 layer of cake on a plate. Pack Lemon Cream Sherbet firmly into one of the layer pans to shape it, then turn out quickly onto the cake; top with second layer of cake. Serve at once at the table, passing Fluffy Orange Sauce. Serves 10 to 12.

LEMON-ORANGE MILK SHERBET

The first time I ate this, at a friend's home, it was with warm Lazy Daisy Cake. I took home the sherbet recipe, of course, and have been making it on frequent occasions ever since.

3 large lemons
1 large orange
2 large or 3 small eggs,
    separated

1 1/2 cups sugar
1 quart rich milk
Dash of salt

Grate about 1 teaspoon each of lemon and orange peel; extract the juices. Beat egg yolks, stir in grated peel and juice, 1 cup of the sugar, and all the milk. Add salt to egg whites, beat stiff, gradually beat in remaining 1/2 cup sugar. Fold into first mixture. Freeze in trays until almost firm, take out, beat with a fork until fluffy, then put back into trays and freeze hard. Makes 2 quarts of fresh-flavored fruity sherbet, serving 12 to 16.

GELATIN ICE CREAM WHIP

Dissolve a package of strawberry-flavored gelatin in 1 1/2 cups hot water. Chill until partially thickened, then add 1 pint vanilla ice cream and beat well. Chill in mold until firm. Turn out and serve, garnish with sugared fresh berries if available, or sprinkled with chopped nuts. Serves 10 or 12.

DESSERT WINE JELLY

1 tablespoon plain gelatin   1/2 cup orange juice
1/4 cup cold water   3/4 cup sherry or port wine
1/4 cup boiling water   1 tablespoon lemon juice
1/2 cup sugar   Dash of salt

Add gelatin to cold water, let stand 5 minutes, then add boiling water and sugar, and stir until dissolved. Add rest of ingredients, and chill in shallow pan until firm. Cut into small squares and heap in dessert dishes; sprinkle servings with coarsely chopped walnuts and garnish with fruit if you wish. Serve with whipped cream or custard sauce. Serves 6.

SHERRIED TRIFLE

In a bowl arrange alternate layers of sliced stale sponge cake or jelly roll and crumbled macaroons, sprinkling each layer with chopped blanched almonds (plain or toasted), and moistening lightly with sherry slightly diluted with water or syrup from canned fruit. Chill 12 hours or longer. Serve with chilled custard sauce.

JUST-RIGHT CUSTARD SAUCE

Old cook books call this soft or boiled custard; it is soft, but it certainly should not be boiled! Do it this way and it will be creamy smooth and delicately flavored; use yolks rather than whole eggs, if possible.

2 cups milk   1/2 teaspoon vanilla
4 egg yolks or 2 whole eggs   1/2 teaspoon lemon extract
4 tablespoons sugar   1 or 2 drops almond extract
Dash of salt   (may be omitted)

Scald 1 3/4 cups of the milk in double boiler. Beat egg yolks slightly with remaining cold milk, sugar, and salt. (This keeps the egg from forming hard little lumps with the sugar.)

Stir into hot milk and cook, stirring constantly, about 5 minutes, testing frequently by dipping a clean metal spoon into the custard. The moment it forms a clinging coat on the spoon, remove custard from hot water. Pour through a fine wire strainer, add flavorings, cover with a damp cloth (to prevent film forming on top), and cool; then cover and keep in coldest part of refrigerator. Serve with canned or fresh fruit, baked apple, prune whip, or other desserts. Makes 2 1/2 cups, serving 4 to 6.

JUST-RIGHT BAKED CUSTARDS

For 5 or 6 cup custards, use amounts given for Custard Sauce. (If custard is to be baked in a casserole or in a ring mold and turned out, use 6 yolks or 3 eggs to 2 cups milk, to make it firmer.) Beat eggs slightly with a little milk, add sugar, salt, and the rest of the cold milk. Flavor with vanilla and lemon. Place ungreased custard cups in a shallow pan. Strain custard into the cups and sprinkle tops generously with nutmeg. Pour about 1/2 inch of hot water into pan, set pan and all in moderate oven (350° F.) and bake 35 to 45 minutes, or until done, testing frequently toward the last by inserting the tip of a knife into the custard. When knife comes out clean, the custards are done. Remove at once from heat, cool, and chill. Serve in the cups, or turn out into shallow dishes and pour port wine around them, or surround them with fresh or canned fruit. Applesauce with a bit of grated lemon rind and chopped candied ginger is especially good with custards. Bake a large custard as directed for cup custards, but allow more time.

ZABAGLIONE

To serve 6, combine in top of double boiler 6 eggs, 4 tablespoons powdered sugar, and a dash of salt; place over hot water and beat constantly with rotary beater for about 8 minutes, gradually beating in 6 tablespoons sherry or white wine. When mixture is stiff enough to hold a coffee spoon upright in the center, pour into tall glasses or sherbet cups and serve, hot or cold.

BAKED LEMON PUDDINGS

3 tablespoons flour
1 cup sugar
3 tablespoons soft butter or margarine
3 eggs, separated
1 tablespoon grated lemon peel
3 tablespoons lemon juice
1 1/2 cups milk
Dash of salt

Mix flour with half the sugar and work this gradually into butter, creaming until smooth. Stir in beaten egg yolks, lemon peel and juice, and milk. Add salt to egg whites, beat stiff, and gradually beat in remaining 1/2 cup sugar. Fold into first mixture. Pour into 6 buttered custard cups, set in pan with 1/2 inch of hot water in it and bake in moderate oven (350° F.) 50 minutes. When done, there will be a cake-like layer on top of a layer of lemon custard. Cool, chill thoroughly, then turn out and serve plain or with lemon sauce or whipped cream. Serves 6.

SEVEN-MINUTE PRUNE WHIP

3 egg whites
1 teaspoon grated lemon peel
2 tablespoons prune juice
1 tablespoon lemon juice
Dash of salt
1/2 cup sugar
1/2 cup chopped cooked prunes

Combine all ingredients except prunes in double boiler, place over boiling water and beat with rotary beater until mixture fluffs up and holds its shape when beater is lifted (about 5 to 7 minutes). Fold in prunes, heap in 4 dessert dishes, or a serving bowl, and chill. Serve with soft custard sauce made with 3 egg yolks, 3 tablespoons sugar, dash salt, and 1 1/2 cups milk, flavoring it with vanilla and lemon extract. (For method see recipe for Just-Right Custard Sauce in this chapter.)

BAKED PRU-NUT WHIP

1 cup chopped cooked
    prunes
1 1/2 tablespoons lemon
    juice
1/2 teaspoon cinnamon
1/4 cup chopped walnuts

1/4 teaspoon salt
3 egg whites
1/2 cup sugar
6 pitted cooked prunes
6 walnut halves

Mix first 4 ingredients. Add salt to egg whites, beat stiff, then gradually beat in sugar. Fold in prune mixture, pour into buttered shallow baking dish, decorate top with 6 walnut-stuffed prunes, and bake in rather slow oven (325° F.) 35 to 40 minutes, until firm. Serve cold (it will shrink somewhat as it cools), with custard sauce. Serves 6.

For Pru-Nut Whip Pie, pour uncooked mixture into a baked 9-inch pie shell, decorate, and bake as directed. Serve cold with whipped cream.

DATE-NUT PUDDING

1 cup sliced fresh dates
1/2 to 1 cup coarsely
    chopped walnuts
1/2 cup sifted flour
1/2 teaspoon salt

1 teaspoon baking powder
3 eggs, separated
3/4 cup brown or granu-
    lated sugar
1 teaspoon vanilla

Mix dates and nuts with flour which has been sifted with salt and baking powder. Beat egg yolks, beat in sugar, stir in date-and-flour mixture. Fold in stiffly beaten whites. Bake in a greased 8-inch square or 9-inch layer pan in very moderate oven (325° F.) about 35 minutes. Serve warm, topped with whipped cream or ice cream; or cool, then crumble and mix with whipped cream. Serves 6.

LEMON BREAD PUDDING

This really shouldn't be called bread pudding, for no one would recognize it as such.

3 cups broken pieces of bread	1/4 teaspoon salt
	1/4 teaspoon nutmeg
3 cups milk	1 1/2 teaspoons grated
3 eggs, separated	lemon peel
1 cup sugar	1/4 teaspoon lemon extract

Pour milk over bread and let stand until very soft. Stir in slightly beaten egg yolks, 2/3 cup of the sugar, and salt, nutmeg, and lemon peel, beat thoroughly with rotary beater. Pour into a well-greased baking dish (1 1/2 quart size) and set in shallow pan containing hot water 1/2 inch deep. Bake in moderately slow oven (325° F.) about 1 1/4 hours, or until pudding is lightly browned and begins to leave sides of pan. Remove from oven and spread roughly with meringue made by beating the 3 egg whites stiff with lemon extract and a dash of salt, and gradually beating in the remaining 1/3 cup sugar. Bake at 350° F. about 15 minutes longer, until firm and lightly browned. Serve cold, decorated with spoonfuls of red jelly. Serves 6.

PEACHY COBBLER

Fruit part:	*Batter:*
3 cups sliced peaches, fresh or canned	1 cup sifted cake flour
	1/2 teaspoon salt
1/2 cup sugar	2 teaspoons baking powder
1 tablespoon lemon juice	3 tablespoons sugar
2 tablespoons melted butter or margarine	3 tablespoons shortening
	1/3 cup milk

Slice peaches into baking dish and add sugar, lemon juice, and melted butter. Make batter: sift flour, salt, baking powder, and sugar, cut in shortening fine, as for biscuits, then stir in milk to make a soft dough. Drop or spread over peaches and bake in fairly hot oven (425° F.) about 30 minutes. Serve warm with top milk. Serves 4 or 5. Berries or apricots may replace the peaches. Leftover cobbler is good warmed in the oven.

BAKED FUDGE PUDDING

Batter:

1 cup sifted flour
2 teaspoons baking powder
1/2 teaspoon salt
1/2 cup sugar
2 tablespoons ground
   chocolate or cocoa

3/4 cup chopped walnuts
1/2 cup milk
1 teaspoon vanilla
2 tablespoons melted
   shortening

Topping:

1/4 cup ground chocolate or
   cocoa

3/4 cup brown sugar
1 3/4 cups hot water

Sift together flour, baking powder, salt, sugar, and chocolate or cocoa into mixing bowl. Add nuts, then stir in milk, vanilla, and melted shortening. Spread in greased 8-inch square pan or shallow oven-glass baking dish. Make the topping: mix chocolate or cocoa with brown sugar, stir in hot water, and pour over batter. Bake in moderate oven (350° F.) about 45 minutes. As the pudding bakes, the batter rises through the rich chocolate sauce. Serve warm or cold with top milk, whipped cream, or ice cream. Serves 8.

STEAMED CRANBERRY PUDDING

No egg, no shortening, no sugar in this extra-good, extra-easy steamed pudding, which serves 6 to 8.

2 cups raw cranberries, cut
    in halves
1/2 cup citron, cut fine
1/2 cup chopped walnuts
1/2 cup molasses

1 1/2 cups sifted flour
1/2 teaspoon salt
1 1/2 teaspoons soda
2 tablespoons cold water

Mix cranberries, citron, walnuts, and molasses. Stir in flour sifted with salt. Dissolve soda in water and add last. Mix well, pour into greased mold or cans, filling them 3/4 full, cover or tie doubled waxed paper over the tops, and place on a rack in a kettle. Pour in boiling water to about half the depth of the cans. Cover kettle and boil steadily 2 hours. Serve hot with Creamy Pudding Sauce.

CREAMY PUDDING SAUCE

1 cup sugar
3/4 cup top milk
2 tablespoons butter

1 egg yolk, beaten
1 teaspoon vanilla

Boil sugar, milk, and butter together 3 or 4 minutes, carefully stir in egg yolk and cook, stirring, a minute longer. Flavor, and serve hot. Serves 6.

OLD-TIMER STEAMED PUDDING

1 cup chopped suet
1 cup chopped walnuts
1 1/4 cups raisins
3/4 cup sugar
2 1/2 cups sifted flour
1 teaspoon salt
1/2 teaspoon cloves

1 teaspoon nutmeg
1 tablespoon cinnamon
2 eggs, beaten
1 cup molasses
1 cup buttermilk with 2
    teaspoons soda

Measure suet, nuts, raisins, sugar, flour, salt, and spices into a mixing bowl. Combine eggs and molasses, stir soda into buttermilk and add, then stir this liquid mixture into dry mixture in bowl. Blend well. Fill greased molds (or bowls, or tin cans) 2/3 full, cover with greased lid or with two or three thicknesses of waxed paper tied on. Place on a rack in a deep kettle, pour in boiling water to come up about half-way on the molds, cover kettle tightly and steam 2 1/2 hours. Serves 8 to 12. Serve hot with a thin hot sauce, and hard sauce, too, if you like. My favorite thin sauce for this pudding is this:

VINEGAR SAUCE

2 cups water
2 tablespoons butter
3/4 cup sugar
2 tablespoons cornstarch
Dash of salt

1 teaspoon vanilla
1 to 2 tablespoons vinegar
    or lemon juice
Dash of nutmeg

Heat water and butter to boiling. Mix sugar, cornstarch, and salt thoroughly, add all at once to the boiling liquid (no, it won't lump, if you stir fast) and cook, stirring, until clear and slightly thickened. Add flavorings and serve hot. Makes enough for the pudding given above.

NO-COOKING ORANGE SAUCE

To serve over rice or tapioca pudding, stir together equal parts of sugar and orange juice, until the sugar is dissolved.

HARD SAUCE FOR PUDDING

1/4 cup (1/2 cube) soft
    butter
1 tablespoon hot water
1 cup sifted powdered sugar

1/2 teaspoon vanilla; or
    brandy, rum, or sherry
    to taste

Add hot water and powdered sugar alternately to butter, creaming and beating until light and fluffy. Add flavoring.

Heap in a pretty bowl or drop by spoonfuls on waxed paper and top each mound with a walnut half. Chill. Makes 4 or 5 servings.

FOAMY SAUCE FOR STEAMED PUDDINGS

1/2 cup soft butter
1 cup brown sugar, firmly
    packed

1 egg, well beaten
1/4 cup brandy or 1/2 cup
    sherry

Gradually work sugar into butter, creaming until fluffy. Add egg and beat well. Just before serving, gradually beat in brandy or sherry, place over hot water and heat, beating constantly, until soft but not syrupy. This takes only a minute or so. Serves about 6.

DEVONSHIRE CREAM

For something out of this world, serve this on warm apple pie, or fresh strawberries. It is definitely not a "thrift" recipe, but it is wonderful.

In a wide pan heat slowly together 5 quarts whole milk and 3 pints cream; keep the mixture just at simmering point for 2 to 3 hours. Cool, chill in refrigerator overnight, then skim off the creamy top, and serve wherever you would serve whipped cream.

EASY BUTTERSCOTCH SAUCE

1/4 cup corn syrup
1 small can (2/3 cup) un-
    sweetened evaporated
    milk

1 cup brown sugar
1 cup granulated sugar
Few grains of salt

Combine all ingredients in double boiler, cover, and let cook, stirring once in a while, about 30 minutes, or until it thickens. Add 2 tablespoons butter and 1 teaspoon vanilla. Turn off heat, but let sauce stand over hot water until wanted. Makes 1 1/2 cups rich, delicious sauce for ice cream, rice, tapioca, or cottage pudding.

HOT FUDGE SAUCE

2 squares (2 ounces) choco- 1 small can (2/3 cup) un-
  late   sweetened evaporated
1 cup sugar   milk

Combine in double boiler and let cook, stirring occasionally, about 30 minutes, or until it thickens. Add 1 tablespoon butter and 1 teaspoon vanilla. Turn off heat, but let sauce stand over hot water until wanted. Makes about 1 1/2 cups rich, thick fudge sauce. If you prefer a thinner syrup, stir in a little milk or water and heat for a moment.

QUICK CHOCOLATE SAUCE

2 squares chocolate   4 tablespoons cream
1 cup sugar   1 egg, beaten
Dash of salt

Melt chocolate in a saucepan, add rest of the ingredients, and cook 2 minutes, stirring. Add 1/2 teaspoon vanilla. Serve hot on ice cream or whatever.

CRÊPES SUZETTE

These thin pancakes, served in a rich liqueur-flavored sauce, are a favorite dessert at French restaurants. These amounts make 12 to 16 cakes, serving 6 to 8. To serve 2, make 1/3 of the recipe.

1 cup sifted flour   3 eggs, beaten
1 tablespoon sugar   1 cup milk (about)
1/2 teaspoon salt   1 teaspoon oil

Sift flour, sugar, and salt into a bowl. Combine beaten eggs and milk and add slowly, stirring until smooth. The batter should be very thin. Add oil. Cook one at a time in a well-buttered 5-inch skillet, turning once. Keep warm in the oven until needed, then reheat in one of these sauces.

CURACAO BUTTER SAUCE

1/2 cup butter
1/2 cup sugar

Grated peel and juice of 1
   orange
1/4 cup Curacao

Melt butter, add sugar, orange peel and juice, and Curacao. Heat and serve with crêpes.

RUM SAUCE FOR CRÊPES

1 cup sugar
1/2 cup water
4 tablespoons butter
1 teaspoon grated orange
   peel

1 tablespoon orange juice
1/4 cup rum

Boil sugar and water together for 5 minutes. Add butter, orange peel and juice, and rum. (Or add any liqueur—anisette, Cointreau, or Grand Marnier, for example—to taste, instead of rum.) Heat and pour over the folded crêpes on a hot platter.

FLAMING CHERRIES WITH ICE CREAM

This requires a chafing dish or an electric table stove. Several hours in advance, drain pitted canned black cherries thoroughly, add 1/4 to 1/2 cup brandy (cherry-flavored Kirschwasser is good to use), and let stand, stirring occasionally, until just before serving; then drain again, and put cherries into chafing dish. Add a few tablespoonfuls of fresh brandy, previously warmed over hot water, stir cherries around a bit, then light a tablespoonful of this hot brandy (from the chafing dish flame or from a candle), pour over the cherries, and continue to spoon the flaming brandy over them until the flame goes out. Serve at once over very hard vanilla ice cream.

FOR BETTER CAKES

Whatever the method you use—traditional or new—have eggs and milk as well as shortening at room temperature when you start mixing a cake. . . .

Measure accurately, leveling off cups and spoons with a straight knife. . . .

If shortening and sugar are to be creamed together, add sugar gradually, and cream the mixture until light and fluffy. . . .

Use cake flour when the recipe calls for it; otherwise, all-purpose flour. Sift the flour once *before measuring*—otherwise you get too much flour in your cake. . . .

Use right size pans; an 8-inch round layer pan has an area of about 50 square inches; a 9-inch round pan, approximately 64 square inches, or same as an 8-inch-square pan. . . .

A cake recipe calling for around 2 cups of flour will make an 8 x 8 x 2-inch loaf, or two 8-inch layers, or 12 cup cakes. . . .

Don't grease the pan for sponge or angel cake. Grease (or grease and flour) bottom of pan only for cakes with shortening; cake can't climb a greased wall! For big sheet cakes (9 x 12 inches or larger) grease bottom of the pan, then line with paper and grease that. . . .

Have oven preheated to the right temperature before putting cake in. Bake until done when tested with a wire cake tester, or until top springs back when dented with finger. Oven-glass pans bake faster, so reduce oven heat by 25° F.

Let cake stand in the pan about 5 minutes, then turn it out on wire rack with paper beneath rack to absorb steam. Cool, brush off crumbs, then frost if and as desired, doing sides first, then top.

BEST WHITE LAYER CAKE

The kind of white layer cake you've always wished you could make—here it is! Get out all the ingredients, grease 2 round 8-inch layer pans on bottoms only, turn on the oven and set it for moderate heat (350° F.), and you are ready to mix the cake.

1/2 cup (1 cube) soft butter or other shortening	1/2 teaspoon salt
1 1/2 cups sugar	3/4 cup milk and water, mixed
2 cups sifted cake flour	1 teaspoon vanilla
2 teaspoons baking powder	4 egg whites

Cream butter, add sugar gradually, and cream until very light and fluffy. Sift flour, measure, sift again with baking powder and salt. Add vanilla to water and milk. To the creamed butter-and-sugar add flour and liquid alternately, a little at a time, beating smooth after each addition. Beat egg whites stiff but not dry, and fold them quickly but thoroughly into the batter. Spread evenly in the greased pans, tap pans sharply on table 2 or 3 times to break large air bubbles, and bake 25 to 30 minutes at 350° F. When done, let stand in pans 5 minutes, then turn out on racks to cool thoroughly before frosting. To make three 8-inch layers, or two 9-inch layers, make 1 1/2 times this recipe.

For Fresh Coconut Cake. Use just 1 1/4 cups sugar in the above recipe, and use half coconut milk, half "regular" milk, for liquid. Sprinkle fresh grated coconut over frosting.

FROSTING SUPERB FOR WHITE CAKE

Bake that Best White Layer Cake. Shortly before serving, put cooled layers together with this filling, and cover top thickly with it.

1 cup moist canned (or
    fresh grated) coconut
3 teaspoons grated orange
    peel

1/4 cup sugar
2 tablespoons orange juice
1 cup whipping cream

Mix first 4 ingredients and let them stand until time to frost the cake. Then whip the cream, fold in the coconut mixture, and spread between the layers and on the top.

PINEAPPLE UPSIDE-DOWN CAKE

First, prepare the upside-down topping: melt 3 tablespoons butter or margarine in an 8 x 8 x 2-inch square or a deep 9-inch round pan, sprinkle with 1/2 cup brown sugar, then arrange over sugar 4 slices or 6 half-slices of pineapple, centered or interspersed with Maraschino cherries or walnut halves, or both. Set aside while you make the cake batter:

1/3 cup shortening
1/2 cup sugar
1 egg, unbeaten
1 teaspoon vanilla
1 1/4 cups sifted flour

1/4 teaspoon salt
1 1/2 teaspoons baking
    powder
1/2 cup pineapple syrup

Gradually add sugar to shortening, creaming until fluffy. Add egg and vanilla; beat well. Add alternately small amounts of sifted dry ingredients and pineapple syrup, beating smooth after each addition. Spread batter over pineapple, and bake in moderate oven (350° F.) 50 to 60 minutes. Let stand 5 minutes, then turn out on big plate. Serve warm. Serves 6 to 8.

BETTER-THAN-EVER ANGEL FOOD CAKE

This is my own new and improved version of the Heavenly Angel Cake which appeared in earlier editions of this book. It is baked at a higher temperature, of course, which in itself makes for a higher, more tender cake. It differs in just a few amounts from the good standard angel foods—but those details make a lot of difference in the result!

For a big, high, 10-inch diameter cake you'll need:

1 1/2 to 1 2/3 cups egg whites (13 large eggs)
1/2 teaspoon salt
1 1/2 teaspoons cream of tartar
1 teaspoon vanilla
3/4 teaspoon lemon extract
1/4 teaspoon almond extract
1 1/4 cups sifted cake flour
2 cups sifted dessert sugar (i.e. extra-fine granulated)

Preheat oven to 375° F. (moderate). Measure egg whites (have them at room temperature) into a *big* (at least 4-quart) bowl; add salt, cream of tartar, and extracts. Sift flour, measure, sift again 3 times with 1 cup of the sugar; set aside in sifter.

With flat wire whip, beat egg whites until foamy throughout. Now beat in, 2 tablespoons at a time, the remaining 1 cup sugar; beat about 10 seconds after each addition, and scrape the bowl frequently with rubber scraper. After last of sugar has been added, continue beating until the meringue will hold up in high, stiff peaks when beater is lifted.

Now sift the flour-sugar mixture, about 3 tablespoons at a time, over the stiff meringue, folding gently each time with wire whip until well mixed, and scraping bowl occasionally.

Empty the thick batter carefully into ungreased 10-inch tube pan. Run a knife around and around through the batter 5 or 6 times to break up big bubbles. Level top of batter. Bake at 375° F. for 35 to 38 minutes, until top will not show dent when touched lightly. (There will be deep cracks in the top, but don't worry about them.) Hang cake upside-down at once on a funnel or bottle for at least an hour, and better yet, 3 or 4 hours or overnight. Then loosen from sides and tube by running a slender knife quickly around the cake close to pan, and remove. Serve plain, or frost with a thin powdered sugar icing.

HOT MILK SPONGE SQUARE

Grease the bottom of an 8 x 8 x 2-inch pan, and turn on oven to 350° F. before you begin mixing the batter:

2 eggs	1/2 teaspoon salt
1 cup sugar	1/2 cup milk
1 cup sifted cake flour	1 tablespoon butter
1 teaspoon baking powder	1 teaspoon vanilla

Beat eggs in mixing bowl. Add sugar gradually, continuing to beat until fluffy and light-colored. Add flour sifted with baking powder and salt, and beat thoroughly. Heat milk and butter just to boiling, add vanilla, stir hot liquid quickly into batter, and beat slightly. Pour the thin batter at once into greased pan, and bake 30 minutes in moderate oven (350° F.). Turn out, cool, and frost as desired. Or, upon removing from oven, spread top of hot cake with this Lazy Daisy Frosting, and broil.

LAZY DAISY FROSTING

3 tablespoons butter or margarine	1/2 cup brown sugar, firmly packed
5 tablespoons cream or evaporated milk	1/2 cup coconut
	1/4 cup chopped walnuts

Heat butter and cream together, add other ingredients and blend well. Spread lightly on hot cake, place low under broiler, and broil slowly until bubbly and lightly browned. Leave in pan to cool. Serve slightly warm, if possible.

BIG CHOCOLATE CAKE

This recipe turns out such a superior chocolate cake, I make it whenever I need a good-sized one. It is perfect for every occasion, from picnics to tea parties, and it keeps wonderfully. Do make it with butter—it's worth it!

1/2 cup (1 cube) soft butter
1 pound brown sugar (2 1/2 cups, firmly packed)
2 eggs, beaten
2 squares chocolate, melted
1/2 cup buttermilk

2 teaspoons vanilla
2 1/4 cups sifted cake flour
1/2 teaspoon salt
1 cup boiling water
2 teaspoons soda

Light the oven, set at 375° F. Cream the butter, gradually add sugar, creaming until light and fluffy. Add eggs and beat hard. Stir in melted chocolate, then buttermilk and vanilla. Gradually add cake flour sifted with salt, beating thoroughly after each addition. Last of all, stir soda into boiling water and stir into the batter. You'll think you are ruining it, but don't be alarmed! Pour the extremely thin batter into a greased 9 x 12 x 2-inch pan and bake at 375° F. for 15 minutes, then reduce heat to 350° F. and bake about 30 minutes longer, until done. Leave cake in pan if you wish; or turn out on rack to cool, then put back into its pan; frost with this delicious uncooked Creamy Chocolate Frosting, or with Nut Cream Frosting.

CREAMY CHOCOLATE FROSTING

1 egg, beaten
1 square (1 ounce) chocolate, melted
1 3/4 cups sifted powdered sugar

1 teaspoon vanilla
1 tablespoon cream

Stir hot melted chocolate into egg. Gradually add remaining ingredients, beating well. Spread on the cool cake and sprinkle with coarsely chopped walnuts.

NUT CREAM FROSTING

1 1/2 cups brown or granulated sugar
1 cup sweet or sour cream
1 tablespoon corn syrup

1 cup coarsely chopped walnuts
1/2 teaspoon vanilla

Boil sugar, cream, and corn syrup together to very soft ball stage. Add nuts and vanilla and let cool to lukewarm, then beat hard, until of right consistency to spread. If it should harden too quickly, stir in a few drops of milk or hot water. Spread on cool cake. Either light or heavy cream works well in this recipe.

FRUIT FILLING FOR LAYER CAKE

Chop fine or grind 1 cup raisins and 1 cup figs or dates. Add 1 cup water, 1/2 cup sugar, and a dash of salt, and cook, stirring frequently, about 10 minutes or until thick. Add 1 tablespoon lemon juice. Cool and spread thickly between layers of cake.

LITTLE CHOCOLATE CAKE

This is ever so simple and quick to do, and the resulting cake is fine-textured and velvety. If you melt the chocolate and butter together in a large double boiler or in a bowl set in hot water, you can mix the entire cake in that same utensil.

2 squares chocolate	1/4 teaspoon salt
3 tablespoons butter or other shortening	1 cup sugar
1 cup sifted cake flour	2 eggs, beaten
1 1/2 teaspoons baking powder	1/2 cup milk
	1 teaspoon vanilla

As soon as chocolate and butter are barely melted, set aside to cool while you sift cake flour, measure, and sift again with baking powder and salt; set aside. When chocolate and butter are lukewarm, stir in sugar, add beaten eggs and beat hard. Add milk and vanilla. Add flour and beat thoroughly. Pour the very thin batter into a greased 8 x 8 x 2-inch pan, and bake in moderate oven (350° F.) 30 to 35 minutes. Turn out on rack to cool, then frost if and as desired.

CRUMB CAKE

2 1/2 cups sifted flour
1 cup sugar
1 teaspoon cinnamon
1 teaspoon nutmeg
1/2 teaspoon cloves
3/4 teaspoon salt

3/4 cup mixed butter anb
   shortening
1 cup raisins
1 egg, beaten
1 cup buttermilk
1 teaspoon soda

Sift flour, sugar, spices, and salt into bowl. Cut in shortening as for biscuits. Take out 1 cup of this crumbly mixture and set aside for topping. To remainder add the raisins. Stir soda into buttermilk, mix with beaten egg, add to flour mixture and stir just until blended. Spread in greased 8 x 11-inch pan, sprinkle reserved crumbs over top and bake in moderately hot oven (375° F.) about 35 minutes. Serve warm, with afternoon coffee or tea, or as dessert.

RAISIN-NUT APPLESAUCE CAKE

1 cup seedless raisins
1 cup chopped walnuts
1/2 cup shortening
1 cup sugar
1 teaspoon cinnamon
1/2 teaspoon nutmeg
1/4 teaspoon cloves

1 egg, or 2 yolks, unbeaten
1 cup thick strained un-
   sweetened applesauce
2 cups sifted flour
1/2 teaspoon salt
1 teaspoon baking powder
1 teaspoon soda

Pour boiling water over raisins, let stand a few minutes to plump them, then drain thoroughly and mix with chopped nuts; set aside. Cream shortening with sugar and spices until light and fluffy. Add the egg (or yolks, saving the whites for frosting), beat well. Blend in applesauce. Add sifted dry ingredients, beat smooth. Stir in the raisins and nuts. Bake in a greased 8 x 8 x 2-inch square pan or an 8 x 4 x 4-inch loaf pan about an hour at 350° F., or in 2 greased 8-inch layer pans 35 to 40 minutes. Cool on racks. Serve plain, or frost thickly with this unusual Applesauce Frosting or Seven-Minute or other frosting.

APPLESAUCE FROSTING

2 egg whites, unbeaten
1/4 cup thick strained
     applesauce
1/2 teaspoon grated lemon
     peel

1 tablespoon lemon juice
Few grains salt
1 cup sugar
1/2 teaspoon cinnamon

Combine all the ingredients in the top of a double boiler, place over hot water, and beat with rotary beater about 5 minutes, or until the mixture holds a point when the beater is lifted. Remove from heat, and beat 2 or 3 minutes longer. Spread on cool applesauce cake.

CALIFORNIA PRUNE CAKE

1 cup chopped cooked
     prunes
1 cup chopped walnuts
1/2 cup shortening
1 cup sugar
1 teaspoon cinnamon
1/2 teaspoon nutmeg
1/4 teaspoon cloves

2 eggs, unbeaten
2 cups sifted flour
3 teaspoons baking powder
1 teaspoon salt
1/4 teaspoon soda
3/4 cup prune juice and
     milk, mixed

Fix prunes and nuts first, and set aside. Cream shortening with sugar and spices until fluffy. Add eggs, 1 at a time, and beat hard. Add alternately, a little at a time, sifted dry ingredients and liquid, beating smooth after each addition. Stir in prunes and nuts. Bake in greased and floured 8 x 8 x 2-inch pan in moderate oven (350° F.) about 50 minutes. Cool on rack. Serve plain or frosted.

SEVEN-MINUTE FROSTING

Don't take that title too literally. The frosting may require altogether anywhere from 5 or 6 to 10 or 12 minutes' beating, depending upon weather conditions, shape of double boiler, kind of beater, etc. But it's easy and dependable, and you'll like it.

For large cake

1 cup sugar
2 egg whites, unbeaten
3 tablespoons cold water
Few grains salt
1/4 teaspoon cream of
    tartar
1 teaspoon vanilla

For small cake

3/4 cup sugar
1 egg white
2 tablespoons cold water
Few grains salt
1/8 teaspoon cream of
    tartar
3/4 teaspoon vanilla

Mix all ingredients except vanilla in top of double boiler, place over boiling water, and beat with rotary beater for 5 to 7 minutes, or until frosting is thick and fluffy and holds up in peaks when beater is lifted. Remove from boiling water, add vanilla, and continue beating until stiff enough to spread on cool cake.

Light brown sugar, packed firmly in the cup, may be used instead of granulated sugar in this recipe. Flavor with a few drops of maple flavoring. If you like, add 1/4 cup halved seeded raisins just before spreading on cake.

FAVORITE FRUIT CAKE

This recipe makes 5 pounds of rich, moist, dark fruit cake. If light cake is desired, simply omit spices. If possible make it at least a month before using.

Get the pans ready in advance, grease them well, then line with two thicknesses of greased wrapping paper, then with heavy waxed paper, also greased. (This greasing helps to hold the layers of paper in place. If the paper is cut in strips, and let extend about an inch above the sides of the pans, it is easier to remove the cakes after baking.) Two 8 x 4 x 4-inch bread loaf pans may be used, or smaller pans, as preferred.

4 cups seedless raisins
1 1/2 cups thinly sliced
   citron
1 1/2 cups thinly sliced
   candied pineapple
1/2 cup sliced candied or
   Maraschino cherries
1 cup chopped candied
   orange and lemon peel,
   mixed
1 cup coarsely chopped
   walnuts
1 cup coarsely chopped
   blanched almonds

1 cup coarsely chopped
   pecans
2 1/4 cups sifted flour
3/4 teaspoon salt
1 1/4 cups shortening
1 teaspoon nutmeg
1 1/2 tablespoons cinnamon
1/2 teaspoon allspice
1/4 teaspoon ground cloves
1 1/4 cups sugar
8 eggs, unbeaten
1/2 cup pineapple juice or
   sherry

Plump the raisins first: cover with water, heat to boiling, then drain well. Combine with other prepared fruits and nuts, add flour and salt, toss until well mixed, and set aside. In a large mixing bowl cream shortening with spices, gradually add sugar, creaming until light and fluffy. Add eggs, one at a time, beating until well blended after each addition. Stir in pineapple juice or sherry, then add floured fruits and nuts and stir until well mixed. Pour the stiff batter into paper-lined pans, filling them almost to the top. Bake in very slow oven (250° F.) with a shallow pan of water on the bottom shelf. Allow 2 1/2 hours for 1-pound cakes, or 3 to 4 1/2 hours for larger ones. Test by touching cake with fingertip; if no imprint is left, the cake is done. If you wish to decorate tops of cakes with almonds and cherries, do so after the cakes have baked 2 hours. After baking, remove cakes from pans to cool, but do not remove paper. When cool, moisten lightly with brandy if desired; wrap in a cloth dampened with brandy, sherry, or cider, and store in a covered container in a cool place. If kept for several months, add more brandy.

PECAN COOKY BALLS

Rich as anything, but wonderfully good for tea party or holiday serving are these crunchy, sugar-frosted little balls.

1 cup soft butter
1/2 cup sifted powdered
    sugar
2 teaspoons vanilla
2 cups sifted flour
1/4 teaspoon salt

2 cups finely chopped
    pecans
More powdered sugar
    (about 2 cups) for
    rolling

Gradually add the 1/2 cup powdered sugar to the butter, creaming thoroughly. Add vanilla. Add flour, salt, and chopped pecans, and blend well. Chill if convenient. Shape into small balls about the size of large marbles, place on a greased cooky sheet, and bake in moderate oven (350° F.) about 15 minutes, until just light brown. Remove from pan and at once carefully roll the hot balls in sifted powdered sugar until well coated. Cool, then roll again in the powdered sugar. Makes 10 to 12 dozen cooky balls; cut the recipe in half, if you prefer!

MY FAVORITE CHOCOLATE DROP COOKIES

1/2 cup shortening
1 cup brown sugar
1 egg, unbeaten
2 squares chocolate, melted
1/2 cup buttermilk

1 teaspoon vanilla
1 1/4 cups sifted flour
1/4 teaspoon soda
1/4 teaspoon salt
1 cup chopped walnuts

Gradually add sugar to shortening, creaming until fluffy. Add egg and beat hard. Stir in melted chocolate. Add buttermilk and vanilla, then stir in flour sifted with soda and salt. Add the nuts. Drop by teaspoonfuls on ungreased baking sheets, and bake 12 to 15 minutes in moderate oven (350° F.). Makes about 3 dozen soft, rich, just-right cookies. While they are still warm, frost them if you wish with that Creamy Chocolate Frosting given with the "Big Chocolate Cake."

FIG-FILLED COOKY SQUARES

These are miniature "sandwiches" of fig-nut filling, baked between crumbly oatmeal crusts. Make the filling first.

1 cup dried figs, chopped
1 cup water
1 teaspoon grated lemon
   peel
1 tablespoon lemon juice

1/2 cup sugar
2 tablespoons flour
Dash of salt
1/4 cup chopped walnuts

(If the figs are a bit too dry, cover them with boiling water, let stand 10 minutes, then drain, snip off stems, and cut fine, using scissors.) To the chopped figs add the cup of water and let simmer until soft. Add lemon peel and juice. Mix sugar with flour and salt, stir in, and cook, stirring, until thick and clear. Add the nuts. Let cool while you mix the crumbly crust.

1 1/2 cups uncooked rolled
   oats
1/2 cup sifted flour
1/2 cup brown sugar

1/2 teaspoon salt
1/2 cup shortening (part
   butter, if possible)

Combine dry ingredients and work in shortening with a pastry blender or your fingers, until crumbly. Spread half the mixture in a 7-inch square pan and pat smooth, using waxed paper to keep the crumbs from sticking to your fingers. Spread with the filling, then cover with the rest of the crumbs, pat smooth and bake in moderate oven (350° F.) about 35 minutes. Let it cool in the pan; cut in small squares or strips.

WALNUT CORNFLAKE COOKIES

4 egg whites	1 cup sugar
1/2 teaspoon salt	2 cups cornflakes
1 teaspoon vanilla	1 cup chopped walnuts

Add salt and vanilla to egg whites and beat stiff with a rotary beater, gradually beat in sugar. Fold in the cornflakes and walnuts. Drop by fat teaspoonfuls on a greased baking sheet. Bake in moderate oven (350° F.) 20 to 25 minutes. Remove from the pan at once. Makes 2 to 3 dozen chewy, candy-like cookies.

EASIEST OATMEAL COOKIES

Among the best of oatmeal cookies are these, which take no tedious creaming:

2 cups sifted flour	2 cups uncooked rolled oats
1 cup sugar	1 cup raisins
1 teaspoon salt	2 eggs, beaten
1 teaspoon soda	3/4 cup salad oil or melted
1 teaspoon cinnamon, or allspice	shortening
1 teaspoon nutmeg	1/2 cup milk
	1 teaspoon vanilla

Sift together flour, sugar, salt, soda, and spices into mixing bowl. Add rolled oats and raisins. Combine eggs, oil or shortening, milk, and vanilla, and stir into dry ingredients. (If you like your cookies rocky-rough on top after baking, stir just until well mixed. If you like them smooth and cakelike in texture, beat the batter hard!) Drop by spoonfuls 2 inches apart on greased and floured baking sheet (or an ungreased one). Bake in moderate oven (350° F.) 15 to 18 minutes. Makes 3 dozen big cookies.

BEST RAISIN DROP COOKIES

2 cups seedless raisins
1 cup water
1 teaspoon soda
1 cup shortening
2 teaspoons salt
1 1/2 teaspoons cinnamon
1/4 teaspoon nutmeg

1/4 teaspoon allspice
2 cups sugar
3 eggs, well beaten
1 teaspoon vanilla
4 cups sifted flour
1 teaspoon baking powder
1 cup chopped walnuts

Add water to raisins and boil 5 minutes; there should be 1/2 cup liquid left. Cool, then add soda. Blend shortening with salt and spices, gradually add sugar, creaming thoroughly. Add eggs, vanilla, and cooled raisin-soda mixture. Add flour sifted with baking powder, mixing well. Stir in the nuts. Chill the dough until stiff, then drop by fat teaspoonfuls on greased and floured baking sheet (or an ungreased one), and bake in fairly hot oven (400° F.) 12 to 15 minutes. Cool on rack. Makes about 6 dozen soft, puffy cookies. Store in covered jar. For extra goodness, warm them before serving.

OATMEAL CRISPIES

1/2 cup seedless raisins
1/2 cup shortening
1/4 cup water
3/4 cup sifted flour
1/2 teaspoon soda
1/2 teaspoon salt
1/4 teaspoon cinnamon

1/4 teaspoon nutmeg
1 1/2 cups uncooked rolled
    oats
1 cup brown sugar, firmly
    packed
1/2 cup chopped nuts
1 teaspoon vanilla

Combine raisins, shortening, and water in saucepan and heat slowly until shortening is just melted (don't boil violently or too much water may boil away). Cool. Sift flour, soda, salt, and spices into mixing bowl, add rolled oats, brown sugar, and nuts, and mix. Add cooled raisin-shortening mixture and vanilla, and blend thoroughly. Shape into a ball, wrap in waxed paper, and chill until stiff. Break off small balls, the size of a rounded teaspoonful, and place well apart on a greased and floured baking sheet. Flatten balls by stamping with the bottom of a drinking glass covered with a damp cloth. Bake in moderate oven (350° F.) 8 to 10 minutes. You'll think they are not done, but they are. Using a spatula or pancake turner, remove the soft cookies from pan to rack. They become crisp as they cool. This small, eggless recipe makes about 4 dozen lacy cookies.

FOR BETTER PIES

A pie is no better than its crust! Accurate measuring and care and skill in handling pastry are as important as the recipe. . . .

Be careful about adding liquid. A few drops too much will make pie crust tough. . . .

Use a canvas cover for your molding board and a stockinet cover for your rolling pin, to save work and achieve more tender crust. Roll lightly, handle lightly. Don't pull and stretch the dough to fit the pan. Relax—and let the crust relax! . . .

To make a pretty pie shell, use scissors to trim edge of crust, leaving a half-inch overhang all around the pan. Fold this under, then with the thumb and first finger of left hand and one finger of right hand, crimp or flute edge to make a high rim. Prick it with a fork, if it's to be baked empty; chill, then bake in very hot oven (475° F.). . . .

For double crust for fruit pies, trim bottom crust even with pan, but leave half an inch overhang on the top crust; moisten the edge of the lower crust, tuck the edge of the top crust under the lower one, and flute the edge, then wrap wet parchment pie tape (it's sold in houseware stores) around edge to keep syrup from boiling out. . . .

Always let pie filling cool before spreading with meringue,

or it will "weep"; spread meringue well onto crust all around, or it will shrink; bake slowly.

EGG AND LEMON PIE CRUST

If you are one who has had trouble achieving really good pie crust, try this one. It's easy to mix, easy to handle, easy to eat!

3 1/2 cups sifted flour	1 egg, beaten
1 1/2 teaspoons salt	3 tablespoons lemon juice
1 cup shortening	3 tablespoons cold water

Sift flour and salt into mixing bowl. Add half the shortening and cut in with pastry blender until finely divided. Add rest of shortening and cut in coarsely, until it is like peas. Mix egg, lemon juice, and water, and stir into flour mixture until well mixed; if necessary, add a few drops more water to moisten dry portions. Roll out about 1/3 at a time on lightly floured canvas.

HOT WATER PIE CRUST

This never-fail pastry is the amateur's joy. To make it, pour 1/2 cup boiling water over 1 cup shortening in mixing bowl and beat with fork until creamy. Add, all at once, 3 cups of sifted flour mixed with 1 1/2 teaspoons salt, and stir until well mixed. Shape into a ball, wrap in waxed paper, and chill thoroughly before rolling out. Makes 3 small (8-inch) single crusts, or 1 double-crust pie and 1 pie shell. This type of crust is tender but not flaky.

BETTER-THAN-EVER APPLE PIE

You think a good apple pie can't be improved? That's what I thought, until I tasted this new kind of apple pie at a picnic in Walnut Creek. The maker's secret, which she generously shared, and which I've adopted as "standard practice," is this:

In the bottom of a pastry-lined pie pan spread crushed canned pears—3 or 4 halves to a pie. Sprinkle 1 to 2 tablespoons rum over the pears. Dice (rather than slice) 4 to 6 firm apples, add 1 cup sugar mixed with 2 tablespoons flour, and 1/2 to 1 teaspoon cinnamon; mix well, and heap over the pears. Dot generously with butter, cover with top crust, and bake as usual—10 minutes at 450° F., then 45 to 55 minutes longer at 350° F. Serve slightly warm. It's superb!

To Thicken Berry Pies. For 4 cups washed and well-drained blackberries, blueberries, huckleberries, raspberries, or cherries, mix 4 tablespoons flour with 3/4 to 1 cup sugar and a dash of salt. Sprinkle over berries in layers in pastry shell. For sweet cherry pie, add 1 tablespoon lemon juice.

SOUR CREAM RAISIN PIE

1 egg or 2 yolks	3/4 teaspoon cinnamon
1 cup sour cream or butter- milk	1/2 teaspoon nutmeg
	1/4 teaspoon salt
1 tablespoon vinegar	2 cups seedless raisins
3/4 cup sugar	1/2 cup chopped walnuts
2 tablespoons flour	Pastry for 2-crust 9-inch pie

Beat egg slightly, add sour cream and vinegar. (Buttermilk makes a slightly less rich but almost equally delicious pie.) Stir in sugar mixed with flour, spices, and salt. Add raisins and nuts, pour into pastry-lined pan, cover with top crust or lattice strips. Bake in hot oven (450° F.) 10 minutes, then reduce heat to 350° F. and bake 30 to 40 minutes longer. Some persons prefer to bake this pie in one crust, then cool it, cover with meringue, and bake 15 to 20 minutes at 325° F. Serves 6 or 7.

BANBURY TARTS

1 1/2 cups seeded raisins
1 teaspoon grated lemon
    peel
Dash of salt
3/4 cup sugar
1 cup water

4 soda crackers, crushed
    fine
1 tablespoon butter or
    margarine
2 tablespoons lemon juice

Mix all ingredients except lemon juice, and cook slowly, stirring frequently, until about like jam. Stir in the lemon juice,
and let cool before using. For the tarts, make your favorite
pie crust and roll it thin. Using a saucer or small bowl for a
guide, cut out circles of the crust. Put a spoonful of raisin
filling in the center of each circle, fold over, moisten edges
with water, and crimp together. Prick the tops, and bake in
hot oven (450° F.) about 15 minutes, or until the crust is
nicely browned. Serve slightly warm or cold, preferably with
cheese. Makes a dozen or more good-sized turnovers. The filling may be kept in a covered jar in refrigerator, ready for use
at any time.

FLUFFY LEMON MERINGUE PIE

1 cup boiling water
1 tablespoon butter or
    margarine
1 teaspoon grated lemon
    peel
1 1/4 cups sugar
3 tablespoons flour

3 tablespoons cornstarch
4 eggs, separated
Dash of salt
1/2 teaspoon vanilla
4 tablespoons lemon juice
1 baked pie shell (8-inch or
    9-inch)

Combine boiling water, butter or margarine, and grated lemon
peel in the top of a double boiler. Mix 3/4 cup of the sugar
with cornstarch and flour, add to the water, and cook over direct
heat, stirring constantly, until smooth and thick. Place over
boiling water, cover, and let cook 10 minutes. Stir in beaten

egg yolks and cook a minute longer. Remove from heat, add lemon juice, and cool. Add salt and vanilla to the egg whites, beat stiff, then gradually beat in the remaining 1/2 cup sugar. Fold about one-fourth of this meringue into the cooked lemon filling, pour into a baked pie shell (the Patty Pie Crust that follows is good to use), and top with the remaining meringue spread in rough swirls. Bake in a very moderate oven (325° F.) about 20 minutes. Cool and serve.

PATTY PIE CRUST

1 cup sifted flour
1/4 teaspoon salt
1/4 cup butter

1 egg yolk
1 1/2 teaspoons sugar

Add salt to flour, cut or rub in butter as for regulation pie crust. Beat egg yolk with sugar, stir into flour mixture, and blend until well mixed and crumbly. Pat into an 8-inch pie pan, and bake in moderately hot oven (375° F.) about 12 minutes, or until lightly browned. Cool, then fill with lemon filling or any cream-type filling. Makes 1 pie.

LEMON PUFF PIE

4 eggs, separated
1 teaspoon grated lemon
   peel
4 tablespoons lemon juice

1 cup sugar
Dash of salt
Baked 9-inch pie shell

Mix egg yolks, lemon peel and juice, and 1/2 cup of the sugar in double boiler, and cook, stirring, until thick. Add salt to egg whites, beat stiff, then gradually beat in remaining 1/2 cup sugar. Fold in hot lemon mixture, heap in a baked pie shell, and bake in very moderate oven (325° F.) 15 to 20 minutes, until lightly browned. Cool. It will sink a bit, but will still be puffy. Serves 6.

YUBA COUNTY PEACH PIE

Peel fresh peaches, cut in eighths and arrange, 1 layer deep, in an unbaked pie shell. Mix together 1/2 cup sugar, 2 tablespoons flour, a dash of salt, 1/4 to 1/2 teaspoon nutmeg, 1/2 cup thin cream, and 1/2 teaspoon vanilla; pour over the peaches. Bake in hot oven (450° F.) for 10 minutes, then reduce heat to 350° F. and bake 40 to 50 minutes longer. Serve warm—small portions, please!—with coffee.

FRESH COCONUT PIE

2 cups freshly grated coco-
    nut
2 cups milk
1/4 cup coconut milk
1/2 cup sugar
5 tablespoons flour
2 tablespoons cornstarch

1/4 teaspoon salt
3 egg yolks, beaten
3/4 teaspoon vanilla
3/4 teaspoon lemon extract
1 drop almond extract
1 baked 8-inch pie shell

Scald 1 cup of the coconut with milk and coconut milk in double boiler about 20 minutes, strain, discard this coconut, and return milk to double boiler. Mix sugar, flour, cornstarch, and salt, add all at once to hot milk and cook, stirring constantly, until smoothly thickened. Cover, and let cook 15 minutes. Stir in egg yolks and cook a minute longer. Remove from heat, add flavorings and part of remaining coconut, and let cool thoroughly before spreading in pie shell. Shortly before serving, cover lightly with whipped cream and sprinkle the remaining coconut over all. Serves 6. This may seem like quite a lot of to-do over a pie, and it is, but it's the Hawaiian way, and the results are worth the effort.

ABOUT NUTS

Nuts of all kinds keep best and cost least in the shell. Keep them in a cool place; keep shelled nuts in covered jars in the refrigerator. Halves of California walnuts measure 4 1/2 to 5 cups to the pound; coarsely chopped, 4 cups. Almond, pecan, and peanut kernels measure about 3 1/2 cups to the pound. . . . To chop nuts, spread on a board and chop-chop with a big knife, steadying tip end of knife on the board with left hand. Leave in good-sized pieces unless directed otherwise. . . . You can add nuts to practically any recipe without changing the recipe. Allow 1/4 to 1/2 cup chopped nuts to each cup of flour; about 1/2 cup nuts to each quart of pudding or ice cream.

ABOUT FLAVORING

A drop or two of almond extract improves cobblers and pies made with peaches or apricots. . . . Cook a few thin slices of lemon with the syrup for pears for canning; it gives them character. . . . Use vanilla and lemon extract, half and half, plus a tiny bit of almond extract, to flavor angel or sponge cakes, custards, and other egg dishes. Covers up that "eggy" taste. . . . Try different flavorings, different combinations occasionally, but don't carry it too far! . . . A good balance of spices for pumpkin pie is 1 teaspoon cinnamon, 1/2 teaspoon each nutmeg and ginger. . . . For spice cake, 1 teaspoon cinnamon, 1/2 teaspoon nutmeg, 1/4 teaspoon cloves. . . . If you're short of cinnamon, use 3/4 teaspoon allspice in place of 1 teaspoon cinnamon. . . . Don't forget salt! Add a dash of it to every sweet mixture; more when needed. . . . Taste things while you're mixing them. You and your family may like different amounts of flavorings or spices than the recipe calls for. And you develop and educate your sense of taste by tasting!

DESSERT THOUGHTS—MISCELLANEOUS

A little on the fancy order: Bring in individual dessert plates each bearing a ball of raspberry ice and a snowball of angel cake frosted with coconut.

Ever serve crème de menthe as a sauce over pineapple ice?

Or use it to color and flavor a transparent fruit sauce, to serve over vanilla ice cream? Little chocolate cakes frosted in white are right with either of these.

Picked up at Pebble Beach: Fold whipped mint jelly into whipped cream, and serve with frosty-cold apricot halves, fresh or canned.

Pitted black cherries, canned or cooked in heavy syrup and well drained, make a marvelous topping for vanilla ice cream.

Pour sherry over canned pear halves, add a few thin strips of yellow lemon peel, and chill well; at serving time, sprinkle a dash of nutmeg on the pears to prettify them.

Dress thinly sliced fresh pineapple with honey and lime juice; combine with sherried fruits. Serve with crisp cookies, not too sweet.

FREEZER FANCIES

Rainbow Ice Cream Cake. Cut a long (9-inch or 10-inch) loaf of angel food cake lengthwise into 3 layers. Spread a pint of strawberry ice cream on bottom layer. Put on second layer of cake; spread with a pint of chocolate or mint ice cream. Put on top layer. Put to freeze while you whip half a pint of heavy cream. Sweeten and flavor it lightly. Quickly frost cake all over with the cream, sprinkle with coconut, and put back to freeze. When hard, wrap and store in freezer. Serves 8. Keeps well up to a month. (Use other flavors and colors of ice cream as you prefer, of course.)

Ice Cream Pies. Use either graham cracker or regulation baked crust. Fill with ice cream; freeze. Serve topped with fruit . . . Make Chiffon Pies as usual. Spread top with whipped cream before freezing.

Whipped Cream Rosettes. Drop mounds of whipped cream on waxed paper, freeze, then wrap. Serve on hot or cold desserts.

By-laws for Beverage Serving

1. Pour hot coffee, tea, chocolate, or cocoa at the table; makes for prettiest and hottest service.

2. Serve iced coffee, tea, or fruit drinks with plenty of ice. Bar sugar, which dissolves quickly, is nicest to offer with these cold drinks. Use good-sized pieces of lemon for garnishing glasses of iced tea and fruit drinks.

3. Follow this simple, sensible guide for serving California wines: As an appetizer before lunch or dinner serve dry sherry or vermouth (at room temperature, or chilled), or perhaps a wine cocktail (very cold). With the main course, serve a table wine, usually a dry wine—that is, not sweet. With red meats and meat dishes, serve a red table wine—for example, claret or Burgundy—at room temperature. With white meats or with fish, serve a white table wine, such as sauterne, Chablis, or Riesling, well chilled. With afternoon or evening refreshments serve a dessert wine, such as port, muscatel, or sherry, at room temperature; or serve a hot wine drink, such as mulled wine. For all types of wines, thin, colorless, stemmed glasses are most popular. Pour wine at the table, first wrapping the bottle in a napkin to prevent dripping on the cloth. Fill glasses only 3/4 full. Hot wine drinks may be served in tea-cups, or after-dinner coffee cups, or small pottery mugs, or preheated small glasses.

4. Have punch well chilled in advance, then use a large block of ice in the punch bowl so that the beverage won't be too greatly diluted by melting ice. Figure on about 1/3 cup per serving and 2 to 3 servings per person, or 1 quart of punch for each 5 or 6 persons to be served.

5. For details on serving cocktails and canapés, see "How to Give a Cocktail Party or Housewarming" (Chapter Twelve).

Chapter 10

Beverages and Accompaniments
as Served by Californians

COLD or hot, soft or hard, whatever the drink you are making, do it exactly right every time. Carelessness has spoiled more coffee, more cocktails, than ignorance. Here is an assortment of especially good recipes for beverages that go well for indoor or outdoor eating.

SUNDAY MORNING ORANGE JUICE

In tall glasses of cold orange juice (fresh-squeezed or diluted frozen) stand swizzle sticks strung with frozen pineapple chunks, plus one or two fresh strawberries or a Maraschino cherry.

SPARKLING LEMONADE

Mix a 6-ounce can of frozen lemonade concentrate with 1 1/2 cups cold water. Pour over ice cubes in 4 tall glasses, then fill with chilled sparkling water. For a pretty topper, add 1 or 2 spoonfuls of bottled cranberry juice (or home-cooked—see recipe for Cranberry Juice Cocktail) or grape juice carefully to each glass so it will float on top. Don't stir. Add sprigs of mint and long straws.

THREE SHORT DRINKS

Grapefruit Juice on the Rocks. Shake canned grapefruit juice. Pour over cracked ice in small glasses. Serve with short straws. . . . *Pineapple Refresher.* Half-fill small (or tall) glasses with chilled pineapple juice, either canned or frozen fresh. Drop a ball of lemon sherbet into each glass. Top with mint, serve with green and white straws. . . . *New Fashioned Old-Fashioned.* Put ice cubes in old-fashioned glasses. Half fill each glass with chilled cider, then add ginger ale to fill. Decorate with swizzle sticks strung with fruit—a cube of unpeeled red apple, a thick quarter-slice of orange, a pineapple chunk, a Maraschino cherry, or whatever you please.

REMINDERS

In punch recipes that follow, you can, of course, use diluted frozen fruit juice concentrates or undiluted canned or bottled juices interchangeably with fresh. You can use instant coffee or chocolate, or canned syrups, et cetera, in place of making your own. And most certainly you can use your electric blender to mix cold drinks in a jiffy to sparkling smoothness.

Pick over and wash cranberries, add water, and boil for about 5 minutes, until berries have all popped open. Strain through cheesecloth. Heat juice to boiling, add sugar, and boil, stirring, for 2 minutes. Cool, chill, and serve with ice, garnished with thin slices of lemon or orange. Makes 10 to 12 small glasses.

MOCK PINK CHAMPAGNE

1 cup sugar	1/2 cup orange juice
1 cup water	1/3 cup grenadine syrup
1 cup grapefruit juice	1 quart chilled ginger ale

Boil sugar and water together 5 minutes, cool. Add grapefruit and orange juice, and chill. At serving time, add the grenadine and ginger ale, stir lightly, and serve in champagne glasses, goblets, or stemmed wine glasses. Makes about 3 pints.

FRUITY PUNCH

1 cup sugar	5 cups canned pineapple
2 cups grapefruit juice	juice
1/2 cup lemon juice	

Combine ingredients and stir until sugar is dissolved. Serve in punch bowl with block of ice, or in tall glasses filled with ice cubes or crushed ice. Garnish with halves of orange slices and Maraschino cherries on swizzle sticks. Serves 12.

COFFEE FOR A CROWD

Simplest way to make a lot of coffee, for a barbecue feast or a club affair, is to tie the ground coffee in a bag or square of doubled cheesecloth or lightweight white muslin, leaving plenty of room for the coffee to swell. (A 5-pound sugar sack, bleached and boiled, works fine.) For approximately 50 servings of 3/4 cup each, use 1 pound (5 cups) of regular-grind coffee. Drop the bag of coffee into a large kettle containing

2 1/2 gallons (10 quarts) of boiling water, cover kettle, turn heat very low, and let coffee stand at just below boiling for about 15 minutes. Move the bag occasionally. (I like to leave long ends of string hanging out over the top, for lifting and moving the bag.) Remove bag, and keep coffee hot but not boiling.

When fewer than 50 servings are needed, figure that 1 cup of ground coffee and 2 quarts (8 cups) of water will make 10 servings.

You can use cold water instead of boiling water in making coffee by this method. The coffee will be stronger, but not quite so good according to most tastes.

Another old-fashioned way to make sparkling-clear, delicious coffee is to use egg white. (The yolks do no good, so don't use them—it's wasteful.) In the coffee pot or kettle, mix 1 cup regular-grind coffee with 1 egg white and enough cold water to moisten it well. Stir in 6 measuring cups of boiling water, and bring just to boiling, stirring occasionally. When it boils up, turn off heat, add a dash (maybe 1/4 cup) of cold water, and let stand 5 to 10 minutes before serving. Makes 8 servings. This method requires using a little more coffee than the bag method.

TEA FOR A TEA PARTY

Tie 1 cup tea leaves loosely in a scalded cheesecloth bag, place in a scalded kettle, and pour 4 quarts of freshly boiling water over the tea, cover, and let stand 5 minutes over very low heat. Remove bag, and pour tea into scalded teapot to serve. Makes about 25 servings.

———————————————————

Take a lemon when you take to the woods. Every good hiker knows that there isn't always drinking water to be had along the trail. A lemon or two in the pocket will provide an "all day sucker" that counteracts thirst.

CHOCOLATE SYRUP FOR CHOCOLATE DRINKS

1 cup ground chocolate
1/2 cup sugar
1/4 teaspoon salt

1 cup hot water
1/2 cup corn syrup
1 teaspoon vanilla

Mix ground chocolate, sugar, and salt, stir in hot water and corn syrup and boil 3 minutes, stirring. Add vanilla, cool, and store in covered jar in refrigerator, ready to use for hot or iced chocolate, or as a sauce for ice cream, cottage pudding, or other dessert. Makes about 1 pint. Cocoa may be used in place of the sweet ground chocolate in this recipe; in that case, use 3/4 cup sugar instead of 1/2 cup.

For hot chocolate, stir 1 to 2 tablespoons of the chocolate syrup into 1 cup hot milk, mix well and serve. *For chocolate milk,* add the syrup to cold milk and stir, or shake in a covered jar. *For frosted chocolate,* add a big spoonful of vanilla or chocolate ice cream to the chocolate milk, and stir well. Minced ham sandwiches, or other salty or savory ones, go especially well with these sweet drinks for lunch or a snack.

MEXICAN CHOCOLATE

2 squares (2 ounces)
    chocolate
1/2 cup hot water
1/4 cup sugar
1/2 teaspoon cinnamon
Dash of nutmeg and allspice

Dash of salt
2 cups milk
1 cup cream
1 egg, beaten
1 teaspoon vanilla

Add hot water to chocolate in the top of a double boiler and cook, stirring, until a smooth paste is formed. Add sugar, spices, and salt, then stir in milk, cream, and beaten egg, and cook for an hour, beating frequently with a rotary beater or wire whip. Serves 4.

This is a California adaptation of the true Mexican method,

which calls for a special Mexican chocolate flavored with cinnamon, and for vigorous beating with a *molinillo* (wooden beater).

MULLED CIDER

1 gallon fresh apple cider　　1 tablespoon whole cloves
3 cups brown sugar　　　　　1 tablespoon whole allspice
5 or 6 inches stick cinnamon　2 pieces whole mace

To cider, add sugar, and the spices tied loosely in cheesecloth. Heat slowly, stirring until sugar is dissolved, and simmer for 20 minutes. Serve hot, with a few thin slices of lemon or apple stuck with cloves, floating in the bowl or pitcher. Crackers and cheese, or little minced ham sandwiches, or plain cookies, go well with this. Makes about 20 servings.

ICED COFFEE

Make double-strength regular or decaffeinated coffee by any method—drip, percolated, glass coffee maker, or boiled—using 1 cup ground coffee to 4 cups water. Pour at once over plenty of ice in tall glasses and serve with cream and sugar.

ICED TEA

Make extra-strong tea, using a rounding teaspoon of tea for each cup of freshly boiling water. Let steep about 5 minutes, then strain over plenty of ice in tall glasses. Serve with quarters of lemon.

CHAMPAGNE COCKTAIL

Thoroughly chill champagne glasses (wide-brimmed ones, if possible; if not, tulip-shaped thin, clear, wine glasses do very well). In each glass put a small cubelet of sugar or 1/2 teaspoon bar sugar. On the sugar drop 4 drops of Angostura bitters. Fill the glass almost to the top with chilled white or pink California champagne. Don't stir, but do add a tiny twist of yellow lemon peel, if you wish, and serve. Some like a cube of ice in this cocktail. It's unorthodox, but good if you like it.

ROYAL HAWAIIAN COCKTAIL

Fill each chilled champagne glass with 1/3 chilled canned unsweetened pineapple juice, 2/3 chilled California champagne; add 4 drops Angostura bitters. Decorate each cocktail with a small cube of canned pineapple on a swizzle stick, stir slightly, and serve.

SHERRY SHAKE

Into a large cocktail shaker (or a 2-quart fruit jar) put:

1 1/2 cups orange juice	Sugar to taste
1/2 cup lemon juice	1 large or 2 small eggs
1 cup sherry	Plenty of ice cubes

Shake hard, until well mixed and frothy. Serve at once. Serves 8 to 12. (If it is more convenient, you can beat the egg, mix in the other ingredients, stir well, and pour quickly.)

Shake? Do you have trouble remembering which drinks should be shaken, which merely stirred? Carlos, of the Back Yard restaurant in San Francisco, puts it this way: "No sugar, no shake!"

50-50 APPETIZER

Mix chilled Dubonnet and dry sherry, half-and-half, and serve in cocktail glasses. Dubonnet and gin, mixed 50-50, or 60-40, make another good and quickly mixed cocktail.

BAMBOO COCKTAIL

To plenty of finely cracked ice in a pitcher, add for each person 1 jigger (1 1/2 ounces) of sherry, 1 jigger of sweet (Italian type) vermouth, a dash of bitters; stir—don't shake! Strain into cocktail glasses. This resembles a good non-dry Martini.

CLARET LEMONADE, HAPPY VALLEY STYLE

For each glass, dissolve 1 tablespoon sugar in 2 tablespoons lemon juice. Pour over crushed ice or ice cubes in tall glass, add plain or sparkling water until glass is 3/4 full, and stir. Add claret wine to fill glass, but do not stir. Garnish with mint sprigs and half-slices of orange, and serve with straws.

WINE LEMONADE SHAKE

Allow 1 tablespoon sugar, 1 1/2 tablespoons lemon juice, and about 1/2 cup red or white table wine per person. Shake or stir with ice until sugar is dissolved. Pour over ice cubes in tall glass, filling about 3/4 full, then fill glass with sparkling water or plain ice water, stir, and serve with lemon or orange garnish.

PARTY PUNCH

1/2 cup sugar	1 cup pineapple juice
3/4 cup water	1 cup orange juice
12 cloves	1/2 cup lemon juice
3 inches stick cinnamon	1 bottle (4/5 quart) claret
6 thin strips yellow lemon peel	1 1/2 cups sparkling water

Boil sugar, water, spices, and lemon peel together 5 minutes. Strain, cool, add remaining ingredients, and pour over a block of ice in punch bowl. Float thin slices of orange and lemon on top. Makes 16 servings of about 1/2 cup each.

For directions for making Orange Toast, Cinnamon Toast, and other accompaniments especially good with afternoon tea or coffee, see Chapter Eight, "Breads and Little Breads."

HONOLULU CHAMPAGNE PUNCH

Just before serving, mix California champagne and dry sauterne in the proportions of 3 large (4/5 quart or 26 ounces) bottles of Champagne to 1 quart of sauterne. Add a little lemon juice, and sugar to taste. Pour over a block of ice in punch bowl, and float a few strawberries and/or small, thin slices of fresh pineapple on the punch.

A Piedmont friend who has lived in the Islands served this punch at a big afternoon party featuring the Hawaiian theme. The hostess and the girls who helped her wore gay print dresses and flower leis, and the house was decorated with arrangements of pineapples, banana hands, gardenias, and hibiscus. For the buffet table, she borrowed an idea from Don the Beachcomber, and served the punch from a hollowed-out block of ice, into hollowed-out tiny fresh pineapples. These were placed on plates, and short straws were provided for drinking the punch.

In some places, a hollowed-out ice block may be ordered from the ice dealer at little cost. Or it's easy to make your own: Order a good-sized block of ice. Set it in a tub or sink, place a round pan of boiling water on top, and let it melt out a hollow as deep as the pan. Refill the pan with boiling water as required. To serve, place the ice block in a deep tray, decorate with leaves and flowers or fruit, and fill with ice-cold punch.

FRUITED CHAMPAGNE PUNCH

Peel and cube a fresh pineapple (about 4 cups). Add 4 cups sugar and 2 cups lemon juice (a dozen large lemons) and let stand, stirring occasionally, until sugar is dissolved. Shortly before serving, put it into the punch bowl with a block of ice, add 1 1/2 quarts ice water and 1 large bottle of chilled sauterne. Just before serving, add a quart of lightly sugared fresh (or thawed frozen) strawberries or raspberries, and 2 large (4/5-quart) bottles of Champagne. Makes about 6 quarts, serving 30.

MULLED WINE

1 cup sugar	6 inches stick cinnamon
3 cups boiling water	2 large (4/5-quart) bottles
Yellow peel of half a lemon	claret or Burgundy
18 whole cloves	Nutmeg

Boil sugar, water, lemon peel, and spices together 15 minutes. Strain into a large double boiler, add wine, and heat piping hot but do not let boil. (Wine boils at a lower temperature than water does, you know.) Serve hot, dashed with nutmeg. Serves 10 to 15.

Simple canapés or sandwiches, salted nuts, and not too sweet cookies go well with this hot spiced wine drink for an at-home or housewarming, or an afternoon or evening refreshment.

TOM-'N'-JERRY

For about 24 servings, you will need approximately 3 pints of batter, plus 2 to 2 1/2 pints of Bourbon whisky and 1/2 cup Jamaica rum. Make the batter as follows:

6 eggs, separated	1 1/2 cups sifted powdered
Few grains salt	sugar

Add salt to the egg whites, beat stiff, then gradually beat in half the powdered sugar. With the same beater, beat the yolks light, and gradually beat in the remaining sugar. Fold into the whites, and pour into a serving bowl. To serve, heat individual cups or mugs by filling with hot water. Empty them, then put a big spoonful of batter into each cup, and stir in slowly a jigger (1 1/2 ounces) of Bourbon and a dash of rum. (Or, a jigger of rum may be used, and 1/2 jigger of brandy.)

Slowly stir in boiling water to fill the mug, sprinkle with nutmeg, and serve.

TOM-'N'-SHERRY

Follow the above recipe for batter. Heat dry sherry in a double boiler. Stir about 1 1/2 jiggers of hot sherry into the batter in each heated cup, add a little boiling water (and a dash of brandy also if wished), sprinkle with nutmeg, and serve.

CHERRY BOUNCE

In cherry time, mix 1 cup fresh (or thawed frozen) sour pie cherries, 1 cup sugar, and 1 cup California brandy. Let stand until around Thanksgiving, then pour off the cherry-flavored brandy, and serve as an after-dinner cordial.

This is an "imported" recipe, brought from the East, since fresh sour cherries are rare in California. Replace the cherries with boysenberries or diced fresh apricots, and you'll have something entirely Californian. (Yes, the sugar is refined here, too!)

FOOD WITH DRINKS

Whatever the drink, a little something to nibble along with it seems to make it taste even better. Nibbles may range from bowls of plain crisp little crackers or pretzel sticks, fresh popcorn, or salted nuts, to trays of fancy canapés and hot and cold *hors d'oeuvres*. (Yes, I know that there really shouldn't be a final *s* on that word, but it's the way we spell it here in America!)

Generally speaking, the simpler these accompaniments are, the better they are likely to be. One most gracious California hostess serves buttered slices of fresh homemade bread with her New Year's eggnog—and a superlative combination it is. Another one features nut bread sandwiches with sherry. Another serves, with cocktails, little hot biscuits which she has rolled in melted butter and grated cheese before baking. Marsh Maslin, San Francisco columnist, tells about a bar across from the Palace Hotel where in the "good old days" a smiling Negro chef served hot baked ham slices in hot biscuits to eat with gin fizzes.

Popular right now is the practice of serving crisp raw vegetables, with or without a dunking sauce, to eat with cocktails. It's pretty to arrange the following in rings in a huge flaring bowl or chop plate: chilled, peeled, small red and yellow tomatoes; spikes of celery and carrot; radishes; and short sprigs of water cress. (As a matter of fact, any of the relish plates suggested in the Salad Chapter will go well with cocktails.)

Then there are, of course, the regulation hot and cold canapés and hors d'oeuvres. If you're interested in the difference between the two, it's this: canapés have a foundation of bread, toast, biscuits, crackers, or the like; while hors d'oeuvres are little appetizers such as dried beef rolls, stuffed pickle slices, or tiny hot sausages, served without bread. Hot canapés and hors d'oeuvres are always popular, but are a bit hard to manage unless you plan just right or have help in the kitchen. If you're doing them yourself, don't try to have more than 1 or 2 kinds, but do have plenty of them, and do rush them from stove to guests. Now, first, some of the hots, then the colds—but instead of calling them canapés and hors d'oeuvres, let's call them "pick-ups."

PICK-UPS—HOT

Cheese Puffies. Blend 1/2 pound grated American cheese with 1/2 cup butter. Work in 1 cup sifted flour and a dash of cayenne. Chill thoroughly. Shape into balls like large marbles, place on a cooky sheet, and bake 12 to 15 minutes in a hot oven (450° F.). Serve warm.

Clamapes. Drain canned minced clams. Mix ad lib. with cream cheese and plenty of Worcestershire, spread thickly on crisp round crackers or toast rounds, and broil until puffy. Serve straight from the broiler.

Cheese Stix. Cut bread slices into sticks about 2 inches long. Mix 2 tablespoons melted butter (slightly cooled) with 1 beaten egg. Roll bread sticks in this, then in grated American cheese. Bake on a greased cooky sheet in a moderately hot oven (375° F.) until lightly browned. Serve hot.

Cheese Brambles. Cream together a 3-ounce package of cream cheese and 1/2 cup (1 cube) of soft butter. Work in 1 cup sifted flour and a dash of salt and cayenne. Chill in refrigerator overnight. Roll thin and cut with a medium-sized cooky cutter. On each round lay a small piece of sharp cheese —such as Old English or New York—and fold over, turnover style; pinch edges, and bake in a hot (450° F.) oven about 8 minutes, until puffed and lightly browned. Serve hot, either freshly baked or reheated. They are delicious—like best puff paste. This dough makes wonderful cheese sticks, too; roll out, spread with grated cheese, fold over, then cut in strips and bake.

Fish Patty-Cakes. Shape canned or homemade codfish cake mixture into tiny patties, pan-fry in butter until crisp and brown, and serve hot on cocktail picks. Or shape into small balls and fry in deep hot fat.

Roll-Ups. Roll pie pastry thin. Skin and mash 5 or 6 slices of liverwurst, and add lemon juice and onion juice to make a spreadable paste. Add about 2 tablespoons chopped parsley and spread carefully over the rolled-out pastry. Roll up as you would a jelly roll. Chill. Slice crosswise, brush with butter, and bake in a hot oven (450° F.) 10 to 15 minutes, or until crust is done. Serve right from the oven, with ice-cold drinks.

Remember that almost any canapé spread can be adapted for use as a filling for regulation sandwiches.

PICK-UPS—COLD

Devils. Cut hard-cooked eggs in halves lengthwise. Mash the yolks with deviled ham, a dash of cayenne, and finely chopped parsley. Fill the whites, heaping them roughly.

Skewers. Use edible skewers for such cold bit-bites as cheese balls, or small cubes of cheese or liverwurst or salami, or spiced ham, or half-inch slices of frankfurters, marinated in French dressing. The skewers? Just slender, crisp, raw carrot or celery sticks.

Chipsos. Sprinkle potato chips generously with grated American or Parmesan cheese, or with paprika, and heat in the oven. Serve hot or cold.

Nut-Tops. Paste California walnut halves onto small rounds of buttered bread, using anchovy paste to hold them in place.

Cheese Log. Mash a triangle of Roquefort cheese (or about 1/2 cup of blue cheese) and blend with 2 cakes (3-ounce size) of cream cheese. Add 1 tablespoon chopped parsley, 2 tablespoons chopped chives or green onions, 3 tablespoons finely chopped celery, a generous dash of cayenne or Tabasco sauce, and mayonnaise to hold it all together. Shape into a long roll on waxed paper, roll up, and chill. Shortly before serving, remove the waxed paper and roll in chopped walnuts or pecans; slice, and serve on crackers. Or shape the chilled cheese into small balls and roll them in chopped nuts or crushed cereal flakes.

Horseradish Rolls. Blend a 3-ounce cake of cream cheese with a tablespoon of horseradish. Spread on slices of dried beef, roll up, and chill. Cut in bite-sized pieces, and serve on cocktail picks.

Crunchettes. Whip 2 cakes (3-ounce size) of cream cheese with 1/2 cup chopped walnuts, 1/4 cup chopped stuffed olives,

1 tablespoon grated onion, 1 tablespoon mayonnaise, and 1 teaspoon Worcestershire or A-1 sauce. Heap on crisp pastry rounds, decorate each top with sliced stuffed olives or strips of anchovy, and serve.

Pickle Canapés. Spread crisp crackers with cream cheese and top each with a slice of sweet pickle.

Popcornies. Add a peeled clove of garlic to the butter when melting it for popcorn; remove the garlic, pour over freshly popped corn. Or sprinkle grated American cheese over hot buttered popcorn, mix well, and set the bowl in the oven for a few minutes for the cheese to melt.

CANAPÉ SPREADS

Zippy Spread. Blend a 3-ounce package of cream cheese with 1 1/2 teaspoons anchovy paste or 1 tablespoon deviled ham. Spread on crackers or toast rounds and garnish with sliced stuffed olives.

Chutney Liverwursters. Skin liverwurst, mash fine, and blend with about 1/3 as much chutney. Spread on thin buttered bread, roll up, chill; cut in short lengths and toast under broiler. Serve hot.

Carmel Special. Chop crisp bacon, blend with peanut butter, and heap on crisp crackers that have been rubbed lightly with a cut clove of garlic. Lots better than they sound!

Unbelievable! Toast thin squares or rounds of bread on one side. Spread the untoasted side with mayonnaise mixed with finely chopped or grated onion. Sprinkle with grated Parmesan cheese. Toast under the broiler and serve hot.

Ham-Nut Spread. Grind about 1 cup cooked ham with 1/2 cup walnuts. Blend with a 3-ounce cake of cream cheese, adding horseradish and mayonnaise to taste just right and hold together well. Serve on strips or rounds of toast.

Snap-Ups. Blend a 3-ounce package of cream cheese with about 2 teaspoons of concentrated meat extract. Add about 2 tablespoons each of finely chopped parsley, carrot, and green pepper, and a generous tablespoon of chopped chives or green onions. Mix thoroughly, and use to stuff short lengths of tender heart-stalks of celery, or spread on crisp crackers. Serve at once.

DIPS AND DUNKS

Cheese Bowl. Mix a cup of grated well-aged American cheese with a pint of fairly dry cottage cheese. Add 2 or 3 tablespoons horseradish, 3 or 4 finely chopped green onions (tops included), 2 or 3 tablespoons mayonnaise, and salt and pepper to taste. Heap in a bowl. Set the bowl on a plate or tray and surround with thin slices of pumpernickel or rye bread (no butter needed), and salted whole-wheat and white crackers; also butter spreaders, so each may spread his own. (This goes well on a picnic.)

Roquefort Whip. Mash 2 cakes (3-ounce size) of cream cheese with a small triangle of Roquefort or blue cheese, or about half a jar of Roquefort spread; fold in 1 cup whipped cream. Heap in a bowl, and dash with paprika. Serve with potato chips.

Guacamole. Mashed avocado, zipped up with tarragon vinegar, grated onion, mayonnaise, and salt and pepper, makes a good-looking, good-tasting spread. (For the exact recipe, which is in the Salad Chapter, see Index.)

Baconized Avocado. Mash ripe avocado and add crumbled crisp bacon, lemon juice, and salt and pepper to taste. Serve in a bowl with crisp crackers or potato or tortilla chips.

When you want to sprinkle chopped parsley or grated cheese or the like on canapés in sharply straight lines, use the edge of a spatula or knife as a guide. When you want to apply them in definite circles, squares or diamonds, cut out paper "stencils" and lay over the canapés while sprinkling.

By-laws for Making Relishes and Sweets

1. In making jams and jellies with commercial fruit pectin, liquid or powdered, be sure to follow the directions carefully and time the cooking exactly.

2. To improve the taste and the texture of most fruit jellies and spreads, add 1/2 to 2 tablespoons lemon juice for each cup of prepared fruit or juice. Your sense of taste will tell you how much to add.

3. When making jellies and jams the old-fashioned way, allow from 3/4 to 1 cup sugar for each cup of fruit juice or prepared fruit. Cook in small batches—not more than 4 cups at a time—in a large kettle. Boil rapidly, stirring almost constantly, until the jelling stage is reached.

4. To tell whether jam, jelly, or marmalade is ready to jell, use the spoon test. That is, dip a clean metal spoon into the boiling syrup; hold it up; when the syrup "sheets" off the spoon, or when 2 heavy drops form on the edge and slide together, the syrup is at the jelly stage. (If you are using a candy thermometer, cook until it registers 219° F. to 221° F.; use the spoon test, too.)

5. Skim. Pour jelly at once into hot jars or glasses and cover with melted paraffin. Let jam, marmalade, preserves, or conserves cool in the kettle, stirring occasionally in order to plump the pieces of fruit and prevent them from floating; then reheat, pour into hot sterilized jars, and seal with lids; or pour into glasses and cover with melted paraffin. (Sealing in jars is preferable, especially in warm, humid climates.)

6. When making pickles or relishes, be sure to use vinegar of at least 5 per cent acidity. Weak vinegar may permit dangerous spoilage. Pack in glass jars and seal with glass or enamel-lined lids—never use zinc lids for pickles.

7. Store all relishes, jams, jellies, et cetera in a cool, dry, dark place—not on the top shelf in the kitchen!

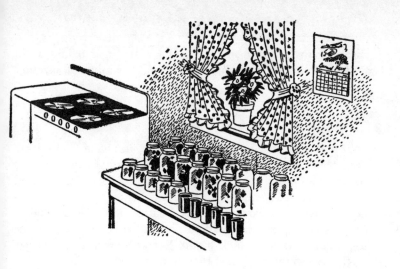

Chapter 11

Relishes and Treats Typical of
the Golden State

THEY aren't included in the "Basic 7" foods, but for most of us they are decidedly important—those pickles and relishes and other tidbits that sprinkle the spice of variety over our everyday meals.

Here are, first, some relishes that can or should be made shortly before serving; then other relishes, pickles, and preserves that are "put up" and stored; and, finally, a few extra-good fruity and nutty confections.

BAKED ORANGE SLICES

Cover 6 whole unpeeled oranges with water and boil about 30 minutes, until tender. Drain and cool, then cut in half-inch slices (or in quarters or halves) and place in a baking dish. Boil the following ingredients together for 5 minutes, stirring:

2 cups sugar   3/4 cup light corn syrup
2 cups water

Pour over the cooked orange slices, cover, and bake in moderate oven (350° F.) for 1 1/2 hours. If syrup does not cover oranges completely, baste them frequently with it. Serve hot or cold with ham, pork, veal, lamb, or poultry, or as a salad with cottage cheese or cream cheese and salted nuts. These baked oranges will keep well without crystallizing, because of the use of corn syrup in their syrup. Keep them in a covered jar in the refrigerator, or seal them hot in sterilized jars.

CLARET SPICED PRUNES

3 cups dried prunes   1/2 teaspoon powdered
2 cups claret   cinnamon or allspice
1 cup water   1/4 teaspoon powdered
1/2 cup brown sugar   cloves

Cook prunes in claret and water in a double boiler about 40 minutes. Add sugar and spices, and cook 15 to 20 minutes longer. Serve cold with meats. For a pretty garnish for the turkey platter, use crisp lettuce cups, each filled with 2 or 3 of these prunes.

GLAZED APRICOTS

Wash dried apricots well and simmer or steam with a little water until tender—about 15 minutes. Drain. Stick a whole clove in each apricot half. For each pound of apricots, prepare a syrup of 1 cup sugar and 1/2 cup water, heat to boiling, add apricots, and simmer until syrup is absorbed. Serve cold with meat. Seal in jars or keep tightly covered in refrigerator.

CRANBERRY RELISHES

These 4 uncooked relishes are made the same way, using different fruit combinations. All keep well in covered jars in the refrigerator.

1. *Cranberry-Apple Relish.* Wash and grind medium fine 1 pound (4 cups) raw cranberries, 1 unpeeled orange (seeded), and 1 unpeeled apple (cored). Stir in 2 1/4 cups sugar. Let stand at least a few hours before using. Makes 2 1/2 pints.

2. *Cranberry-Orange Relish.* Omit apple from above recipe, and use just 2 cups sugar. Makes 2 pints.

3. *Cranberry-Pineapple Relish.* Grind 1 pound raw cranberries, add 1 cup drained crushed pineapple, 2 tablespoons lemon juice, and 1 1/2 cups sugar. Stir well. Makes 1 1/2 pints.

4. *Cranberry-Prune Relish.* Simmer 1 cup dried prunes in water for 10 minutes, cool, pit, and grind with 2 cups raw cranberries and 1 small orange. Stir in 1 tablespoon lemon juice and 1 cup sugar. Makes 1 1/4 pints.

JELLIED CRANBERRY SAUCE

Cook 1 pound (4 cups) cranberries with 2 cups water about 5 minutes, until most of berries have popped. Stir in 2 cups sugar, and boil 2 or 3 minutes. Pour into bowl or mold. For clear cranberry jelly, force berries through a wire strainer before adding sugar.

WHOLE CRANBERRY SAUCE

Boil 2 cups sugar with 2 cups water 5 minutes, add 1 pound cranberries and boil 5 minutes, or until most of the berries have popped. Let cool in the pan, undisturbed.

CATSUP APPLES

Make these fresh to serve hot with ham, pork, or baked beans. Wash apples, cut in halves crosswise, remove cores, and place, cut sides up, in shallow pan. On each half, put a tablespoon of brown sugar, a tablespoon of catsup, and a dot of butter. Pour a little water around them and bake in a moderate oven (350° F.) for about 30 minutes. When serving, spoon the liquid from baking pan over them.

REALLY SPECIAL APPLESAUCE

Wash and pare 2 apples and cut them in fairly thick slices. Heat a good tablespoon of butter in a heavy saucepan, add the apples and 1 to 2 tablespoons of water, cover, and cook for a few minutes, until the slices are almost tender but not cooked to pieces. Now remove the cover, sprinkle the apples generously with sugar—about 1/4 to 1/3 cup—and a good dash of cinnamon; cook, stirring occasionally, until the apples are fairly transparent and beautifully glazed. Serve hot or warm, with ham or pork chops or other meat. Serves 2 or 3. These are definitely unusual and superlatively good.

GARLIC OLIVES

Drain canned ripe olives and put into a glass jar. Add several peeled and sliced cloves of garlic (perhaps 5 or 6 for a pint of olives), and a few slices of lemon. Pour in enough olive oil or other salad oil almost to cover the olives. Cover the jar and keep in the refrigerator a day or longer. Just before serving, drain the olives and sprinkle with chopped parsley. Remove the garlic and save the oil to use for green salads.

GINGERED PEARS

4 lemons	4 pounds (8 cups) sugar
1/2 cup water	1/4 pound green ginger
8 pounds firm Bartlett pears	root

Chip off yellow peel of lemons rather coarsely, add water, cover, and let simmer until the peel is tender. Wash and peel pears, and cut into medium-fine chips. (There should be about 4 quarts after cutting.) Add sugar and lemon juice, and cooked peel. Scald ginger root, scrape or peel it, then grind medium fine. Add to pears, and cook gently about 45 minutes, until fairly thick. Seal in small jars. Makes about 8 pints.

BRANDIED CHERRIES

Pit 3 pounds large black cherries, cover with 3 pounds (6 cups) sugar, and let stand an hour or longer. Heat slowly, stirring, and cook gently until cherries are tender, about 20 minutes. Remove cherries to hot sterilized jars. Cook down the syrup slightly, until rich and fairly thick. Pour over the cherries, filling the jars 3/4 full of the syrup. Add brandy to fill jars, seal at once, invert to mix brandy and syrup. These make a marvelous topping for ice cream.

For *Brandied Peaches,* cook peeled whole cling or halved freestone peaches almost tender in a little water, add sugar to make a fairly heavy syrup, and finish cooking. Pack peaches in jars. Add more sugar to the syrup and boil until heavy, fill jars 3/4 full of syrup, finish filling with brandy, seal. Let stand several weeks before using.

CHERRY OLIVES

These uncooked pickled cherries are the simplest things possible to make. They are perfect with meats, casserole dishes, or sandwiches. Select large perfect sweet red or black cherries. Leave stems on. Wash carefully, and fill into quart jars, keeping stems upright, if possible. To each quart jar add 1 tablespoon salt, 1 cup vinegar, and cold water to fill the jar. Seal. Store in a cool place for at least a few weeks before using.

PRIZE CUCUMBER PICKLES

These crisp, crunchy, sweet-sour pickles are extremely easy to do, taking only a few minutes' attention each day for about a week.

14 large (dill size)
   cucumbers
Boiling water
1 quart vinegar

8 cups (2 quarts) sugar
2 tablespoons mixed
   pickling spices
2 tablespoons salt

Wash cucumbers, cover with boiling water and let stand 24 hours; drain, again cover with boiling water and let stand 24 hours; repeat for 2 more days. The fifth day slice the cukes about 1/4 inch thick. Boil together for 5 minutes the vinegar, sugar, spices, and salt. Pour hot over the sliced cukes, let stand 24 hours. Drain off the syrup, reheat to boiling; again pour over the slices and let stand. Repeat for 2 more days. On the last day, drain, heat the syrup to boiling, put in the cucumber slices, bring to boiling, pack hot in glass jars, and seal. Makes about 8 pints.

BREAD-AND-BUTTER PICKLES

I've tasted some rather sad specimens of homemade bread-and-butter pickles. But this recipe turns out really good ones every time.

1 gallon medium-small
   cucumbers, sliced thin
8 or 10 small white onions,
   sliced thin
1 green pepper, cut in strips
1 sweet red pepper or
   pimiento, cut in strips
1/2 cup salt
Cracked ice

5 cups sugar
5 cups cider vinegar
2 tablespoons mustard seed
2 teaspoons celery seed
1 1/2 teaspoons turmeric
   powder
1/2 teaspoon powdered
   cloves

Mix the sliced cucumbers, onions, peppers, salt, and plenty of ice in a large kettle and let stand 3 hours. Drain. Mix the remaining ingredients, pour over the cukes, heat just to boiling, and seal at once in hot sterilized jars. Makes 8 pints.

"CHICAGO HOT" (UNCOOKED RELISH)

Some time during late summer we are almost sure to make a batch of this delicious uncooked tomato relish. It's so good to serve in place of a salad at autumn barbecues. Good, too, as a relish all through the fall and winter. It keeps almost indefinitely in a refrigerator or other cool place. These amounts make about 6 pints.

8 pounds ripe tomatoes
2 cups chopped onions
2 cups chopped celery
2 green peppers, chopped
2 cups sugar

2 cups cider vinegar
2 tablespoons mustard seed
2 tablespoons mixed
   pickling spices
4 tablespoons salt

Remove stem ends and any hard bits from tomatoes; cut up coarsely. Chop onions, celery, and peppers—not too fine. Combine all vegetables in colander and let drain several hours. Mix sugar, vinegar, spices, and salt in saucepan, heat to boiling, cool, then pour over drained, chopped vegetables in a big bowl. Let stand several hours, stirring occasionally. Pack cold in jars; cover but do not seal; store in refrigerator.

SWEET RED PEPPER MARMALADE

12 sweet red peppers
1 tablespoon seeds from
   peppers
1 1/2 teaspoons salt

2 cups vinegar
3 cups sugar
1 tablespoon grated lemon
   peel

Wash peppers, and remove seeds, reserving 1 tablespoon of seeds. Put peppers through food chopper. Add the seeds and remaining ingredients, and cook to the consistency of marmalade—about 30 minutes. Makes about 2 pints. This is a delicious accompaniment for meats or served with crackers and cheese.

CALIFORNIA APPLE CHUTNEY

2 pounds (4 or 5) apples,
    chopped
1/2 pound (1 cup) dates,
    chopped
1/2 pound (1 1/2 cups) figs,
    chopped
1 large onion, chopped
1/2 pound (1 1/2 cups)
    raisins
1 cup chopped chives

2 tablespoons salt
1/2 pound (1 1/2 cups)
    brown sugar
1 ounce (4 1/2 tablespoons)
    ginger
1 teaspoon nutmeg
2 or 3 whole cloves
2 or 3 peppercorns
3 cups cider vinegar

Combine all the ingredients and boil, stirring frequently, until thick. Seal in small jars. Makes about 4 1/2 pints.

PICKLING SYRUP FOR FRUITS

3 cups sugar
1 1/2 cups water
1 1/2 cups cider vinegar

1 tablespoon whole cloves
1 tablespoon whole allspice
2 inches stick cinnamon

Combine sugar, water, and vinegar in a large kettle. Tie the spices loosely in cheesecloth and add. Boil 10 minutes, then put in fruit and cook gently until tender. This syrup may be used for apricots, peaches, pears, apples, crab apples, plums, and other fruits.

GUAVA JELLY

Select guavas that are slightly underripe. Wash, cut off the stiff blossom ends, and slice the fruit into a kettle. Add enough water so that the fruit is almost but not quite covered, and boil slowly, stirring occasionally, for 30 to 45 minutes, until soft. Strain through wet jelly bag or doubled cheesecloth, without squeezing the bag. Taste the juice; if it is not sharply tart, add lemon or lime juice to taste. Measure not more than 4 cups of the juice into a large, wide kettle or saucepan, add an equal measure of sugar, and boil rapidly, stirring almost constantly, until the syrup will sheet from the spoon (or to 222° F. to 224° F. on a candy thermometer). Skim and pour at once into hot jelly glasses.

GUAVA JAM

Wash guavas, remove blossom and stem ends, and cut out any blemishes. Cut the fruit in halves and scoop out the soft pulp and seeds from the center. (You can force this pulp through a food press or wire strainer to remove the seeds, and serve it as a sauce for ice cream or cake, or serve it with cream for dessert.) Cut the guava shells in small pieces, and weigh. For 2 pounds, add 3 cups sugar and 1/2 cup water and let stand overnight. Next day add 1/4 cup lemon juice or lime juice and 1 teaspoon grated fresh ginger root, and boil until the jelly test is almost reached. Seal at once in small hot jars. Makes about 2 pints.

PERSIMMON JAM

Use persimmons that are so ripe they are like jelly. Wash, cut up, and press the pulp through a wire strainer. Measure 2 cups of pulp into a heavy saucepan, add an equal amount of sugar, and simmer slowly for 20 minutes, stirring constantly. (If kept below boiling point the jam will not become bitter. Some persons use a double boiler for cooking this delicate sweet.) Pour into small hot jars or glasses and seal. Excellent with hot biscuits or toast. Makes about a pint.

DIFFERENT STRAWBERRY JAM

2 cups strawberries, washed and hulled
2 1/2 cups sugar

1/2 teaspoon cornstarch
1/4 teaspoon butter
1/2 cup lemon juice

Mix sugar and cornstarch, pour over berries, and let stand several hours to draw the juice. Add butter and half the lemon juice, heat to boiling, and boil vigorously for 10 minutes. Add the remaining lemon juice and boil 2 minutes longer. Skim. Let stand in the kettle overnight, to plump the berries. In the morning, pour the cold jam into sterilized jars. Arrange uncovered jars and sterilized covers on baking sheets, and place in fairly hot oven (400° F.) 3 minutes. Put the covers on the jars and seal tight. Makes about 1 pint.

SUNKISSED STRAWBERRIES

This is my own new version of Strawberry Sunshine.

4 cups sugar
1/4 cup lemon juice

1/4 cup water
4 cups strawberries

Mix sugar, lemon juice, and water, heat slowly, stirring, and boil 4 minutes. Add the berries, heat to boiling, and boil 10 minutes. Pour out into shallow pans or platters, cover with glass (slightly raised to permit evaporation), and let stand in hot sunshine 3 or 4 days, stirring occasionally, until syrup is rich and thick and berries are plump and translucent. Seal in small jars or glasses. Makes about 2 pints.

YOUNGBERRY JAM

4 cups youngberries or boysenberries

3 1/2 cups sugar
3 tablespoons lemon juice

Wash berries quickly, drain well, put into a large kettle and mash rather thoroughly. Add sugar and heat slowly to boiling, stirring. Boil hard, stirring constantly, about 8 to 10 minutes, until almost ready to jell. Add lemon juice and boil a few minutes longer, stirring, until syrup jells when tested with a spoon. Stir and skim; let stand in the kettle several hours or overnight, stirring occasionally while cooling. Seal in sterilized jars or glasses. Makes about 2 pints.

Use the foregoing recipe for raspberries, strawberries, loganberries, or mixtures of berries; also huckleberries and other wild berries; increase or decrease the amount of lemon juice according to the tartness of the fruit. (Loganberries, for example, take very little. Personally, I prefer logans mixed with red raspberries or peaches, or other mild-flavored fruits.) Reason for mashing the large seedy berries is that they sometimes form rather tough, hard knots in the syrup. It isn't necessary to mash strawberries.

GINGERED CHERRY PRESERVES

2 pounds sweet black
    cherries, pitted
1/4 cup preserved ginger
1 No. 2 can crushed pine-
    apple

5 cups sugar
1/4 cup lemon juice
1/2 cup sliced blanched
    almonds

Grind cherries and ginger medium coarse, add pineapple and sugar, and cook, stirring frequently, about an hour, until fairly thick. Add lemon juice and cook a few minutes longer, until of the consistency preferred. Stir in almonds and seal in small jars or glasses. Makes about 2 1/2 pints.

Sweet Cherries are inclined to turn into hard knots when cooked whole in heavy syrup. So are cling peaches when left in large pieces. They should be either ground or chopped fine, or cooked tender with a very little water before adding the sugar.

CHERRY-O PEACH CONSERVE

5 pints (10 cups or 5
    pounds) finely chopped
    freestone peaches
5 pints (10 cups or 5
    pounds) sugar
1/4 teaspoon salt
1/2 pint (1 cup) Maraschino
    cherries

Juice of 1 large lemon
Juice of 1 large or 2 small
    oranges
2 cups coarsely chopped
    nuts (1 1/2 cups wal-
    nuts and 1/2 cup pecans
    or almonds, is a good
    mix)

Scald and peel peaches, remove pits, and chop fine before measuring or weighing. Put into a large kettle, add sugar, salt, syrup from the cherries, and juice of the lemon and orange. Heat, stirring, until the sugar is dissolved, then boil fairly rapidly, stirring often, until the syrup will drop off a clean metal spoon in 2 thick drops that run together. This will take about 45 minutes. Add finely chopped cherries and chopped nuts, let boil up once, then remove from heat. Skim off the foam, and let the conserve stand in the kettle for several hours or overnight, stirring occasionally while it is cooling. This prevents the fruit and nuts from floating. Reheat to boiling, and seal hot in small jars. Makes about 12 glasses. Half this recipe may be made if preferred. This conserve makes a perfect sauce for ice cream.

Ripe cling peaches also are good to use in this. Don't expect to peel clings successfully by scalding them; pare by hand. Californians use a spoon-shaped pitting knife to remove the pits.

BLACK FIG JAM

4 pounds small black fresh
    figs
2 1/2 pounds (5 cups) sugar

2 whole lemons
1 teaspoon coriander seed

Wash but do not peel the figs. Cut off the stems and slice each fig into four pieces. Slice the lemons thin and cut into small pieces. Combine all ingredients and cook in a preserving kettle to jam consistency—from 30 to 40 minutes. Seal in small hot sterilized jars. Makes about 4 pints.

To peel or not to peel figs? Do as you like! They keep their shape better (whole for pickles, sliced for preserves) if you don't peel them. If you do peel them for pickling, lay them in the sun for a few hours to dry slightly before cooking, and they will look more attractive.

FRUIT IN WINE AND HONEY

1 cup honey
3/4 cup port wine (red port for dark fruits, white for light)
1/2 cup lemon juice
8 whole cloves

2 inches stick cinnamon
1 quart drained canned fruit, or quartered apples or pears, or peeled fresh figs
Few drops of vanilla

Simmer together for 10 minutes honey, wine, lemon juice, and spices. Add prepared fruit (one kind, or mixed) and simmer 15 minutes (or until uncooked fruits are tender but not broken). Lift out the fruit into small hot jars. Boil syrup down fairly thick, add vanilla to taste and pour over the fruit. Seal. Makes about 2 pints.

SIX-CITRUS MARMALADE

1 lemon
3 medium-sized or 2 large oranges
2 limes

1 medium-sized grapefruit
2 tangerines
6 kumquats

Cut fruits in halves lengthwise, place cut side down on a cutting board, and slice as thin as possible, then cut the slices into small pieces with scissors. Remove all seeds. Measure, and add 4 times the amount of water. Boil vigorously, uncovered, for 40 minutes. Measure again. To 7 cups of the boiling cooked fruit mixture, add 1 package powdered citrus pectin. Stir until dissolved, then add 8 cups sugar and 4 tablespoons lemon juice. Boil 5 minutes after boiling begins. Skim. Partially cool, stirring occasionally while cooling to distribute fruit throughout the jelly. Pour into sterilized jars or glasses. Seal or paraffin at once. Makes about 4 pints.

QUICK ORANGE MARMALADE

Boil 4 whole oranges and 1 whole lemon in water to cover for about 30 minutes. Drain, discarding water. Cut the oranges and lemons in quarters, removing the seeds, and run through food chopper. Add 2 cups water, measure, and add 1 cup of sugar for each cup of fruit and liquid. Cook to jelly test—about 10 minutes. Add 2 tablespoons lemon juice. Boil 1 minute longer. Pour into hot sterilized jars or glasses. Makes about 1 1/2 pints.

For variety, add a few slices of kumquat, tangerine, or lemon or lime when adding the sugar. Or add a tablespoon of freshly grated lemon peel with the lemon juice before the final minute of boiling.

CANDIED PEEL

Better make 2 or 3 times this recipe at once, for the candied peel keeps very well in jars or covered tin boxes. If it should dry out, put a whole orange in with the peel in the covered container, and it will soften again in a few days.

Use the peel from 3 oranges, or 2 grapefruit, or 6 lemons. Remove all membranes. Cover peel with cold water, add 1/2 teaspoon salt, and boil 1/2 hour. Drain, cover with cold water, and boil until tender. Drain, and cut peel in strips. Heat together:

1 cup sugar   2 tablespoons light corn
3/4 cup water   syrup or honey

Add the peel, and cook gently over low heat until most of the syrup has been absorbed. Cover and let stand overnight. Next day, reheat very slowly to simmering point. Cover and let stand again. Repeat this heating and cooling for 2 or 3 more days, if possible, until practically all the syrup is absorbed. Drain if necessary, and spread to dry on rack or waxed paper for a day or more, until syrup on surface has been absorbed. Store in covered containers.

STUFFED DRIED FRUITS

Stuffed Prunes. Wash, place in a colander over boiling water, cover and steam 10 to 15 minutes, until plumped and soft enough to pit. Dry well, slit sides carefully and remove pits. Stuff with one of the fillings suggested below, then roll in granulated sugar, and store in tin containers lined with waxed paper to ripen for at least a few days before using.

Stuffed Figs. If too dry, steam figs as directed for prunes until pliable. Slit, stuff, and roll in sugar. Store, as for prunes.

Stuffed Dates. Fresh dates need only to be pitted before stuffing.

FILLINGS FOR STUFFED FRUITS

(1) Cut marshmallows in halves or thirds, stuff fruit, and dip the sticky side in chopped nuts or coconut. (2) Grind equal parts candied cherries, coconut, and nuts; mix well. (3) Grind or chop equal parts walnuts and candied orange peel, moisten with orange or lemon juice, or with sherry. (4) Use fondant mixed with nuts. (5) Use walnut halves. (6) Use peanut butter blended with chopped candied orange peel.

DRIED FRUITS NATURAL

Dried fruits make delightful confections without stuffing. Big prunes, soaked for 15 minutes in hot water, then drained and placed in a covered casserole in a moderate oven until they are plump and tender, make wonderful eating. Dried pears, simply cut into strips, are excellent by themselves or with cheese and crackers for dessert; so are dried apricots, steamed until tender, but not soft, then cut into strips and rolled in granulated sugar. Dried figs and dates, of course, need no pretreatment.

FRUIT PATTIES

1 cup dried figs
1 cup raisins
1 cup pitted dates
1/2 cup candied or
    Maraschino cherries

1/2 cup candied orange peel
1 cup walnuts
2 to 4 tablespoons orange
    juice

Grind fruits and nuts, mix thoroughly, moistening with orange juice to right consistency for shaping into small patties or balls. Roll in granulated or powdered sugar if desired.

UNCOOKED FRUIT CAKE

1 pound dried prunes
1 pound dried apricots
1 pound dried figs
1 pound seeded or seedless
    raisins
1 pound dates, pitted
1 pound candied orange
    peel
1 pound candied pineapple

1 pound candied cherries
1 pound candied citron
1 cup blanched almonds
1 cup walnuts
1 cup pecans
1 cup filberts or Brazil nuts
2 to 3 cups sugar
1 cup orange juice
1 cup brandy

Pour boiling water over prunes, apricots, and figs in separate bowls and let stand just until pliable, then drain well. Pit the prunes. Put all the fruits and nuts through food chopper, using the medium blade. (Do a few of one kind, then of another, in order to mix them more evenly and easily than otherwise.) Add sugar, orange juice, and brandy, and mix well with the hands. Pack tightly into tins and cover snugly, or shape into not too large rolls or loaves and store in tightly covered containers in a cool place before using. The loaves may be sliced, using a sharp knife dipped in hot water. Or the mixture may be shaped into balls or patties, rolled in granulated or powdered sugar or in chopped nuts or coconut, and served as candy. Makes about 12 pounds; divide as desired.

SPICED LOQUATS

This decorative small golden fruit appears on ornamental trees and in the markets of California in early summer. For 4 pints of sweet pickles, wash 3 pounds of firm loquats and remove the stem and blossom ends; do not peel them. Drop them into the pickling syrup on page 318 and cook until tender. Remove the fruit to hot jars, fill almost to overflowing with the hot syrup, and seal.

SALTED NUTS

Oven Salted. Rinse walnut halves, pecans, blanched almonds, or filberts in cold water, spread in a shallow pan, sprinkle lightly with salt, and bake in moderate oven (350° F.) about 20 minutes, stirring frequently, until golden brown. If you prefer, add 1 tablespoon butter for each 2 cups nuts before baking.

French Fried. Blanch almonds, filberts, or raw peanuts (that is, cover nuts with boiling water and let stand until skins loosen, then slip them off). Dissolve 1/2 cup salt in 1 1/2 cups boiling water, and simmer nuts in this 10 minutes. Drain and let dry. Put into a frying basket and fry in deep hot (370° F.) olive oil or other salad oil until light brown. Drain. No additional salt is needed.

ROASTED WALNUTS

Spread unshelled California walnuts in a shallow pan and bake in hot oven (450° F.) 12 to 15 minutes, stirring occasionally. Serve hot or cold, with the dessert course.

SUGARED WALNUTS

There are so many good ways to fix these that it is hard to say of one, "This is the best." Here, then, is an assortment of 5 excellent recipes.

Orange Sugared Walnuts. Boil 1 1/2 cups sugar and 1/2 cup orange juice to the "soft ball" stage (240° F. on candy thermometer). Remove from the heat, add 1 teaspoon grated orange peel and 2 to 3 cups walnut halves. Stir until the syrup begins to look cloudy; before it hardens, drop by spoonfuls on waxed paper, and separate the nuts.

Sherried Walnuts. Boil 1 1/2 cups sugar and 1/2 cup sherry to the soft ball stage (240° F.). Remove from the heat, add 1/2 teaspoon cinnamon and 2 to 3 cups walnut halves, stir well until cloudy. Turn out on a buttered pan and separate the nuts.

Honey Sugared Walnuts. Boil 1 1/2 cups sugar, 1/4 cup honey, 1/2 cup water to the firm-soft ball stage (242° F.). Remove, add 1/2 teaspoon vanilla and 3 cups walnuts. Stir until creamy and thick. Turn out and separate.

Cinnamon Sugared Walnuts. Boil 1 cup sugar, 1 teaspoon cinnamon, dash of salt, 6 tablespoons milk to very soft ball stage (236° F.). Remove, add 1 teaspoon vanilla and 2 to 3 cups walnuts. Stir until creamy. Turn out and separate the nuts.

Panoche Walnuts. Boil 1 cup brown sugar, 1/2 cup granulated sugar, 6 tablespoons top milk and 2 tablespoons light corn syrup to very soft ball stage (236° F.). Add 1 teaspoon vanilla, 1 tablespoon butter, 2 to 3 cups walnuts. Beat until creamy. Turn out and separate.

CONFECTION FRUIT CAKE

For this different and extravagantly good fruit cake, you'll need:

4 eggs, beaten	2 teaspoons baking powder
1 cup sugar	1/2 teaspoon salt
1 teaspoon vanilla	4 cups pecan halves
1 cup flour	3 cups pitted dates

To the eggs, add sugar and vanilla and mix thoroughly. Sift flour, baking powder, and salt into the mixture and stir to make a smooth batter. Add nuts and dates. (No, don't chop them.) Blend with spoon until well mixed. (You may think this a strange-looking dough, for the batter will scarcely cover the nuts and dates.)

Spread the mixture in two 9-inch square pans or one larger pan. Be sure pans are well buttered. Bake in a moderately slow oven (325° F.) for 40 to 45 minutes. Let stand in pan until partially cool before turning it out onto a cake rack. Cool thoroughly before storing. Slice very thin for serving.

P.S. Some good cooks that I know add 2 tablespoons butter to this batter. Some use more nuts and more dates. Some add candied pineapple and cherries. Some are surprised to find that the cake is not very thick. But all are delighted with the cake's goodness and long-keeping quality.

By-laws of Outdoor Cooking and Serving

1. Start with enough charcoal to make a good bed of coals—much better than adding fuel later. A bed 2 to 3 inches deep is right for most grill cooking, but a deeper one is needed for meats that require long roasting or slow broiling.

2. Let fire burn down past the "red-coal" stage before starting to cook. (Count on at least 45 minutes from starting time to grilling time.) Big error in barbecuing is trying to broil before coals are ready.

3. Choose thick cuts of steaks or chops for grilling—thin pieces of meat are likely to dry out or get crusty. Make hamburgers thick for the same reason. When broiling thin ham slices or bacon, let fire burn almost to ashes, then broil quickly and watch carefully. With all meats, have water at hand to put out flames caused by grease drips. (A toy water pistol works fine.)

4. Depend on the grill primarily for cooking meat. Don't overload it with other foods to the sacrifice of perfect meat results.

5. Give special thought to barbecue sauces. Use them only when they improve the meat, or (as in the case of broiled chicken or turkey) keep it from drying out during cooking.

6. Keep outdoor meals simple. A practical pattern consists of: Grilled meat; hearty casserole; zippy salad; bread or rolls, heated last few minutes over coals; simple dessert; drink.

7. Set up a table near the scene of action. Even though you serve on trays, you'll need that table to hold foods and dishes. Avoid running back and forth from kitchen to grill.

8. Give everyone a job! That's half the fun of cooking and eating outdoor style.

Chapter 12

Outdoor Cook Book

IN READING through the preceding chapters, you have (we hope!) come across many recipes that you will want to try out on your garden grill or serve at your next picnic or patio party. And if you have, we hope you are now saying to yourself, "But I want more—and really new—ideas for cooking and eating blue-sky style." Because that's what this chapter is about.

In it you'll find only the dishes we like best when we cook the charcoal way at our week-end place in Inverness. While they seem to be—and are—completely casual, they are planned for easy managing as well as good eating.

APPETIZERS TO ENJOY WHILE THE CHARCOAL BURNS

As every outdoor cook knows, one of the first rules in barbecueing is to wait until the charcoal burns down to a bed of gray-red coals (which in most grills takes from 45 minutes to an hour) before you broil those steaks or chops or hamburgers. But there's no rule that says you must go hungry or thirsty while you wait!

During the "waiting hour" it's fun to provide simple munchies or pick-ups to go with frosty fruit punch or cold beer or spirited cocktails. Of these munchies, one of our favorites is popcorn, done either indoors on the old wood-and-coal range, or in a long-handled popper on the grill, or in the electric popper plugged in on the back porch. Sometimes we dress the popcorn with garlic butter or grated cheese as suggested on page 307. More often we serve it, salted and buttered, to eat with crisp radishes—a wonderful combination—or, in summer, with cubes of cold watermelon or cantaloupe impaled on toothpicks.

When bread is not to be included in the meal that follows, we like to round out the cocktail hour (and ourselves) by bringing out a basket of thinly-sliced and lightly-buttered sour-dough French bread from the kitchen. Occasionally we mix Vegex or other meat extract with the butter, and then heat the bread. But with or without, the bread tastes mighty good with a refreshing drink at the end of a day of gardening or pine-knot gathering.

If the meat of the meal is to be grilled ham or barbecued fish, we frequently bring on a skillet of blazing beef balls for an appetizer. So easy—when all you need do is open a can of cocktail beef balls without gravy (we use Yak Yaks); brown them quickly in a little butter in a skillet; pour in a few spoonfuls of brandy, light it for all to see and sniff, then pass the skillet around, along with cocktail picks, so that each can spear a meat ball and mumble, "These are wonderful."

There are times, of course, when it works out better to make appetizers in advance. Such as:

SURPRISE CHEESE BALLS

For these, cream together 4 tablespoons soft butter and 1 cup grated sharp Cheddar cheese. Blend in 1/4 teaspoon each salt and paprika, a dash of cayenne, and 1/2 cup sifted flour. Have ready about 24 pimiento-stuffed olives or pitted ripe ones, well drained. Wrap a teaspoon of dough around each olive, covering it completely. Arrange on cooky sheet. Bake in 400° F. oven (hot) 10 to 15 minutes. Serve hot, either freshly baked or reheated. Makes about 24.

BABY PIZZA PIES

These can be fixed several hours in advance, ready for last-minute baking. They're especially good for outdoor serving. To serve 8 to 12, cut 3 English muffins in halves. Brush cut surfaces first with olive oil or soft butter, then spread lightly with anchovy paste. Snip 8 or 9 thin slices salami into bits and scatter over paste; slice 6 to 9 stuffed olives and arrange over salami; then scatter drained chopped mushrooms (half of a 2-ounce can) over olives. Put a slice of well-aged sharp Cheddar cheese on top of each. Arrange on baking sheet and keep in refrigerator until about 20 minutes before serving time. Heat oven to 350° F. (moderate) and bake 10 minutes. Cut each "pie" into 4 or 6 wedges and bring them on. (See also page 232.)

DOTTY'S SAUSAGES AND MUSHROOMS

Melt 1 or 2 tablespoons butter in a small skillet, or in the chafing dish. Put in a tiny bit of fresh or dried marjoram, summer savory, rosemary, and thyme—or use a pinch of mixed dried Italian herbs if you have them. Open a 9-ounce can of Vienna sausages, cut them in halves, and add with their jellied juice. Drain and add a 3-ounce can of whole mushrooms. Add 3 or 4 tablespoons of Cabernet or other dry red or white wine. Heat gently. Bring on in the skillet or chafing dish, with cocktail picks for spearing, and plenty of paper napkins. Makes enough for 5 or 6.

BUONA CULDA—"GOOD GRAVY"

This savory dunk, introduced to us by a young Italian friend a few years ago, is fun to fix when appetites are lusty and the day is cold and foggy. Ideal for serving out of doors around the grill. It's gooey and drippy and horribly rich—an experience to fix and to eat!

Chop 3 cloves garlic very fine and cook until lightly browned in 1/2 cup melted butter (1 stick or cube). Stir in 2 or 3 tablespoons anchovy paste or finely chopped anchovies, and a few pickled mushrooms if you have them. (We usually use about 1/4 cup chopped mushrooms marinated half an hour or so in wine vinegar.) Add 1 cup whipping cream. Heat, stirring. Serve very hot, right in its saucepan (a chafing dish can be used, of course). With it pass a bowl of crisp carrot and celery strips and inner leaves of romaine, and a basket of chunky finger-length strips of sour French bread to be dunked in the hot savory mixture. Makes enough for 8 to 10.

SALAD BAR LUNCHEON

Bowl of Crisp Lettuce Garnished with
Tiny Red Tomatoes

Bowl Salad of Shrimp, Crab, and Shredded Chinese Cabbage
with Thousand Island Dressing

Platter of Celery Victor   Cottage Cheese

Baby Pizza Pies (Hot)

Coffee

PICKLED EGGS

When the day is warm and the pre-supper drink is tomato juice or beer, these eggs are just right. To make them, heat 2 cups cider vinegar with 2 tablespoons sugar, 1 teaspoon salt, 1 teaspoon mixed pickling spices and a sprig of dill or slice of garlic or onion; simmer about 8 minutes. Have ready

12 to 16 hard-cooked eggs (shelled). Put eggs into quart jars. When vinegar mixture is ready, pour it hot over the eggs. Cover and let stand in refrigerator for two days before using. Serve eggs icy cold, either whole or cut in halves. Especially good when barbecued salmon is part of the meal to follow. For pink pickled eggs, use the spiced vinegar left over from pickled beets; heat and proceed as above.

FRESH WAYS TO FIX GRILLED MEATS AND FISH

(In Addition to Those Given in Chapters 3, 4, and 5.)

BEST-EVER GRILL-BURGERS

Hamburgers broiled on a charcoal grill present two problems. (1) The meat is inclined to stick. (2) Ground meat cools down pretty fast after outdoor broiling. Doing 'burgers the following way not only gets around those difficulties, but produces super results. Here's how:

Allow 1/3 to 1/2 pound ground beef (lean chuck or round steak) for each serving. Form into thick, soft patties, and arrange in folding wire toaster. When charcoal has burned low, set toaster on grill, with a small stone under each corner to prop it up so that meat does not come in direct contact with grill. (This prevents sticking.) Flop toaster occasionally to brown meat evenly on both sides; season to taste with salt and pepper while cooking.

Meanwhile, at back of grill heat a skillet containing a generous chunk of butter and about an equal amount of Worcestershire sauce. When patties are ready, transfer them to the hot buttery skillet and turn them over once to coat both sides. Serve direct from skillet.

Skillet Notes. Standard equipment for every outdoor grill is a heavy skillet (iron or stainless steel), preferably one with metal handle. If skillet is light weight, watch out for scorching of food. If handle is of wood or plastic, better wrap it in 2 or 3 thicknesses of heavy foil to prevent its burning. To protect skillet from rusting, rub it with oil before storing for winter.

HAMBURGERS HAWAIIAN

1 clove garlic, peeled and mashed	1 tablespoon vinegar
	1/4 teaspoon black pepper
3 tablespoons salad oil	1 1/2 pounds ground beef
3 tablespoons soy sauce	4 slices canned pineapple
2 tablespoons catsup	

Combine first 6 ingredients in shallow pan; mixing well. Shape ground beef lightly into 4 thick patties; turn them over in the mixture, and let stand 30 minutes, or so, until time to cook. Broil on outdoor grill. When you turn the patties for the first time, dip pineapple slices into remaining sauce and put on grill to broil with the meat. Makes 4 large servings. Good with toasted slices of French bread, potato chips, and a green salad.

WAYS WITH SPARERIBS

Important points in doing spareribs on the outdoor grill are to broil them slowly, high above a deep bed of coals; cook them thoroughly; and allow plenty—a pound per person is about right. With these in mind, you are ready to proceed in any one of various ways.

Select as many "sides" of spareribs as required and have them cracked down the middle. Cut into serving size (or larger) pieces, sprinkle generously with salt and pepper and let stand until cooking time.

If you like the flavor of smoky ribs, spread them in wire toaster. Broil slowly about 5 inches above the bed of coals, turning frequently. Allow 45 minutes to an hour of cooking

time. During the last few minutes of cooking, lay a few
sprigs of rosemary, thyme, and/or bay leaves on the coals and
let the fragrant smoke permeate the meat. Or sprinkle meat
with hickory smoke salt or other smoke salt or liquid smoke
during cooking.

If you prefer ribs with barbecue sauce, follow the basic
rules just given for preparing and broiling, but omit the
smoke seasonings and, instead, swab the meat as it cooks,
with barbecue sauce. The barbecue sauce given on page 107
is a good one for spareribs. Or marinate the ribs in any zippy
sauce, then broil as usual.

If your idea of ribs is to have them moist and tender as
well as savory, broil them over coals until brown on both
sides, then brush with barbecue sauce and pack into covered
roasting pan at back of grill. Let steam for at least an hour,
adding more sauce as needed.

If your grill is small or if time is an element to be consid-
ered, pre-bake ribs in kitchen oven or simmer them on top of
range until almost tender, then finish over the coals, with or
without barbecue sauce. Incidentally, when doing that pre-
baking, use an open pan and pour off the fat as it accumulates.

HAWAIIAN SPARERIBS

Peel and chop or mash an egg-sized piece of green ginger and
2 or 3 cloves of garlic in a big shallow pan. Add 1/2 cup soy
sauce and 1 cup catsup. Mix well. Have 2 sides of pork spareribs (3 1/2 to 5 pounds) cracked down the center, to make the
ribs a more manageable length. Coat the strips of ribs all over
with the soy-catsup mixture and let stand overnight. Roast in
an open pan in 300° F. oven for 1 hour; finish over garden
grill, basting with the drained-off sauce as they cook. Serves 4.

For a sparerib supper we like to serve either the Mixed
Bean Casserole given on page 169 or the Kraut Noodle Casserole on page 344, plus celery and carrot sticks.

ABOUT LAMB BREAST

Can breast of lamb (which resembles spareribs in form) be barbecued in the same manner as pork ribs? Yes, but naturally the results are not quite the same. Also the marinade (or barbecue sauce) for lamb should be quite different from that used with pork. Our favorite is the following mixture: 4 tablespoons salad oil; 6 tablespoons soy sauce; 1 onion, grated; 3 tablespoons lemon juice or wine vinegar, and plenty of coarsely ground pepper. Enough for 4 pounds of meat. Since lamb breast is inclined to be fat, we usually roast it in a 325° F. oven for about an hour (pouring off the fat as it accumulates), then finish on the garden grill, basting the meat with the marinade. Incidentally, when the budget is a consideration, it's smart to serve some lamb breast along with the spareribs. A happy combination.

SHISH KEBABS WITH LAMB AND HAM

1 5-pound leg of lamb, cut in 1 1/2-inch slices, then in cubes (Makes about 60)

2 thin slices smoked ham, cut in 1-inch squares

3 large onions, sliced

3 cloves garlic, crushed in bowl with 3 teaspoons salt

1/3 cup oil

1/3 cup Port wine

1/3 cup tarragon wine vinegar

1/3 cup soy sauce

1/2 teaspoon pepper

2 teaspoons seasoning salt (such as Beau Monde or Lawry's)

Arrange lamb, ham, and onions in shallow pan. Mix sauce and pour over all; cover and store in refrigerator overnight. String lamb cubes alternately with ham squares on long skewers. Broil over coals 15 to 20 minutes or longer. At same time heat onions and remaining sauce in skillet to spoon over the meat when ready to serve.

What's left of that leg of lamb? After slicing off the meat, wrap up the bone and store in refrigerator. Then a day or so later, saw or chop it up so it will fit into a big kettle, and use it as the basis of a good soup.

SKEWER STORY

When buying skewers look for square ones with sharp points. Be sure the metal is non-rusting. If you live in California or other semi-tropical area, look around for a clump of growing bamboo. The hard green growth (not too mature) makes excellent skewers when stripped of leaves, cut into usable lengths, then sharpened in a pencil sharpener. They do not burn, can be discarded after using.

TERIYAKIS (MEAT ON STICKS)

1 pound tender top round or sirloin of beef, cut 3/4 inch thick
1 No. 2 can pineapple chunks, drained
1/2 cup syrup from pine-apple
1/4 cup soy sauce
1 teaspoon chopped fresh ginger root, or 3/4 tea-spoon ground ginger
1 clove garlic, chopped fine
1 small jar stuffed olives, drained (about 22)
Thin bamboo sticks (6 inches long)

With a sharp knife, cut meat into cubes about the size of the pineapple chunks. Combine pineapple syrup, soy sauce, ginger and garlic; pour over meat cubes and let stand at room temperature about an hour. Alternate cubes of meat and pineapple on the sticks, then finish off with stuffed olives. Broil 3 inches from coals, for 10 to 12 minutes, turning once. Serve hot as an appetizer; or allow 3 or 4 sticks per person to accompany a hearty casserole for a main course. Makes enough appetizers for 10 to 12; enough full-size servings for 4.

VEAL CHOPS INVERNESS

4 veal chops, 3/4 inch thick   3 tablespoons soy sauce
2 cloves garlic, peeled and   2 tablespoons catsup
    mashed   1 tablespoon vinegar
1/3 cup salad oil   1/4 teaspoon black pepper

Arrange chops in big pan. Mix together the saucy ingredients.
Pour over chops and let stand overnight in refrigerator. Broil
over coals about 15 minutes, turning occasionally.

SALT-ROASTED POT ROAST

First important point in this recipe is to let the charcoal burn
down to a deep bed of coals. While fire burns, prepare the
meat. Start with a *thick, chunky* piece of beef chuck weighing
4 to 5 pounds. This is important, too. Don't try to use a thin
blade pot roast. Spread meat generously with prepared mustard so that all of the outside is coated. Then into the mustard
pat all the coarse salt (ice cream salt) that will stick. When
fire has burned really low, put meat right down into the
coals; cook 30 to 40 minutes, then pull it out, using long
tongs or a clean shovel. Turn roast carefully, return to fire
and cook 20 to 30 minutes longer. Lift onto a platter. Break
off the charred salt, and serve. Enough for 6 hungry folks.

OUR SMOKE-ROAST SPECIALS

Because we are particularly fond of the smoky taste in meats
cooked out of doors, we have rigged up a sort of "Rube Gold-
berg" device that makes it possible for us to smoke-roast to
perfection.

What it is, briefly, is a tunnel of bricks—set right on the
ground—5 or 6 bricks long, 3 bricks high, and one-brick-
length apart, with a 12 x 12 x 30-inch drain tile standing

upright on the bricks at back of tunnel, and a portable oven on top of the tile.

The idea is to start a charcoal fire on the ground at the front end of this tunnel. When fire gets going, lay a piece of sheet metal over the tunnel, then block up the front and back ends of tunnel with bricks. This forces all the smoke and heat back through the tunnel, up the drain tile, and into the oven where the spareribs or whatever are spread on the racks. There they roast gently, their grease dripping down through the tile onto the ground, but not onto the fire.

To make the smoke, feed the fire frequently with sticks of green apple or hickory wood, leafy twigs from alder, or bay leaves.

Spareribs smoke-cooked in this way are wonderful. Equally delicious is corned beef, pre-cooked on range, then smoke-roasted an hour or more. Capons are good, split like broilers, and roasted (cut-side up) about 2 hours, with butter and herbs in their cavities.

In fact, an entire book could be written on this interesting way of cooking out of doors—but half the fun of it comes in trying it out for one's self, working out details as you go!

BARBECUED CHICKEN

Having been brought up in the "fried-chicken belt," we are likely to serve a big basket of crispy, fried chicken, hot (or at least warm) from the kitchen range, rather than to broil it over the garden grill. On the occasions that we do go in for barbecued chicken, we usually do it the following way:

Have medium-size frying chickens (2 1/2 to 3 1/2 pounds) disjointed or quartered, as you prefer. For each chicken mix 1/3 cup salad oil with 1/3 cup Bourbon. Pour over chicken and let stand 4 hours in refrigerator; turn pieces occasionally if convenient. Arrange pieces on grill set high over coals, and broil very slowly 45 minutes to an hour, turning frequently with kitchen tongs and brushing with oil-and-Bourbon mixture that remains.

Sunday Dinner in the Country. Bourbon-broiled chicken; big dish of potato salad; sliced tomatoes on watercress; chocolate cake (see page 273) with ice cream. Iced tea or coffee.

BROILED SALMON STEAKS

Allow 1 thick salmon steak or fillet per person. Brush both sides with melted butter, arrange in folding wire toaster, and prop up on grill as described for hamburgers (page 335). Broil slowly, brushing occasionally with more melted butter, and seasoning with salt and pepper. During last few minutes of broiling, lay a few sprigs of fresh rosemary and thyme on the coals to smudge and smoke and flavor the fish. Serve with lemon wedges. With this I like best to serve potato salad made with plenty of hard-cooked eggs, and enough boiled dressing and mayonnaise to make it really moist. Grill-toasted bread is a good addition to the meal.

SAUCE FOR GRILLED FISH

Grilled fish of any kind—halibut, bass, salmon steaks—takes on new flavor when served with a delicate sauce brought hot from the kitchen. See pages 88 and 89 for recipes.

FOIL-BAKED FISH

For each serving, allow:

1 fillet of flounder, sole, or other flat fish
1 slice red or white onion
1 bay leaf
1 tomato slice
1 slice lemon
Dash of salt
Coarsely ground black pepper

Lay fish in center of square of aluminum foil, top with onion, bay leaf, tomato, and lemon. Season with salt and pepper. Wrap in neat bundle, using the double-fold "drugstore wrap" to keep moisture in. Cook on grill about 15 minutes, turning occasionally.

BIG FISH BARBECUE

Whether your "big fish" is a bass or a rock cod, a salmon, or a big chunk of any one of these, the following sauce is a good one to use.

1 cup salad oil
Juice of 1 lemon
1 tablespoon chopped
    parsley
1 teaspoon salt
1 teaspoon orégano

1/2 teaspoon basil
1/4 teaspoon thyme
1 clove garlic, mashed
2 tablespoons Worcester-
    shire sauce
3 tablespoons wine vinegar

Mix ingredients in quart jar and shake well before pouring it over the prepared fish. Let stand an hour or more before barbecuing. When ready to go, spread a sheet of heavy aluminum foil on grill over glowing coals. Lay fish on it carefully, and cover fish with sliced onions. Cook slowly, basting frequently with the sauce and/or sauterne wine. Turn fish when lower part appears light in color (about half an hour). Continue to cook and baste until done. Cooking time for a medium-sized salmon is 1 to 1 1/2 hours.

DINNER IN COFFEE CANS

This is a good way to handle certain types of outdoor meals, even though the meat does lack the "browned" flavor of grilled meats. The cans are fun—and everyone seems to like the idea of having his "meal in one dish." For each person, allow:

1/3 to 1/2 pound ground beef
Pepper and seasoning salt
2 small, white onions
1/2 a good sized, pared potato

1/2 a carrot, cut in chunks
1/4 a green pepper, cut in strips
1 ear of corn
2 tablespoons sherry wine
1-pound coffee can, with lid

Mix meat with seasoning salt and pepper; form into a patty and put in bottom of a buttered coffee can. Press the peeled onions into sides of meat. Tuck in carrot and green pepper. Break ear of corn into 3 pieces and fit it in on top. Pour in sherry. Put lid on firmly. Cook slowly 45 minutes to an hour on grill. Turn out onto plates to serve, or let everyone eat direct from can—hobo style. Pass heated hard rolls and small bowls of cabbage salad.

CASSEROLES TO ROUND OUT OUTDOOR MEALS

Yes, indeed, with big, thick, barbecued steaks very little else is needed for a perfect outdoor feast. But what about those many times when the "steak" turns out to be fish or frankfurters or chops or hamburgers—and not giant-sized servings, either. On such occasions best plan is to bring on a good hearty casserole from the kitchen to round out the meal. To go with whatever meat is on the grill, casseroles are usually made up largely of beans, pastes, or potatoes. Especially good bring-out-from-kitchen specials include: Easy Cheesy Macaroni (page 154); Italian Risotto (page 155); Mixed Bean Casserole (page 169); Barbecue Beans (page 172); Mushroom Scalloped Potatoes (page 201). And the following ones.

KRAUT NOODLE CASSEROLE

Cook 2 cups (about 1/4 pound) noodles in boiling, salted water according to directions on package. Drain, add 3 tablespoons butter and mix lightly. While the noodles cook, open a No. 2 can of sauerkraut, drain, rinse in cold water, then drain again and spread about three-fourths of it in a shallow baking dish. Over this spread the hot noodles. Sprinkle generously with cubed or grated sharp Cheddar cheese (about 1 cup), then put on the rest of the kraut. Cover the dish and bake at 350° F. (moderate) about 40 minutes. Makes 4 or 5 good servings. Especially good with grilled ham.

Notes: If you use a baking dish without a cover, spread a piece of heavy foil over the top. And if you have an electric bean pot, let the mixture cook in it for an hour or longer, instead of in the oven.

WHISKEY BAKED BEANS

Directions for this hospitable casserole came to us from a friend in Washington, D.C., but it's equally at home on the West Coast, East Coast, or in between. Into a big casserole empty 4 or 5 one-pound cans of New England style baked beans. Add 1/4 cup really strong coffee and 1/4 cup Bourbon, or rum if you prefer. Mix well and let stand in kitchen a few hours, then bake "quite a little while," said the friend who passed along the recipe. In other words, bake at 300° F. for 1 1/2 to 2 hours, or at 325° F. to 350° F. about an hour. The dish is an accommodating one, and will wait until you are ready for it. Makes about 12 servings.

BAKED CHEESE-CREAMED POTATOES

Potatoes in cheese sauce can be very ordinary, or they can be positively de luxe, as these are. A cateress who served them at a super supper in Al and Dora McCann's garden in Yonkers, New York, generously told me how to do them.

Boil 7 or 8 medium potatoes in their jackets, then peel and dice fairly fine—in about 1/2-inch cubes. (There'll be somewhere around 2 quarts after dicing.) Spread them in a big 13 x 9 x 2-inch shallow pan.

Make a medium-thin cream sauce of 4 tablespoons each of butter and flour and 3 cups milk. When it's smoothly thickened, add 2 to 3 cups diced, sharp, well-aged Cheddar cheese —a pound or more. (Yes you can cut down on the cheese, but it won't be as good!) Let melt, slowly stirring. Add salt and white pepper to taste. Pour over the diced potatoes. Cover with about 1 1/2 cups buttered fluffy crumbs. Dash with paprika. Bake 1 hour at 325° F. (moderate) or until bubbling hot and browned. Makes 12 servings.

MEXICAN BORDER CASSEROLE

1/2 a green pepper, chopped
1 medium onion, chopped
3 tablespoons bacon
    drippings
1 pound can chili con carne
    (without beans)
1-pound can red kidney
    beans, drained

12-ounce can whole-kernel
    corn
3-ounce can mushrooms,
    drained
1 cup grated sharp cheese

Cook green pepper and onion in bacon drippings in small skillet about 5 minutes. Empty into 2-quart casserole and swish around to grease bottom and sides. Put in rest of ingredients in layers, sprinkling cheese over top. Cover and refrigerate until about 1 1/2 hours before serving. Then bake, covered, 1 hour at 325° F. (moderate); uncover and bake 30 minutes longer. Makes 10 servings.

WHITE AND YELLOW HOMINY

Here's a hearty that's done in the double boiler—a good one to serve to a small group outdoors or in. To make: Drain

1 No. 2 can yellow hominy and 1 No. 2 can white hominy. Empty into top of double boiler, add 1/2 teaspoon salt, 2/3 cup light cream, 2 tablespoons butter, and a dash of pepper. Heat over boiling water about 30 minutes. Add 2 tablespoons chopped parsley, mix lightly, and serve to 4 or 5.

TOMATO CORN CASSEROLE

1 No. 2 1/2 can solid-pack tomatoes	1 teaspoon sugar
	1 teaspoon cornstarch
1/4 pound bacon, cut in small squares (about 1/2 cup)	3/4 teaspoon salt
	1/4 teaspoon pepper
1 small green pepper, seeded and diced	1 No. 2 can whole-kernel corn
1 large onion, chopped (1 cup)	2 slices toast
	1 clove garlic, peeled

Pour tomatoes into wire strainer to drain. Cook bacon in large skillet until light brown; remove. To fat in skillet, add onion and green pepper and cook gently 5 minutes, stirring. Stir in cornstarch, salt and pepper; add drained tomatoes and bacon and cook, stirring, 3 or 4 minutes. Add corn. Rub toast slices with garlic, cut into cubes, and add to mixture. Pour all into a 1 1/2-quart casserole, cover, and bake in 350° F. (moderate) oven 30 to 40 minutes, until bubbling hot. *Note:* In this, as in all casseroles, increase baking time 10 to 15 minutes if mixture has been made in advance and refrigerated.

CALEXICO CORN BREAD CASSEROLE

This decidedly unusual—and unusually good—"soft" corn bread came to us from a friend on the Mexican border. It sounds strange, but is wonderful eating:

1 cup yellow corn meal
1 1/2 teaspoons salt
12-ounce can cream-style
  corn
1/3 cup melted shortening
  or bacon drippings
1/4 cup milk
1/4 pound Cheddar cheese,
  sliced or grated
2 canned green chile pep-
  pers (1/2 of a 4-ounce
  can)

Mix first 5 ingredients. Spread half the mixture in lightly greased shallow 6 x 10 or 8 x 8-inch pan. Cover with the cheese, then cover cheese with long strips of chile pepper. Spread rest of batter over all. Bake at 375° F. (moderate) 35 to 40 minutes, or until lightly browned. Makes 6 to 8 servings, about right for 4.

SHELL BEACH SPECIAL

Having tried cooking at the beach in a sandstorm too many times, we have come to the conclusion that such picnics are only for the stalwart. On occasions when we do go down to the sea with potato chips, we like to take along a dish of this. It's an easy recipe to remember—and to double and redouble as needed.

1 pound ground round
  steak
1 cup fluffy bread crumbs
1 cup chopped celery
1 onion, chopped
1 egg
1 teaspoon salt
Pepper
Dash of sage
1 can cream of mushroom
  soup

Combine meat, crumbs, celery, onion, and egg; season with salt, pepper, and sage, and form into 6 patties. Arrange in small casserole, pour soup over patties. Bake about 30 minutes at 350° F. (moderate). Wrap casserole in several thicknesses of newspaper to guarantee its staying hot en route to the beach. Serve with buttered buns, pickles, and such.

WHAT ABOUT VEGETABLES?

When it comes to vegetables for serving out of doors, why not face facts? And the main fact is that most vegetables—whether kitchen-cooked or done on the grill—cool down too fast for good outdoor eating. For that reason, we usually serve our green-and-leafies raw (as in salads) or work them into casseroles. There are, however, these exceptions.

FROZEN FRENCH FRIES

Simplest way we've found is to empty potatoes into a metal corn popper and shake them over the hot coals until thoroughly heated, then season with salt and serve. Or heat a little salad oil in a heavy skillet, put in the potatoes, and heat at edge of grill. Heat canned shoestring potatoes same way.

GRILL BAKED POTATOES (2 WAYS)

For these, use either coffee cans with tight-fitting lids, or heavy aluminum foil. Either way (with air excluded) potatoes bake perfectly in 45 minutes to an hour over hot coals.

When coffee cans are used, pack 2 medium-sized scrubbed baking potatoes into each one-pound can, put on lid, and set cans on grill as soon as the charcoal is burning briskly. Check occasionally to see that they are not sticking or burning. By the time the coals are ready for the meat, potatoes will be about done. That is a good time to prick each potato with a fork. (Sweet potatoes, by the way, bake faster than white ones.)

For baking in foil, select large baking potatoes, wrap each in foil, and let bake on grill until done, following same general principles as for tin can baking. To test, run a skewer or fork right through the foil into the potato.

SPUDS ON SKEWERS

Cook small new potatoes in their jackets until almost tender. Lift out, string carefully on skewers (4 or 5 to each one), brush with butter and broil slowly over hot coals. Chunks of carrots can be done the same way.

BACON FRIES

To serve 4, fry 4 strips of bacon in a heavy skillet at edge of grill. When browned—watch out for burning—take out bacon and set it aside. Have ready 4 large new potatoes, sliced thin. (Do not pare them.) Dump them into the hot fat, cover skillet for the first few minutes of cooking, then remove lid and continue frying until tender and delicately browned, turning frequently. Season with salt and pepper as they cook. When they're done, crumble bacon into bits and scatter over them.

OUTDOOR CORN—THE EASY WAY

It's fun to broil ears of corn in their husks (see page 190). But it's simpler—and equally good—to prepare the corn as for kitchen cooking, brush with butter or garlic butter, then wrap each ear snugly in foil. Grill over hot coals about 10 minutes, turning frequently. Serve a silver-wrapped ear on each plate. Have salt and pepper and more butter at hand, of course.

JULIA'S CORN FOR A CROWD

Fit husked ears of corn snugly together with small ends down in a wide kettle that's deep enough to hold the ears of corn upright. About 10 minutes before it's to be served, salt corn and pour over it enough rapidly-boiling water to cover it completely. Put lid on kettle and let stand 5 to 10 minutes off the heat. Cooking time will depend on freshness and age of corn. For informal outdoor eating, drain corn and take out one ear. Then carry kettle around for guests to help themselves.

FRENCH FRIED ONION RINGS

Is there anything better than delicately browned French fried onion rings with grilled steaks or hamburgers? Easy to do out of doors, too, if you follow the recipe on page 196, and do the cooking in an electric French fryer right on the porch or deck. Simpler, of course, is to use canned French fried onion rings and heat them on a sheet of foil on grill.

SOYA FRIED ONIONS FOR HAMBURGERS

While hamburgers broil, heat salad oil or butter in a heavy skillet at back of grill. In it cook sliced onions gently 10 minutes or so, until fairly tender. Just before serving, douse liberally with soy sauce and heat a jiffy longer. Big thing in this recipe is to use lots of onions and plenty of oil or butter. The soy sauce adds just the right amount of salt.

FRIED TOMATOES, A LA GRILL

In a heavy skillet with heatproof (or foil-wrapped) handle, melt 3 or 4 tablespoons butter. Slice firm-ripe, unpeeled tomatoes crosswise. Dip each slice in corn meal, coating both sides. Fry gently, a few at a time, seasoning with salt and pepper. Serve hot from skillet to eat with broiled chicken livers and/or Canadian bacon for a sunny morning breakfast in the garden.

RIGHT SALADS FOR BLUE SKY EATING

Almost any of the salads described in Chapter One are equally good served outdoors or in. To that long list of favorites, you may like to add the following:

"OLD COUNTRY" SALAD

For one of those good-neighbor garden-get-togethers when guests come in slacks or shorts, it's fun to surprise them with this surprising "hot and cold" salad. For 4, you'll need:

4 or 5 raw potatoes	Bunch of green onions
Head of iceberg lettuce	2 cups sour cream (from
1 or 2 cucumbers	dairy)
Bunch of radishes	

Salt and coarse black pepper

About 20 minutes before serving, pare potatoes, cut in halves lengthwise and put to cook in boiling salted water. Shred lettuce (previously washed and crisped) into salad bowl; slice and add the cucumbers, radishes, and onions. (Do not add any dressing.) Stir up cream, empty it into a small bowl and put on table. When potatoes are tender, drain, dump immediately on top of lettuce, etc., in bowl, and serve at once. Each person takes some of the lettuce mixture and a hot potato, spoons sour cream generously over all, sprinkles on coarse black pepper and salt—and eats with gusto. Cold meat loaf is a good accompaniment.

CRUNCHY KIDNEY BEAN SALAD

1 pound can kidney beans, drained, rinsed in cold water, drained again	2 tablespoons chopped green onions
1/2 cup diced celery	1/3 cup mayonnaise
1/3 cup diced sweet pickles	3 tablespoons chili sauce
1/2 cup sliced stuffed olives	Salt and pepper to taste

Combine chilled ingredients, mixing well. Serve in lettuce cups with parsley garnish. Good with hamburgers. Makes 6 servings.

PARSLEY-FROSTED CABBAGE BOWL

3 cups shredded, crisp, raw
  cabbage
1 cup shredded raw carrot
1/2 cup sweet pickle relish
1/2 cup mayonnaise

3 or 4 tablespoons vinegar
  from sweet pickles
Salt and pepper to taste
1 cup chopped parsley

Mix all ingredients except parsley. Heap in serving bowl.
Cover top with parsley. (Garnish with a flower design made of
carrot slices, if you like.) Makes 6 to 8 servings.

STUFFED HEAD LETTUCE

1 small, firm head iceberg
  lettuce
1/4 pound blue cheese
2 3-ounce packages cream
  cheese

2 tablespoons milk
2 tablespoons chopped
  chives
1 pimiento, chopped

Hollow out lettuce from stem end, making a space to hold
about 2 cups. Mash both kinds of cheese together with fork,
blend in milk, and whip smooth. Add chives and pimiento;
mix well. Pack into lettuce. Chill 2 to 3 hours. Cut head crosswise into slices 3/4 to 1-inch thick, and serve with French
dressing. Makes 4 to 6 servings. Pretty—and good—for a garden
luncheon or supper.

SUMMER RELISH SALAD

1 peeled cucumber
4 medium stalks celery
4 green onions (with tops)
3/4 cup parsley (packed)

2 tablespoons salad oil
3 tablespoons lemon juice
Salt and pepper to taste

Grate cucumber and celery into a bowl. Chop onions and
parsley fine. Combine; add oil and lemon juice, and seasonings to taste. Makes 8 servings.

MOLDED MUSTARD RING WITH CABBAGE SALAD

This is beautiful to serve for an outdoor luncheon or garden buffet. Mighty good, too. To make it, you'll need:

1 envelope gelatin	2 1/2 tablespoons dry
1/4 cup cold water	mustard
1 cup vinegar	1/2 teaspoon salt
3 eggs	1 cup sour cream
1/4 cup sugar	

Add gelatin to cold water; set aside. Heat vinegar in saucepan. While it heats, beat eggs slightly, and stir in sugar mixed with mustard and salt. Gradually add boiling vinegar, stirring briskly; then pour all back into saucepan and cook gently, stirring constantly, until mixture barely comes to a boiling point. Remove from heat, stir in softened gelatin, and cool until beginning to thicken. Then fold in the sour cream. Pour into a 1-quart ring mold, and chill. Shortly before serving, toss 4 cups crisp, shredded cabbage with 1/2 cup French dressing, arrange on a big chop plate, then turn the mustard ring out onto the cabbage. Garnish with parsley and radish roses. Makes 6 to 8 servings.

SALAD STREAMLINERS

Rare is the gathering that isn't made up chiefly of calorie-counters—or at least calorie-talkers. Facing that fact, we often serve what we call our "Long Salad." For it, we use a long, narrow, wooden salad bowl, well rubbed with garlic. In the center goes a big mound of watercress, with an assortment of raw vegetables at each end—sticks of carrots, short stalks of celery, florets of cauliflower, green onions, cucumber chunks, and radish roses. For those who wish dressing, we have at hand a tray containing three different types: French, Mustard Cream, and Roquefort Cheese Dressing (as described on page 35). Easy to fix and to serve—and especially appropriate, we think, for casual outdoor meals.

THERMOS JUG SALAD

2 cups cold, cooked green beans (or drained, canned green beans)
1 package frozen mixed vegetables, cooked and cooled (or 2 cups mixed cooked carrots, peas, celery)
1/2 cup sharp French dressing

2 tablespoons anchovy paste or minced anchovies (may be omitted)
1/2 cup grated Parmesan cheese
Salt and coarsely ground pepper

Combine ingredients; add seasonings as needed. Chill thoroughly. (Chill thermos jug, too, with ice water, before putting salad into it.) Carry chilled tomatoes, lettuce, and green onions separately, wrapped in damp paper towels, then in plastic, then in layers of newspapers to keep them cold. At serving time, dip bean salad out of dressing onto lettuce on paper or foil plates. (Don't forget to pack forks, and salt and pepper for the tomatoes.) Makes 6 to 8 servings. Just right for picnics at the beach.

ADDITIONS AND SUBTRACTIONS

When you are in a mood to vary your salad pattern, you may like to try these: In the Green Salad Bowl given on page 5, cut down on the oil a bit and, for seasoning, add some chopped flower-heads of fresh dill—very refreshing. . . . To the Raw Broccoli Salad on page 8, add half an unpeeled lemon, cut into tiny bits. . . . When serving sliced tomatoes, have them very cold; serve on bed of watercress, and top each tomato slice with a slice of hard-cooked egg.

HOT BREADS FROM GARDEN GRILLS

Ask any garden chef. He'll tell you that bread for outdoor meals must be hot, and preferably done on the grill. All-time favorite here in California, of course, is Garlic French Bread.

GARLIC FRENCH BREAD, GRILL STYLE

Peel and mash 1 or 2 cloves of garlic with 1/2 teaspoon salt, using flat side of knife blade to reduce that garlic to nothingness. Mix with 1/2 cup soft butter and let stand half an hour or longer. Cut a loaf of French or Vienna bread in two lengthwise. Spread cut surfaces of upper and lower halves with the garlic butter. Now, run 2 long skewers through each piece (end to end), leaving enough of the handles for easy management. Just before the call goes out to "Come and get it," toast the bread slowly over the remaining coals by propping the skewers on bricks or stones over the grill.

CHEESE-SPREAD LOAF

Prepare the loaf of French bread as suggested above, but mix a small jar of sharp cheese spread with the soft butter. Spread as usual, then sprinkle thickly with minced parsley. Put halves of bread together, wrap loaf in foil, and heat at edge of grill (or in kitchen oven) 5 to 10 minutes.

ROQUEFORT ROLLS IN FOIL

For these, use butter-flake rolls—the ones with 6 or 7 little folds in them. Mash Roquefort cheese to a paste, mixing it with a little soft butter for easy spreading. Separate the folds of the rolls enough to poke in some of the spread. Wrap in foil, putting 2 or 3 rolls into each bundle. Heat on grill. Delicious with steak or any other grilled meat or meaty casserole.

HUSH PUPPIES TO GO WITH
   BARBECUED FISH

When it's a fish or seafood supper, these always make a hit.
Try them out of doors in an electric French fryer! Easy to do.

1 pound corn meal	1/2 teaspoon soda
(preferably stone	1/2 teaspoon garlic salt
ground)	1 egg
1 tablespoon salt	1 cup buttermilk
1 tablespoon sugar	

Stir ingredients together, then add just enough water to make
a mixture that will drop easily. Drop by spoonfuls into hot
fat (375° F.) and cook till brown. (Or shoot the mixture
through the large tube of a pastry bag, as they do in many
restaurants in the Deep South). Serve hot, or at least warm.
Makes quite a few!

RUTH'S HOT CAKES

These hot cakes, which are put together in a most unusual
way, are our top favorites. To serve 2 or 3, you'll need:

1 cup sifted flour	1 egg, unbeaten
1 teaspoon salt	1 cup buttermilk
1 teaspoon soda	2 tablespoons melted butter

Sift flour, salt and soda into a bowl. Add the egg. Stir in buttermilk and butter. Stir lightly and little, leaving the mixture
lumpy and streaky. Bake (outdoors or in) on piping hot,
lightly-greased griddle. It's best to drop just a spoonful in a
spot, then spread the thick batter with a spoon. Turn almost
as soon as you can get a spatula under the cakes. (Don't wait
for bubbles to break on top.) Elegant with browned butter.
For this, heat butter in a small skillet until it fizzes and turns
a light golden brown, and practically sizzles. Serve syrup or
jam or jelly with the cakes. Don't be skimpy!

OUTDOOR OVEN BREADS

With a small portable oven, it's relatively easy to bake biscuits or corn bread at the grill. Tricks are: (1) prop up the oven on bricks to raise it a little above the grill, in order to eliminate too-fast baking on the bottom; and (2) keep a thermometer in the oven in order to judge and control the temperature. If it registers too high, put more bricks under oven to keep it farther from the heat; if it registers too low, try wrapping oven in foil to keep in the heat. For biscuits, use your favorite recipe or packaged mix or ready-to-bake biscuits. For corn bread, the recipe on page 239 is a good one to follow. Or, use corn-bread mix, with a little sour cream in place of part of the liquid called for.

REMINDERS

Try the Toasted English Muffins (page 225) in folding wire toaster over coals on garden grill. A real treat for a garden breakfast . . . Make Buttery Bread (page 225), wrap in foil and heat on grill about 10 minutes . . . Serve Fugacio (page 233) home-made or bought. Heat a sheet of it, wrapped in foil, to serve with grilled chops or steaks . . . Bake the "Cheese-Frosted Biscuits" (page 236) in portable oven on grill. . . . Heat those Tortillas (page 243) on griddle on grill to eat with the Barbecue Bean Casserole given on page 172.

DESSERTS TO TOP OFF GARDEN MEALS

Since outdoor appetites usually go with outdoor meals, everyone enjoys a "happy ending" to those meals. Often chilled fresh fruit (with or without cheese) is the answer. Sometimes the right dessert is just-right pie or cake or frozen special, for which you will find any number of ideas in Chapter 9 (page 247). Other times you'll want to try one of these.

"TIN CAN COBBLERS"

During wild blackberry season, we make a production of these. To do, allow a one-pound coffee can with tight-fitting lid for each 2 persons to be served. Put 1 1/2 to 2 cups blackberries (or boysenberries, fresh or frozen) in each can. Add 1/2 cup sugar and a generous dab of butter. Set cans on grill. When boiling, drop in 2 big spoonfuls of soft shortcake dough, right on top of the hot berries. (We use biscuit mix with light cream for a mixer.) With juice-can opener, punch 1 or 2 small holes in lids so a little steam can escape. Cook, covered, 18 to 20 minutes. Serve with light cream.

TIN CAN BAKED APPLES

In late summer and early fall when winter apples are so very good, we like to feature grill-baked apples. Here, allow 1 coffee can per big apple and per person (regardless of size). Brush insides of cans with butter. Beginning at stem end of apples, take out cores almost, but not quite, to blossom end. Fill cavities with sugar, then pour in 2 or 3 tablespoons rum. Put on lids (first punching holes for steam to escape) and set cans on grill to bake 30 to 45 minutes.

FLORENCE'S BLACKBERRY MUSH

1 quart blackberries	3 tablespoons cornstarch
1/4 cup water	Dash of salt
1 cup sugar	3 tablespoons orange juice

Cook berries with water 5 to 10 minutes, till soft. Press through wire strainer to remove seeds, forcing as much pulp through as possible. Heat to boiling. Mix sugar, cornstarch and salt, add all at once to boiling juice and stir briskly until smoothly thickened. Remove from heat. Stir in orange juice. Cool and chill. Serve with light cream. Makes 4 or 5 servings.

APPLE AND PEAR CRISP WITH ICE CREAM

Work together with fingers or pastry blender until crumbly: 1/2 cup each brown sugar and granulated sugar; 3/4 cup flour; 1/4 cup butter. Spread 4 cups coarsely sliced apples and pears (4 apples and 1 or 2 pears) in a greased shallow 1 1/2-quart baking dish. Pour over them 2 tablespoons lemon juice mixed with 1/4 cup water. Sprinkle generously with cinnamon, lightly with nutmeg. Bake uncovered in 350° F. (moderate) oven 50 to 60 minutes, until apples are tender and crust is lightly browned. Serve warm, topped with ice cream. Makes 6 servings. A great favorite with outdoor meal-planners.

BETH'S CHEESE CAKE

Small servings of this delicious cheese cake are perfect to finish off a garden supper featuring broiled chicken. Make it the day before, then refrigerate, of course.

1 1/2 cups graham cracker crumbs (15 or 16 crackers)
1/4 cup melted butter
1 cup sugar

2 eight-ounce (or 5 three-ounce) packages cream cheese
3 eggs
2 teaspoons vanilla
1 pint sour cream (dairy made)

For the Crust. Lightly butter sides of a 9-inch spring form pan and sprinkle with 2 tablespoons of the cracker crumbs. Set aside another 2 tablespoons to sprinkle on top of pie. Mix remaining crumbs thoroughly with melted butter and 1/4 cup of the sugar, and spread evenly over the bottom of the pan, pressing firmly with fingers.

For the First Layer. Beat cream cheese until smooth and fluffy (2 to 3 minutes on electric mixer at low speed). Gradually beat in 1/2 cup of the sugar, 1 teaspoon of the vanilla, and the eggs, one at a time; continue to beat until creamy and light. Pour mixture over crumbs and bake at 375° F. (moderate) 20 minutes. Remove from oven and let stand at room temperature 15 minutes. Turn oven to 475° F. (very hot). Stir sour cream with remaining 1/4 cup sugar and 1 teaspoon vanilla, until sugar is dissolved; spoon onto first layer and spread evenly. Sprinkle reserved crumbs on top. Bake at 475° F. for 10 minutes. Let cool at room temperature, then chill thoroughly before cutting. (The sour cream will be soft when removed from oven, but becomes firm as cake cools.) Makes 8 to 10 servings.

LIGHT-AS-A-FEATHER GINGERBREAD

1/4 cup shortening	1/4 cup dark molasses
1 egg	1/2 cup buttermilk
1/4 cup sugar	1 cup sifted flour
1 teaspoon ginger	1/2 teaspoon soda
1 teaspoon cinnamon	1/2 teaspoon salt

Turn on oven to heat to 350° F. (moderate). Put shortening in 8 x 8 x 2-inch pan and set in oven to melt. (Easy way to grease pan.) Beat egg in mixing bowl. Sift in the flour, soda, and salt; beat smooth. Pour into the greased pan and bake 20 to 25 minutes, or until done. Serve warm, topped with whipped cream cheese or whipped cream mixed with apricot jam. Or serve as is, with mugs of cold buttermilk for an under-the-trees lunch on a warm summer's day.

OUTDOOR WAYS WITH ICE CREAM

(1) In advance, spoon ice cream into little freezer pans of aluminum foil. Set on tray. Cover each serving with grated sweet chocolate and store, tray and all, in freezer until serving time. (2) Put slices of sponge or angel food cake together with peppermint or other ice cream between. Freeze quickly, then wrap and store. Serve with choice of sauces. (3) Cut tops off big cup cakes; hollow out. Fill cavities with ice cream, replace tops, and freeze. Serve plain to eat out of hand, or on plates, with a sauce, to eat with fork.

Additional Menus for Special Occasions

WEEK END AT THE CABIN

Saturday Breakfast-Lunch

Grapefruit Halves

Fried Corn Meal Mush   Fried Ham or Sausages

Blackberry Jelly   Coffee

Sweet Rolls for Dessert

Saturday Night Dinner

Green Salad Bowl

Assorted Cold Luncheon Meats   Buttered Peas

Piping Hot Ravioli in Tomato Sauce

Spice Cake   Apple Sauce

Tea or Coffee

Sunday Breakfast

Chilled Tomato Juice

Ready-to-Eat Cereal with Country Cream

Scrambled Eggs   Toast   Bacon

Doughnuts   Coffee

Sunday Dinner

Cold Roast Beef or Lamb

Creamed Potatoes   Green Beans

Cabbage and Pineapple Salad

Spice Cake   Homemade Ice Cream   Coffee

GARDEN GRILL DOUGHNUT PARTY

First Course Salad of Mixed Fresh Fruits Topped with

Cottage Cheese

Hot Doughnuts   Coffee

Serving Suggestion. Provide the picnic table with a number of shallow bowls of sugar in which guests pre-dunk their hot doughnuts before doing the coffee-dunking. . . . Better assign one person to watch the fire constantly; you'll need steady heat to fry those doughnuts just right.

DUDE RANCH SUPPER

Chilled Tomato Juice

Country Sausage with Scrambled Eggs

Cottage Fried Potatoes

Leaf Lettuce with Sour Cream Dressing

Dessert Pancakes with Maple Syrup   Coffee

CHUCK WAGON SUPPER

Tortilla Roll-Ups
(Buy tortillas at Mexican store. On each tortilla lay a slice of cheese, fold over, pin with toothpicks; heat thoroughly on grill over glowing coals. Serve piping hot.)

Chili Beans   Barbecued Lamb Breast

Buckaroo Tomatoes

(To well-seasoned canned tomatoes add chunks of peeled avocado and plenty of chopped green onions; serve chilled, in paper serving dishes)

Fresh Fruit   Coffee

To Manage. Bring hot chili beans and barbecued lamb from home; heat the tortilla roll-ups and make the coffee over the camp fire; reheat the beans and lamb if necessary.

GARDEN FIESTA WITH MEXICAN TOUCH

Appetizers: Guacamole; Cheese-Stuffed Celery; Pickled Peppers; Salami; Sliced Tomatoes; Ripe Olives

South of the Border Chili

Tortillas, Heated   Cabbage Slaw

Caramel Pudding Topped with Whipped Cream and Coconut

Small Cakes or Cookies   Coffee

Note. If tortillas are not available (they're usually to be found in Mexican grocery stores), substitute corn sticks or corn bread. Make generous amounts of the chili—it's amazing what a fiesta crowd can eat.

Index